Church Transition Through the Princple of 12

By
Dr. Kim Sam-Seong

Church Transition through the Princple of 12

By

Dr. Kim Sam-Seong

Copyright © Kim Sam-Seong 2008

ISBN # 1-931178-10-0

All rights in this book are reserved. No part of this book may be reproduced in any manner whatsoever without the written permission of the author except brief quotations embodied in critical articles or reviews.

FOR ORDERING INFORMATION, PLEASE CONATCT:

VISION PUBLISHING
1115 D STREET, RAMONA CALIFORNIA 92065
www.visionpublishingservices.com
1-800-9-VISION

Foreword

"The church worldwide is in a time of transition. A generation of spiritual leaders is moving on, and new leadership is stepping up. Strategies from the past that have been effective are being reevaluated, and a re-visitation of biblical principles has become a mandate. In light of this, men of God such as Dr. Kim Sam-Seong, dynamic missionary pastor to Kazakhstan, have restructured their ministry with a renewed passion for souls and for church planting. The New Testament model for revival has always been to plant churches everywhere. Utilizing the Principle of 12 and Cell church structures, Dr. Kim has already planted hundreds of indigenous churches along the Silk Road, and has a strategy to plant churches all the way back to Jerusalem.

In this book, Dr. Kim explores the dynamics of church planting utilizing the Principle of 12 (discipleship), and gives testimony to the struggles and joys of finding and mentoring committed leaders, faithful men and women, who will teach others also for the glory of God. This book is more than theology, it is living Acts 29 testimony of the grace and power of God to transform whole communities by implementing a strategy that is for our time, yet rooted in biblical history".

Stan DeKoven, Ph.D.
President
Vision International University

Table of Contents

FOREWORD 3

Part 1: Principles of *PRINCIPLE OF 12* Church 7

Chapter 1: From a Traditional Church to a Cell Church 7

Part 2: Biblical Background of *PRINCIPLE OF 12* Church 57

Chapter 2: Government Order of the Kingdom of God 57

Chapter 3: Holy Vision 83

Part 3: Spirituality and Anointing of a *PRINCIPLE OF 12* Church 117

Chapter 4: *PRINCIPLE OF 12* Spirituality 117

Chapter 5: Anointing for Explosive Growth 151

Chapter 6: Restoration of Anointing 199

Part 4: How to Develop the *PRINCIPLE OF 12* Church 229

Chapter 7: Ladder of Success 229

Chapter 8: Process of Choosing and Developing the 12 Disciples 271

Chapter 9: The Power of Mentoring 289

Chapter 10: *PRINCIPLE OF 12* Ministry is a Team Ministry 311

Chapter 11: How to Convert to *PRINCIPLE OF 12*? 335

Questions and Answers 361

Part 1:
Principles of PRINCIPLE OF 12 Church

Chapter 1:
From a Traditional Church to a Cell Church

Introduction

It has been nearly 20 years since I left Korea. I have been commissioned as a missionary, serving for the last 13 years in Kazakhstan, in Central Asia. On the mission field, a pastor and his wife work together more often as co-pastors. While it is a core element of PRINCIPLE OF 12 ministry, rather than distinguishing us as a pastor and pastor's wife, the couple works together as one, with the idea that they are both senior pastors. Ultimately, the major difference in the ministry climate between Korea and the mission field is that on my mission field, the children have their own vision for ministry as well. Therefore, the whole family is working together towards a clearly articulated vision.

Specifically, Almaty Grace Church has a Men's network, Women's network, Young Adult network and Children's network. While the women's network has 630 cells, the men's network has only 70. We started the men's ministry last January. I oversee over 70 cells while my wife supervises over 630 cells. Thus, one can see how much impact women have at Almaty Grace Church. Young Adults have about 210 cells and recently, we launched a children's cell which numbers at 40. In total, about 950 cells are striving to grow and mature like that of the early church for the sake of Jesus' ministry.

An important biblical text for understanding the PRINCIPLE OF 12 church and its ministry is found in Numbers 1:1-4. The Israelites were traversing the desert when God gave them a revolutionary command. In essence, they had formed some semblance of a church. As I[1] read, I came to understand it as the Old Testament model of the PRINCIPLE OF 12 church.

> [1] The LORD spoke to Moses in the Tent of Meeting in the Desert of Sinai on the first day of the second month of the second year after the Israelites came out of Egypt. He said:
> [2] "Take a census of the whole Israelite community by their clans and families, listing every man by name, one by one.
> [3] You and Aaron are to number by their divisions all the men in Israel twenty years old or more who are able to serve in the army. One man from each tribe, each the head of his family, is to help you. (Nu. 1:1-4)

In verse 20, it reads, "All the men twenty years old or more who were able to serve in the army were listed by name,

---

[1] First person will be frequently used in this book, as this book is more than principles, but the principles have been worked out with great success in the life and ministry of the author.

one by one, according to the records of their clans and families…" Even in verses 22, 24, 26, 28 and 30, the command was to call out, from 12 specific tribes, men who were able to fight in the army. Within this text, God reveals a picture of what the church should look like in the last days.

There are 3 stages to the church. The first is the traditional church. This is depicted through the leadership of one man, Moses, who was called by God to lead the church of two to three million Israelites out of Egypt. They left in a dignified fashion and organized itself into God's church and army. This is the traditional view of the first stage of church.

The second stage can be found in Exodus 18. Even though Moses was able to lead the Israelites out of Egypt, in spite of his excellent leadership, it was impossible for one man to keep a governing order over 2 to 3 million people. So, initial wisdom was given through his father-in-law Jethro. They established officials over 1000, 100, 50, and 10 people. Even though nearly 10,000 leaders were created in a moment, most with little training in leadership, nevertheless through this organization, the church of God was able to go forth. This is a picture of a cell church. The organization brought fragmented people together systematically and they were able to realize the need for organization through fellowship. This picture of church is the Old Testament model for cell church.

The third stage emerged in preparation to leave the wilderness and enter the land of Canaan, after having lived in the desert following the advice of Jethro. It is not enough to merely systematize or remain with God's church. It is crucial to have devoted people form God's army to fight against enemies found in the wilderness. Also, in order to enter into the land that flows with milk and honey, we have to have a clear vision and goal. To achieve such goals, simple organization is not enough. Until the organization becomes a dedicated army of God, they cannot accomplish the will of God. Today's church cannot just stay where they are at; they need to become a church that accomplishes the will of God by becoming the army of God as shown in the Old Testament.

To summarize, the first stage, the traditional church was depicted by the escape of Egypt. In Exodus 18, we see the second stage or the reorganization of Israelites; this is a spiritual picture of a cell church. Thirdly, according to Numbers 1-11, they reorganized once again, but this time into an army under truly anointed leader (the 70 elders).[2] This cannot be accomplishedwithout dedication and devotion. It is devotion to the leader, devotion to each other, devotion to commit to battle, and to follow the vision and purpose. God has presented this picture of a devoted church through many events in the book of Exodus, from the wilderness and the conquest of Canaan. From this point of view, it can be the most suitable metaphor for the church. During the last two years of transitioning from a traditional church to a cell church to a PRINCIPLE OF 12 church, God has shown me these three types of leadership models during my intimate

---

[2] For more information on this concept, see Dr. Stan DeKoven's book "Visionary Leadership" by Vision Publishing. Then put this in the back of the book to order.

times of prayer with him. The book of Numbers helped me realize that in the government of God's kingdom, numbers are very important. As a whole, this is the Old Testament model of how to view the church of God.

If you were to study the growth process of Almaty Grace Church (the church where my wife and I serve), you will understand the reason why we went with the PRINCIPLE OF 12 Church model. You'll also understand the difference between a traditional church, a cell church and a PRINCIPLE OF 12 church.

Commissioned as a Missionary: History of Almaty Grace Church's Cell Ministry

I was commissioned to Kazakhstan by Grace Korean Church of Los Angeles in October of 1990. As the first Korean missionary in Kazakhstan, during the first 3-4 years I ministered based on what I had seen and learned in the past. In Korea, I studied at the Theological Seminary of the Korean Presbyterian Church for a year and a half. I was born again at Dong-An Church in Seoul. At that church, I experienced and learned the different facets of church ministry as the president of the young adult group, a Sunday school leader, a choir member, and a Jr. High Youth Pastor. Based on what I learned, I started my ministry in Kazakhstan, leading Sunday service, Wednesday service, and Friday night service. I served God through traditional methodology, giving it my all. After about three years, the church grew to about 1000 members. It can only be explained as the grace of God. It is not as though I had any special talent; the Lord did it by Himself. Thus, personal experience and encounters with God is very important. I was able to throw my life away for Jesus because of my relationship with the Lord. Because my encounter was so real, that experience has helped me to overcome countless difficulties and tribulations.

The three years of my ministry consisted of witnessing to the natives. All were unbelievers, so I started the church with a couple of people I met in my apartment complex. Not only did people receive Jesus as their Lord and Savior, their lives were visibly transformed. Seeing this, whenever people came, be it the Bible Study or healing sessions, I didn't hesitate to use whatever methodology to help them personally feel the presence of the Holy Sprit and to confess Jesus Christ as their Lord. I would not let them go until I was certain of their salvation and transformation. Over the years, my efforts have helped to pass on my spiritual DNA to the church members. I have never expressed it in words but they saw through my actions that evangelism required relentless passion and dedication. As a result, they accepted me as their role model of how to evangelize and walk with God. People who accepted Jesus through me began to bring other people to me as well. Because I'd studied liberal theology based on rational logic for six years in Germany, for the first 3 to 4 years in Kazakhstan I tried to remove "rationality" from my principle focus. I realized that the Word of God is about simple proclamation and not logical persuasion. I discovered that the faith of people who received the gospel through logical persuasion didn't last long. The reason for that is because it was not based on their personal experience with God. Nowadays, young people ask, "Show me your faith." It was the same in my case. Because of my personal encounter with God, I wanted every member of my church to have a personal encounter with Christ. In the mission field, I clearly discovered that I had one gift, found among gifts listed in 1 Corinthians and Romans. It was the gift of faith. I healed people with faith; I delivered people with faith, and I ministered with faith. Through faith, God allowed many miraculous healing of sick people.

For example, in February of 1991, there occurred a transformational event. A young woman told me that she'd been suffering from epilepsy for 16 years. She had finished reading the gospel of John and saw that Jesus was not only able to heal people but raise the dead as well. She asked me to pray for healing. When I prayed, God healed her completely, on the spot. As a result of her healing, it seemed like all the sick people from Almaty started coming to our church. As the word began to spread, many people began to come seeking healing. One person brought a small bottle of honey; others brought other valuables, looking to be healed. I knew that I didn't have the gift of healing but I had courage. It was my conviction that if the people are not healed, it was God's problem and not mine. So, I prayed, "God, please use me so your name won't be put to shame." God answered prayer in a very special way and we experienced an amazing amount of healing. The presence of the Holy Spirit was so powerful within the church. Even though the church had the look of a traditional church, it grew to about 1000+ members after 3-4 years of ministry.

    I was extremely happy, but after three years, I was completely worn out. My wife was completely worn out as well. On the mission field, ministry is very difficult without the dual efforts of husband and wife. After the third year, my health had deteriorated. I felt so weak that I could not last ten seconds in the pulpit. The reason for this burnout can be attributed to the fact that Kazakhstan has been known to be the hotbed of shamanism in the world. In actuality, Russia's Siberia and Altai Republic are the hotbeds of Shamanism, but Kazakhstan shares its borders with both Russia and China. As a result, there are many who are spiritually oppressed and demonized in this region.

    I was seeking to do deliverance ministry, but because of the circumstances, the three-fold ministry of Jesus (preaching, healing and deliverance) was established in our church early on. I was completely exhausted and my wife experienced partial paralysis of her body for a while, due to exhaustion. I worked day and night for three years straight. On Friday night services, the service would begin at 10 PM and last until 6 AM the next morning. When the Word of God was preached, demons would manifest, causing people to scream or collapse. We would take the people into prayer rooms to cast out demons. The deliverance ministry consisted of six or seven teams praying all night. After three years of doing this non-stop, I had no strength to continue. I needed to be continuously recharged, but no matter how much I prayed, I found it impossible to overcome the overwhelming oppressing climate of the evil spirit of communism, the Islam religion and shamanism. I desperately realized the importance and need for intercessors.

Completely exhausted, I prayed to the Lord, "God, show me. What must I do? You know that I cannot stand to just bring up a ritualistic religious person in the church. I desperately want to help them love with passion and devotion, but I am not able to. What should I do?" My questions to God may have been very simple, but when I asked these questions seriously, God gave me a clear direction. I only had nine months of evangelism experience in Korea; I had not learned the different church systems. However, when I prayed, seeking God's direction, He moved my heart deeply to begin a cell ministry. He said, "Make all lay people into a minister like you!" That was a very important turning point for me. "Yes, God I understand now. Everything that I've been doing, all my passion, all the anointing on me, and the fire that you've given me, I will impart to many small group leaders and cause them to be a minister like me."

After making the decision, I came to Korea and bought every Christian book regarding cell ministry. I studied them for six months in my office in Almaty. How can I prepare people to become passionate ministers? After months of diligent study and research, I proclaimed to the church, "From now on, our church will do cell ministry." Following the proclamation, we started the cell ministry, but because we had very little experience, I was afraid it wouldn't last long. In order to prepare the shepherds to lead the cell groups, I asked for volunteers. At the time, about 80 people signed up. There was a significant response to the call.

I prepared the 80 leaders for about a year, yet not one of them was thinking about starting a cell group. They were fearful. They had the crippling mindset that preaching was only for the pastor and not them. When I went before the Lord regarding the situation, the Holy Spirit gave me assurance saying, "When two or three of you are gathered in my name, I will be with you." This is a very significant basic truth. This means that when two or three believers are gathered, they become the church of God. So, I made that proclamation. When the 80 shepherds in training were gathered, I proclaimed a very simple message saying that when two or three gather to worship, that becomes a place of God's presence and blessing. After the message, 8 out of 80 people started their cell groups. I asked those 8 leaders to prepare to share what blessings they received from the Lord as they gathered together as a cell group. After making such a request, I spent the week prayerful and anxious. However, when we gathered to share, their testimonies were amazing.

They shared that when they got together as a cell group, God spoke to them according to His promise. They witnessed many miracles, such as the transformation of an alcoholic husband. They also experienced healing as they laid hands on the sick. Other members, motivated by the testimonies, began to join in and within months, the cell groups increased from 8 to 60. People need to be motivated. God works more powerfully when we join God in what He is doing. That is how we started the cell ministry. God is truly wonderful. God leads those who trust in him without fail. He leads them perfectly according to his plans. I experienced many difficulties and surprises in ministry due to its nature and my inexperience. Yet, every time I knelt down to pray, Holy Spirit allowed me to hear his voice. The voice of God transformed my life and my ministry. God has been guiding my footsteps and ministry through the process of answered prayers.

In 1993, God sent Pastor Ralph Neighbor to us. At the time, I didn't even know who he was. So God had Pastor Neighbor call me. He called and said, "I have heard that your church in Almaty is growing and is a role-model for other churches. I would like to visit your church and do a seminar." I asked about the kind of seminar he wanted to do and he said it would be a seminar on cell churches. At that time, because I didn't know who he was, I said, "I will pray about it and get back to you." He probably thought I was an arrogant person. After the conversation, I felt that it would be great to have him since we were having a difficult time solidifying the cell church model. We hadn't fully grasped the concept of cell church.

He lectured for the whole day on a Wednesday, and it was very helpful. I asked him if he would come back the next day, and he said that he would. He was having a wonderful time as well, so he spent many days teaching the whole congregation about the need for the church of God and its members to be armed to serve. On the last day, after he finished his lecture, I asked him a question, "Pastor, you have shared exactly what we needed to hear at this crucial transitional time of our church. In your opinion, how can we most effectively transform ourselves into a true cell church?" Then he asked, "How many services do you have during the week?" I answered, "We have Sunday service, Bible study, prayer meetings, and on Friday night, we have an all night prayer meeting." "Do you really want to transform your church into a cell church?" he asked. "Yes," I answered, "I made a commitment to do so." "Then remove everything except for the Sunday service." "Oh, that would be impossible. Sunday services serves to cast vision and direction. Wednesday services are for the newcomers to tangibly experience the infilling of the Holy Spirit by the laying on of hands. This is where people receive the gift of tongues as well as healing, and the Friday night prayer meeting helps to maintain the spirituality of our church where we do deliverance ministry, which is desperately needed. If we were to take away all these services, wouldn't we lose our vitality?" I explained. Then he answered, "All those ministries should take place in the cell groups." I was greatly encouraged by his answer. I am not one to wait to obey when God speaks. The very next Sunday, I made the announcement: "Starting this week, we will no longer have Wednesday or Friday services." The members were up in arms over the announcement. I reassured them, "I will help to make it possible for you to perform and experience every aspect of my personal ministry, the healing, deliverance and everything else." Then they seemed to calm down. "Therefore, I will pour my life into the 80 shepherds who are in training. I will make sure that through these shepherds, God will continue to work and minister to us. If we don't make this decision to change, our church will not grow and the kingdom of God will not expand. This church is not my property. It is my goal to see every single one of you minister along side me as a disciple of God. Please honor the decision I made as your senior pastor."

The members of my church are very devoted. They number in the thousands, but if I were to announce that we are going to quit PRINCIPLE OF 12 ministry tomorrow and move to another town, they would all follow. Without exaggeration, every one of them would follow. I am truly grateful. It is the result of personally leading the majority of them into salvation. Even though the people are highly cultured and proud, they chose to trust and love me. This has been a great source of blessing. Our church has been doing this ministry for the last seven years, with dynamic results.

Pastor Ralph Neighbor came back two more times. In the meantime, Faith Community Baptist Church of Singapore, led by pastor Lawrence Kong was in the process of transitioning into a cell church through clinical trials. Pastor Ralph Neighbor was serving them as an associate pastor. Pastor Neighbor introduced us to the church. For the following seven years, they sent upper level leaders and ministers who were in charge of training, bimonthly, in order to help us get on track with Cell Church Ministry. That was a tremendous help to us. We were helped financially and spiritually. As a result, we experienced explosive growth and established a framework to transform completely into a Cell Church Ministry.

During those seven years of ministry, I discovered that while the cell church movement, started by Pastor Ralph Neighbor, is important enough to be called the "second religious reform," it lacked one key aspect of a whole or complete ministry. In many cases, there were tendencies to concentrate more on fellowship, lacking in spiritual fervor, devotion, and evangelism.

Jjust one of the major differences between Eastern and Western religion is that Western Christianity is based on knowledge and logic. The post renaissance period saw the establishment of universities in the western hemisphere, which led to the solidification of the basic truths of Jesus through knowledge, enabling people to logically explain the gospel. I acutely realize that while Christianity is based upon the Truth, the expansion of the kingdom of God must come through the sharing of life, such as occurs through mentoring relationships, peer to peer life sharing, apprenticeships and prolonged connectedness. Western Christianity's faith places more emphasis on intellectual agreement and understanding. (I'm not saying that all churches are this way). The belief that one would study and gain more information through lectures in classrooms, even evangelism methods have changed. Some believe that a person has been born again if he or she intellectually agrees with the logically presented gospel. However, this method is missing an important truth. Such methods do not transform lives. Evangelism Explosion, Four Spiritual Laws, Navigators' Discipleship, etc... are all excellent evangelism programs. However, such programs only help solidify the faith of someone who has been a Christian for a period of time. I have clearly discovered that the frequency and importance of personal encounters with Jesus decreases and the people fail to bear fruit when the acceptance of Jesus is limited to the mere logical understanding of the gospel.

The Korean style (Asian style) of Christianity considers the emotional dimension as equally important. To clarify, not just emotions but the emotional dimension along with personal encounters is important. Jesus Christ, who is God, is still with us through the Holy Spirit. Even though God desires to come into our lives and work in us, he is left standing at the door; he is not personally invited into our hearts. As a result, even Korean Christianity is experiencing the loss of its passionate prayer movements. The emotional aspect is disappearing. Excluding the underground churches of China, not only Korea but most of the churches around the world have changed, placing an over emphasis on logic. The advantage of Western Christianity is that they were able to organize the truths of Christianity clearly. It is good to see movements focused on strategy, but its flaw is that they abandoned their passionate hearts. I discovered this myself.

Unfortunately, the cell church system does not solve this problem. Actually, most church systems have their foundation in the Western thought process. As a result, the church is focused on organization and logic. It is good, probably necessary to adopt certain business strategies. How well could gthe modern mionisgter function without logic and the internet? Christianity must keep spreading powerfully, even without the internet. You can easily fall into a trap of becoming a church with zero spirituality and knowledge. I realized that a church without fervency will lose the passion for evangelism. Such churches will lose the passion to accomplish the vision of God.

At the time, Pastor Lawrence Kong, who taught our church about the cell church system, introduced us to a church in Bogotá, Columbia in South America, called ICM (International Charismatic Mission), led by Senior Pastor Cesar Castellanos and his wife, Claudia Castellanos. Pastor Castellanos received a vision after attending a church growth seminar (CGI: Church Growth International) at Yeido Full Gospel Church in 1985. Initially following the implementation of the Korean-style zone organization, his church experienced a brief period of growth. However, the church soon became stagnant. Afterwards, through the vision God had given him, he started a new ministry called G-12, or Government of 12, a ministry that initially lead to explosive growth through the apostolic anointing of 12 disciples, modeling Jesus' example with his twelve disciples.

When I heard the report that, as a result of G-12

ministry, his church grew from 2000 members in 1988 to 300,000 members; I was deeply challenged. I felt that God could accomplish such works at our church as well. I am a man who is easily impressed, so I began to pray immediately after hearing their story, "God, help me to go to Bogotá." After about a month, a pastor who visited Almaty asked, "Pastor, how can I help you?" I asked for the expenses to travel to Bogotá. With his help, I was able to visit Bogotá with my wife, in April of 2000. To my amazement, at that conference they did not teach about G-12 at all. In my mind, the best representation of Korea's spirituality and prayer was Yeido Full Gospel Church. From what I witnessed in Bogotá, it felt as though the church in Bogotá was 10 times more fervent. They held services at an indoor gymnasium that held about 20,000 people. When they were interceding for their city and for the nation, I literally felt the gymnasium shake. Oh, how fervent their prayers were!

    Since then, every time I visited that church, I realized time and time again that God's church is led by spirituality. The explosive work of God takes place when spirituality and the PRINCIPLE OF 12 strategy of Jesus are coupled. I realized that more than countless methodologies, we must restore our spirituality. Even after my visit, there was no literature explaining PRINCIPLE OF 12. Actually, there was one book written about PRINCIPLE OF 12, by an American, Joel Komesky. I read that book but I heard Pastor Cesar say, "That is not an original. It is written by an observer of the PRINCIPLE OF 12 and that's like someone describing an elephant by only feeling the elephant's legs. Don't take the book too seriously." "Then what should I do," I asked. But he would not give me an answer. Therefore, I had no choice but to keep meeting with him. My relationship with him grew closer when I met him at a conference that was held in America. Pastor Cesar Castellanos chose twelve disciples from around the world for his G12, which was established to broaden and activate the PRINCIPLE OF 12 ministry all around the world. Thankfully, he asked me to be his disciple to be in charge of the Silk Road region of Central Asia. I said, "Thank you. I truly want to learn. Please be my mentor."

As his disciple, I learned under him for about two years. With the inspiration of Bogata, and the real help of Pastor Larry Stockstill and his team, our church was able to convert itself into a PRINCIPLE OF 12 church. It's been about two years since the conversion. Right before the conversion, in the mode of the traditional cell church, we had approximately 300 cells. Within two years, we have grown to about 950 cells. This is truly explosive. If a pastor truly loves God's church, he would desire the growth of the church. Church growth is definitely not man's desire. A good pastor would continuously want to see the kingdom of God expanded. I believe that the moment that the desire leaves the pastor, that is when the anointing leaves as well. Thankfully, God has given continued this passion and expectations. We have experienced a small growth, but nevertheless, we have already grown to 950 cells. I am confident that within one to two years, it will be possible to make thousands of cells. It is not just me who believes in this vision, but all of my disciples believe it as well. I sincerely hope that this ministry can take root in other parts of the world as well, in Jesus' name. It will not be easy. There must be strong determination and resolve.

A Premise to the Conversion of a PRINCIPLE OF 12 Church

The most crucial part in transformation is the will of the senior pastor. How passionate are you about making your entire congregation into devoted disciples? Jesus did not command us to go and evangelize in Matthew 28:19-20 but he commanded us to go and make disciples. The phrase "make disciples" itself is important. To make disciples is a process and requires complete dedication. What kind of vision do you have for making disciples? Are you endlessly pursuing the vision to make disciples for such growth? Do you have an unwavering determination? Are you prepared to give up your life for the fact that it is the will of God to make disciples of all nations? This is the pivotal point, I believe. If the senior pastor has such determination, the church can overcome any obstacles, no matter what the cost. Even if there is opposition from the ruling board, the pastor would continue to do such work and ministry even if he has to resign and plant a new church. I speak of such extremes because it is my desire to see many of you find rest in his will.

Discernment of the senior pastor is very important as well. Decision making comes from discernment. We are able to make decisions when we have the discernment of the Holy Spirit, when we can see how the Holy Spirit is leading the church, and when we can see where the growing churches of the world are headed. We suffer from indecision because we just don't know. If an associate pastor, elders or deacons attend a PRINCIPLE OF 12 Conference instead of the senior pastor, this ministry will not likely be successful. The senior leader has to be convinced that the PRINCIPLE OF 12 is the ministry needed for the local church. God can work through anyone, but generally He works when the senior pastor, having heard from the Holy Spirit, determines a direction with clear vision and determination. Only then will the senior minister and the church accomplish the will of God without wavering.

Let us think about the flow of the churches in the past. During the 70's and 80's, there were many movements to make disciples in the Korean Church through various para-church organizations. At that time, "making disciples" meant bible study. PRINCIPLE OF 12's definition of "making disciples" is not bible study. The greatest contribution of the 70's and 80's bible study and "making disciples" movement is that it led to an awakening of the existing churches. God considers established churches to be very important. One important work of God was to birth the church through Jesus Christ. The Gates of Hell cannot prevail against it. God wants to strengthen the church and the church must exist as the church. When a countless number of young people became pastors through the commitment they made during the Bible

Study and Discipleship Movement, Korean churches were able to grow up as disciple makers. Also, the trend around the world demonstrates that Holy Spirit has been working in new and unexpected ways to invigorate traditional churches.

Remember, there was the Azusa street revival in the 1900's. In the 1960's we saw the emergence of the Healing Movement, and the Prophecy Movement marked the 1970's and 1980's. In the 1990's the church began to be impacted by the Apostolic Movement. Truly, the Holy Spirit is doing something in our day. Many movements, some of which we cannot fully grasp the meaning of, have taken place. I firmly believe that somewhere down the road, all these movements will be embraced by the church. These changes are currently taking place, leading us to a movement of Disciple Making of Lay People, and the Lay Ministry. This is the key to the future growth of the church. Disciple making is not about people who passively do what they are told by the church. It is a Discipleship Movement of people who minister, with ownership, as true disciples of Jesus Christ. The prominent emergence of such a movement is earmarking the 21st century. I am convinced that people of all nations will rise with Apostolic Anointing to carry on the ministry of making disciples all nations. I am also convinced that God is raising PRINCIPLE OF 12 churches for such purposes. God uses the ministry of PRINCIPLE OF 12. Frankly, PRINCIPLE OF 12 may be the solution God will use for the fulfillment of our endtime commission. No one knows. I cannot be certain. However, I am certain for now that the leadership of the

Senior Minister is of vital importance.

    The spiritual atmosphere of the church is also important. It is closely related to the role and function of the senior pastor. The senior pastor's development of the right spiritual atmosphere is a vital factor. The spiritual atmosphere of the church is especially important when a church is transitioning into a new structure or a new ministry system. I like to use the expression, "Church is led by atmosphere." If the church is made up of the elder board, then the church is run by the elder board. If the church is composed by the vision, direction and strategy of the senior pastor, then the church is led by the senior pastor. This truth is very important. What type of atmosphere does the elder board create? What spiritual atmosphere is the senior pastor helping to anchor? These are the core factors that determine the future and the direction of the church. There are churches that are stagnant and churches that are future-oriented. The Senior Pastor can continue on with creative ministry when he does not settle into the comfort zone of the present. God moves forward, without ceasing. God wants to share his creative ideas with us, at every hour, at every season. God hates tradition. God continues to create new things by transforming the outer appearance, while retaining the core base of the gospel. This gives us joy. One of the reasons why I am so fascinated with God is that He continues to create anew. I also like to experience transformation in my life. Are you stagnant or future-oriented? This is an important question. Is your church under a Maintenance System or a Multiplication System?

Are all your efforts spent on maintaining the church members or does your church have a passion to see your members grow explosively? According to your answers, systems can experience change. Depending on the vision, strategy and direction, the church can change 100%.

The growth process of our church was not an easy one by any means. People in our community heard of Jesus for the very first time. You may think that they would be completely loyal and obedient to my leadership, because I'm their spiritual father. However, I have had my share of difficulties. These people love culture. The Kazak People were under the rule and domination of Russia. One characteristic of all ex-satellite nations of the Soviet Union is the love books. Whether they are on a train or a bus, they always have a book in their hand. It takes about 8 hours to go from Moscow to St. Petersburg by train. Russians stay awake the entire journey reading books. They cherish their culture. However, the biggest difficulty with the Kazak people is that they do not open their hearts. They lived under fear of being expelled by the communist party, so they do not express their intentions openly. Some people say, "It must be easy for them to open their hearts because they are simple people." Nothing could be further from the truth. Russia is famous for Matryshka, or nesting dolls. Open one, and there is a smaller one inside. Open that and another one comes out, and so on. These dolls depict well the complexity of Russians. You can peel off layer after layer but you'll never know their true intentions or thoughts.

Russians were not always like this. Years of oppression under the communist regime closed their hearts and destroyed their marriages. 70% of their marriages experienced failure. Due to this, the next generation of families will also fail due to the breakdown of the family structure. They lost faith in their parents, so they don't have any faith in each other. They do not open their hearts to anyone. This is why their cultural and sociological background is tailor made for PRINCIPLE OF 12. PRINCIPLE OF 12 is impossible in the midst of a closed-hearted community. However, I came to observe the fact that people are hungry to find the archetype of man created by God, especially in a society needing inner healing in the midst of all their brokenness, despair and unbelief. Because a man is created in God's own image, we all have a longing to discover our original image, no matter how badly our lives have been broken. However, human beings were designed by God to desire a life that enables him to love, trust, restore relationships, become united, live in the midst of a vision, be creative, and to be positive. I proclaim such things endlessly. As a result, I discovered that the church members began to open their hearts. So again, I must reiterate that the senior's minister's determination is important. The direction of the church changes based on what the leader presents to the congregation.

3 Stages of Church Growth

As mentioned earlier, there are three stafes of church growth. They are: a traditional church, a cell church, and a

PRINCIPLE OF 12 church. Many growing churches naturally follow this progression. It would be good to start as a PRINCIPLE OF 12 church, but this is an difficult task for a many. Even in God's model, God used Moses to lead the people out of Egypt. After many conflicts surfaced, He created a cell system. Finally, He organized a PRINCIPLE OF 12 army structure. When Jesus started his ministry, he did not start by choosing the twelve disciples. He started by proclaiming his messages, healing and delivering people, and performing miracles. When many people began to follow him, he chose his twelve disciples for a new ministry out of the crowd of followers. Many churches, whether they are in the mode of a traditional church or a cell church, must go through these stages in order to develop into a PRINCIPLE OF 12 church.

Characteristics of a Traditional Church

Obviously, not every traditional church can be categorized under this definition. However, generally, the traditional churches are mostly seeking to maintain the status quo. They are Maintenance Oriented, and often stagnant. Their cells exist to maintain the members and most are focused on church programs such as special morning prayer, bible studies, etc. The programs exist to keep the remaining church members content, rather than looking for ways to facilitate revival and to evangelize the lost.[3] Because most of

---

[3] The author realizes this is a description of stereotypical traditional churches. Many traditional churches are growing, but do so primarily through transfer growth.

these programs are bent on maintaining the status quo, most church members have a mind set of "I need to go to church for..." Today's church members are experiencing a loss of passion for the church because they experience a lack of spiritual formation in their lives. Many church members are discovering that their own church falls short of what they are searching for such as anointing, passion, hunger for the presence and work of God.

The key is for churches to receive a fresh vision and direction from God through prayer and by moving into the realm of God's anointing and presence, rather than becoming satisfied with the status quo. If your church is in this situation, you are likely still in the first stage of a traditional church.

Secondly, a traditional church is bound by the institution they are affiliated with. Often, a deacon or an elder's board works to frustrate a pastor who has fresh vision, just by the sheer makeup of the hierarchy. In such cases, the pastor has difficulty implementing and following through with his vision. Therefore, he becomes incredibly discouraged to the point that he is ineffective or he ends up leaving the church. The problem is that church members with vision end up leaving because they feel restricted and bound by tradition, by the way things have always been done.

When I was visiting different churches worldwide, I heard on many occasions that dedicated members were leaving their churches because their pastors lacked vision. This is unfortunate. This is causecd by a reliance on the institution of church and therefore we feel restricted, lacking freedom to follow God where He is working. We must do our very best to be set free from such bondage. We need to be a church that is alive and vibrant, not one whose faith is in the organization itself, instead of the living God. We need to be a church that moves forward, overcoming mistakes and financial difficulties. Such churches will experience the activation and growth of church and its members.

Thirdly, a traditional church is marked by a lack of vision. A traditional church is not future-oriented but remains in its comfort zone. Many Korean churches experienced powerful spiritual movements, but have also become stagnant, remaining in a traditional mode.

When a church experiences a spiritual truth, the church must move forward, embracing newly discovered truths. Unfortunately, most churches are satisfied with the present and choose to remain there. If the church is not able to continuously cast new vision, members with vision will leave the church. They know that God is a God who endlessly creates new vision for us. If you can take this truth to heart, it will help your ministry significantly. Borrowing an over used expression; lack of vision can be defined as a "church without purpose." Church members, who do not know the direction of the church, simply lend their bodies. They merely attend worship services, which leads to legalistic church attendance on Sundays. There is no goal of saving souls. There is no vision to break the stronghold on the city to bring revival. There is no dream to evangelize to the nation. They have no hope for world missions. There is no confession from church members saying, "This is it. This is the image of church in its essence. This is true church. I am willing to bet my life on it. I am willing to invest my time and finances."

On the other hand, many churches are making vision statements, borrowing them from leading churches in America. In most cases, because they don't have a personal vision, they end up with a vision statement but no real vision. As a result, the church members think that their church has a vision. Vision is received from the Lord when we seek his will. Every church is to have a vision that is tailor made just for them. You must not move before God gives you a vision. The hearts of the members begin to beat the moment you proclaim God's vision received in faith. The church of God begins to come alive at that moment. Otherwise, the church will revert back to being a traditional church.

Fourthly, a traditional church is program oriented. A traditional church has a need for programs but doesn't have a goal or direction. Programs are needed but without a goal, programs become meaningless. A program follows another program but there is no tangible fruit such as making disciples. In order to overcome such difficulty, the key phrase must be "ministry with a focus." Leaders must help the church members to become immersed in the same vision of God through continued repetition. This is what causes a church to be a church. This is what causes a church to become a part of the army of God. If not, countless programs, seminars, and bible studies only increase church members' capacity for criticism. There is no devotion. As a result, they don't know how to evangelize and they don't know how to nurture. The reason for lack of nurturing among Christians is due to confusion. Even senior pastors are confused after having so many programs and seminars. We need focused nurturing and focused ministry. We must dig one deep well, until water gushes forth. Dig until you can see fruit. If not, you will remain as a traditional church, satisfied with maintaining the status quo.

Fifth, a traditional church relies on its senior minister's sermon making ability. If a church is relying solely on the sermon of its senior pastor, then the lay ministry of that church has not been activated. Even at my church, many people call the church asking who will be giving the message when I'm traveling. The attendance goes down when I'm not speaking. The offering drops significantly as well. That is why I don't leave the church without casting God's vision. I try to go only where there is vision. These days, even when I'm traveling out of sheer necessity, people are being blessed more by the sermons of my 12 disciples or my wives 12 female disciples, as when I preach. I am so thankful. In the beginning stages, my disciples preached out of knowledge and not of the Spirit. Now, feedback tells me that people are deeply blessed by their sermons. This fills my heart with joy. What greater blessing is there than to see disciples who are just like you? The blessings and rewards for the senior pastor in heaven will come from this. That is why Jesus was faithful to his twelve disciples' and they multiplied twelve-fold.

In a traditional church, the church members remain as

spectators. Instead of joining in ministry, they end up passively filling seats. Even if there is ministry for the lay people, there is no sense of ownership. They absolutely cannot voluntarily join in ministry because it is a church with hands and feet without leadership.

Lastly, a traditional church is isolated from society. A traditional church is very defensive. Legalism causes high walls to be built. There is no ministry that infiltrates the depths of society. A traditional church rarely learns Christianity as a way of life. It is very restrictive. Such loss of contact and relevancy with society limits Christians from actively ministering and evangelizing the world. These are the general characteristics of a traditional church.

Characteristics of a Cell Church

It is important to understand the cell church model. A cell church has many special traits. First of all, it has the mandate of edification. Cell church can be defined as "edification in relationship." On the other hand, to express PRINCIPLE OF 12 in another way, it would be "commitment in relationship." It is a picture of church requiring devotion within relationships. This is the difference between edification and commitment. We must have the ultimate goal of edifying one another in relationship, or moving beyond it to train, rebuke,[4] and equip them to be devoted followers of Jesus

---

[4] Rebuke does not mean punish, but to correct for the benefit of the disciple and the mission.

Christ. The difference lies in whether the character of the church is strong or weak.

Secondly, it is the activation of the lay ministry. Cell church is about the activation of lay people through small groups. On a smaller scale, it can be defined as small group discipleship or small group movement. This is the end result of the discipleship movement, once popularized by para-church organizations. In this model, small group discipleship tends to remain as a small group focusing on various curriculum based bible studies. As a result, lay leaders serve as ministers, not with a sense of ownership, but with an attitude of an employee. In such cases, there can be too many reporting structures. The cell church has many advantages over a traditional church. The fact that all members can have their own ministry is an obvious advantage, thus all churches should go through this process.

Thirdly, it requires anointed leaders. When a church uses the title "Zone Church," it requires all members of the church to belong and function within the zone groups. However, a traditional church with only the cell system, where not all members are required to be part of the zone district, cannot be called a pure cell church. That is, a cell church must have every member belong to the zone district. The senior pastor casts vision and gives direction to the church through Sunday sermons. Other lay leaders serve to fulfill the role of spreading the vision of the anointed senior pastor. In that sense, the cell church is highly upgraded from the traditional church. It is a church with good soil, where lay members can minister, use their gifts and live out their calling, at least within the context of their small groups.

The fourth characteristic is that cell church moves with the vision. Cell churches usually have similar visions. The vision is to restore the original essence of Christianity through fellowship of the saints. Cell churches srongly present vision and direction. They even begin to take on the appearance of a full-fledged church that infiltrates, co-exists, and transforms society. Not only that, but a cell church seeks growth through doubling. It is a model that seeks church growth through continuous multiplication.

Characteristics of a PRINCIPLE OF 12 Church

The traits of a PRINCIPLE OF 12 church are as follows:

First, a PRINCIPLE OF 12 Church seeks to make lay members into disciples rather than seeking to make them into lay ministers. (Mark 3:13-15) In other words, instead of simply requiring works of edification, a PRINCIPLE OF 12 church requires a higher level of devotion in order to produce true disciples of Jesus who are proactive and have a sense of ownership that allows them to carry on God's ministry.

The second trait of a PRINCIPLE OF 12 church is discipleship through mentoring. (John 17) Relationships are very important in PRINCIPLE OF 12. In the cell church model, due to the multiplication process, pre-existing relationships are broken down through the continuous division of cells. It is difficult because the relationships end as soon as they begin to deepen. Many problems arise because of it. During my 7 years of involvement with the cell church model, I discovered that multiplying actually caused a weakening in both cells. There are cases where the atmosphere of a cell group is quite loving and warm, due to the personality of its leader. In such cases, the atmosphere, then, is the vision for the cell group. For the newly divided cell group with a new leader, members discover the change in atmosphere and philosophy, which usually raises doubts about the new leader's ability. Even the other cell with the existing leader goes through a change in dynamics and sometimes, stagnation, leading to a loss of passion towards evangelism and fellowship. Consequently, both cells are adversely affected.

In order to overcome such obstacles, PRINCIPLE OF 12 must be formed. The transformation in character and life of each member needs to take place through continued relationship and commitment. Mentoring plays a key role here. Mentoring is discipleship. When Jesus called Peter, and further called the twelve disciples, he did not increase the number of the disciples and then divide them into two groups. That was not the model that he used. Rather, he established a lifelong relationship with those 12. When he called his disciples, Jesus basically made them his disciples for life. Who would be the twenty-four elders of John's Revelation- twelve elders of Israel and twelve elders of gentiles? Quite possibly, wouldn't they be the twelve disciples (elders) whom Jesus chose and twelve elders from the gentiles? This signifies a lifelong relationship. Through a lifetime of mentorship, even the deepest areas of our lives can be transformed. Leadership preparation, in a word, is transformation of character. Ministry and anointing must take a backseat. Spirituality of life and spirituality of character has to be the highest priority. In PRINCIPLE OF 12, the collective focus is on the maturation of life and the maturation of the spirituality of the disciple. By asking, "How much transformation took place in my disciple's life? Has my disciple's devotion shown any increase?" We continue to exam and nurture their progress. Afterwards, the anointing of God follows. This is PRINCIPLE OF 12's discipleship through mentoring. A reed like Simon transformed into Peter; the solid rock was formed through the encounter with Jesus. Because Jesus knew this truth, when he first met Peter, he declared, "You are Simon son of John. You will be called Peter." The will of Jesus to transform lives through mentoring was present from the beginning of their encounter. This is the work that transformed Abraham. This is the work that transformed Jacob into Israel. When the Bible speaks of many name changes, the Bible is talking about character transformation. Because Simon's character was not capable of coping with God's apostolic ministry, God wanted to transform the character through the mentoring of Jesus.

Third, a PRINCIPLE OF 12 church has a clear goal of missions as its vision. (Matthew 28:19-20) What is the goal of our ministry? What is our concept of missions? Is the evangelism of other nations the only means to do the work of missions? As we continue to broaden the definition of missions, we can see that expanding the kingdom of God within the confines of the same culture can be considered as missions. There is a huge difference between churches with a specific vision for missions versus a church that seeks to maintain its status quo. A PRINCIPLE OF 12 church firmly establishes the vision for missions as its goal.

Fourth, it is devoted to honest and open relationships. In 2 Timothy 4:2, Paul tells Timothy,

"Preach the Word; be prepared in season and out of season; correct, rebuke and encourage – with great patience and careful instruction."

This is a process of transformation, as a father corrects and rebukes4 his child. Without this type of relationship, one cannot become a disciple. Even Jesus rebuked his twelve disciples when he noticed their lack of faith and corrected them when they displayed wrong motives. Discipleship is impossible without this type of relationship.

Fifth, a PRINCIPLE OF 12 church pursues a Christian lifestyle. A cell church also pursues a similar lifestyle. The early church found in Acts 2:42-47 was praised even by people outside the church. It was due to the fact that people's lives were transformed and they became admirable people, even in the eyes of the general public. One of the most difficult obstacles to overcome when evangelizing is when people say, "I don't want to become a Christian because of such and such Christians…" In other words, many Christians have not incorporated their faith to everyday living. Also, if a cell group is not able to multiply or disbands, 90% of the blame lies with the cell leader. The cell leader's life has not matured. You must mature in quality in order to grow quantitatively. PRINCIPLE OF 12 not only pursues, but also requires such maturity in order for it to be successful.

Sixth, PRINCIPLE OF 12 enables a group to have team ministry. This is a very important concept. Only when twelve disciples are formed, when these 12 specific people have been given to me, can the team ministry in the truest sense begin. Before the establishment of the twelve disciples, groups keep forming. Groups can form anytime a need arises, but such groups cannot develop into devoted long-lasting relationships. One's gifting cannot be developed through individual ministries. Gifts are not developed through seminars but they are developed through team ministry. Gifts are developed through the continued team ministry of twelve disciples.

The leader and disciple discover together who has the gift of preaching, who has the gift of teaching, and who has the gift of healing as they minister together as a team. Thus, the gifts are developed in the truest sense. Once each of the twelve disciples has developed their gifts, they become a ministry team with apostolic anointing that produces an explosive change into local and greater parts of society.

Seventh, a PRINCIPLE OF 12 church is established within the context of society. A PRINCIPLE OF 12 church can effectively infiltrate deep into society through its team ministry. Ministry takes place in the midst of everyday life. My church has an Alpha Course team deployed into every part of society, like a spider's web or octopus tentacles. We have Hospital Alpha, Market Alpha, Bank Alpha, and School Alpha. We even have Alpha for senior citizens. After seeing positive results and changes in people, the city hall has requested that we hold Alpha courses at their offices. We take the Alpha courses deep into every segment of society, turning non-believers into Christians. Then we gather them into a cell group. Once in a cell group, we help to transform them into devoted disciples. We systematically repeat this process.

Lastly, it is about explosive growth through the multiplication of 12. Most mission organizations follow the process of one to one relationship, which doubles in number. However, through the PRINCIPLE OF 12 system of 12 disciples, explosive growth takes place by the multiplication of 12. This may seem difficult but once the twelve is established, the dynamics within the team wields explosive power. Once you experience such power, you also want to form your own team of disciples as well. Therefore, the team exponentially becomes 144. It is not about a mathematical formula but the power of forming your own team with a common and clear vision. You can truly have the power of an army, through the implementation of the Principle of 12.

7 basic principles of PRINCIPLE OF 12 Ministry

All over the world, the PRINCIPLE OF 12 ministry utilizes the same principles. It may be a difficult concept to understand initially but in the midst of ministry, you will discover that the principles are the most important.

PRINCIPLE OF 12 is established through the following principles. The most common question asked is "How do you select the twelve disciples? How can cells grow explosively?"

The first basic principle of PRINCIPLE OF 12 ministry is that everyone is a potential leader. This is a core principle. Because we are created in the image of God, we are all potential leaders. We are not created in the image of apes. We do not believe in evolution. We believe in the God of creation. We are made in the image of God. That means the image of God is within us. The fact that the image of God is within us means that tremendous potential for leadership is hidden in us. The only problem is that our own self-worth and identity have been torn down due to the wounds and scars we've received from Satan. If we can restore them, if we can retrieve and develop the potential within us by restoring the broken self image, anyone can become a leader for God. But, it will take time to heal. It all depends on how deep the wound is or what kind of distorted self-image one may have. By the mighty power of the Holy Spirit, anyone can be restored into a leader. David's greatness lies in the fact that he turned all the wounded and failed people who came to him into great warriors. 1 Samuel 22:1-2 records this;

> *"David left Gath and escaped to the cave of Adullam. When his brothers and his father's household heard about it, they went down to him there. All those who were in distress or in debt or discontented gathered around him, and he became their leader. About four hundred men were with him." (1 Sam. 22:1, 2)*

David fled from Saul to the cave of Adullam. This is why I like to use the expression, "The Leadership School of the Cave of Adullam." If we are to examine the people who came to David, they were, "those who were in distress or in debt or discontented" people. These are the people who were severely wounded by the world. These were people who experienced despair in the world and the Bible tells us that he became their leader. David became their mentor. There were about four hundred men, and through them David united all the tribes of Israel and Judah. According to worldly standards, the men who came to David had some severe deficits. This included a lack of education and serious debt, resulting in a sense of failure and despair. However, David was able to transform them into mighty warriors. David had the ability to transform and unite all Israel into a nation of vision. David's ability came from God. As we all know, David himself did not have such abilities. God chose and gifted him because of David's vision and courage to rely only on God. As a result, the four hundred who were in distress, in debt or discontented also transformed into similar leaders. In other words, everyone has leadership potential.

The truth is, troublemakers have greater potential. They simply do not allow society to dictate their behavior. They do not follow norms just for the sake of following. That is why they cause trouble. We must be able to discover their potential and develop them, instead of looking only at external issues. This is the basic picture of the PRINCIPLE OF 12 ministry. In order to develop their potential, first leaders must being healing to their wounds. We have to help them experience God on a personal level so that He can heal their brokenness. Then we must impart to them God's vision and help them to be filled with the Holy Spirit.

In summary, every potential leader needs deep repentance, healing of wounds, a personal experience with God, a filling of the Holy Spirit, and casting of the vision of God. These 5 factors are crucial. Then, no matter how fragile and wounded a soul may be, they can become great for God and fulfill a purpose in His Kingdom. Many people, who gather at church, though they may not express it outwardly, live a life of despair and woundedness. Divorce, marital conflicts, and a damaged self image must be rehabilitated within the church. Instead of simply being rehabilitated, the people must be transformed, becoming able to live a life of new vision. This is the most important part of our ministry.

To help us accomplish this calling, God built His church, poured out his Holy Spirit, and gave us new vision. Thus, God caused the church to become an organism that infiltrates and transforms society. This is why it is so important to recognize that everyone has God-given potential for leadership. From the moment of this realization, the church will begin to experience explosive growth. From that moment on, the senior pastor's perspective on people will begin to change. What God's people must realize is the fact that their senior pastor possesses incredible potential. It may be merely being frustrated at the moment. It may be frustrated due to the church system or the haunting memories of past failures. Knowledge does not make someone into a great leader.

As the hidden potential and giftings are developed, as the leaders receive healing, as the leadership team is developed, the senior pastors of the local church can become powerful visionaries. This generation needs desperate intercession for its people. Intercession rather than complaining about a pastor makes the church move forward unimpeded. The reason why I am being used as God's vessel, the reason why I can minister through the strong anointing of God is because my twelve disciples are praying for me with passion. Each of my twelve disciples, along with their twelve disciples pray for me throughout the night when I minister. This is where my power comes from. This is why I don't want to disappoint them. This is why I beat my body to submission. This is why I hunger to cast new vision and new anointing. When the church members become passionate, the senior pastor will be transformed. I pray that your church's spiritual atmosphere will be transformed through your prayers. I pray that the amazing potential hidden in your senior pastor's soul can be developed.

The second basic principle of PRINCIPLE OF 12 ministry is that anyone can make disciples. Someone may have had a dream of making thousands of disciples, but this is not realistic. Jesus determined that the optimum number of disciples for the expansion of His kingdom was 12. Jesus did not choose 11 or 13 disciples but he chose 12, because there is a certain dynamic within the number.[5]

In Acts 1, after the death of Judas Iscariot, they did not leave his spot void, but they restored the twelve apostles by selecting Matthias. The number is important. When the twelve disciples are determined, their level of devotion to the leader will also deepen. Though not everyone can make 12 disciples, this is the goal for my disciples. Then explosive, exponential growth begins. Every believer's ultimate goal is to make twelve disciples by evangelizing twelve people. Because you are the one that leads them to Christ, you are able to strongly impart to them the vision and anointing. You would be the person who makes the strongest impression and impact.

Third, everyone ministers and everyone is ministered to. One person makes twelve disciples. I have twelve male disciples. Then, each of my twelve disciples also chooses their twelve. My twelve disciples receive the impartation of the anointing through me and they receive the word. They learn to become sensitive to the voice of the Holy Spirit through me and their lives are transformed. Because they impart to their disciples what I've imparted to them, they can continue to receive and impart simultaneously. They don't merely receive like the Dead Sea, but they receive and give like the Sea of Galilee, maintaining a fresh spiritual state. In most cases, the saints are in the state of spiritual stagnation. They take in volumes but they have no one to pass on the manna to.

---

[5] Not all can develop 12, but all can develop some, according to gifting and the measure of faith.

Their knowledge increases, often becoming critical; but their lives remain unchanged. The word of God truly becomes my own not when I receive and understand the word, but when I begin to share that word with others. That is when you are able to have a responsible teaching ministry.

This principle of PRINCIPLE OF 12 allows everyone to minister and be ministered to. It's important to teach what you have learned. Apostle Paul told Timothy, "Teach what you have learned to the faithful." The same basic principle applies here. I carry on the ministry of choosing my disciples and teaching them the right way as Jesus chose his twelve disciples. This enables the discipleship ministry to make an impact through out the generations. The first generation has 12, and the second generation has 144. The third generation has 1728, etc. Theoretically speaking, a PRINCIPLE OF 12 church can have exponential growth as they follow the principles presented here. The true significance of such multiplication enables the church to have a channel and system of impartation; the pastor imparts to his disciples, and then the disciples impart to their disciples, and so on and so on. In that sense, the PRINCIPLE OF 12 ministry has a strong impartation effect.

Fourth, only those who start "Open Cell" can belong to the twelve disciples. We consider fruit to be very important. Even Jesus said, "You will know them by their fruit." We're talking about two types of fruit here. First is the fruit of life; it is the fruit of character. Secondly, if there is fruit in the quality of life, then there must be quantitative fruit. People are drawn to a leader with character and leadership skills. There is no doubt about it. It is a risky proposition to use someone as a minister simply because they have graduated from a seminary.

A few years ago, Grace Seminary in Moscow was founded. During the first 3-4 years, we sent about 100 people to the seminary. When they graduated, we brought them back to our church to try and use them as ministers. Unfortunately, out of those 100 people, none of them knew what ministry was all about. Out of the 100 people who were trained, we now have only 1 who is serving with us as a minister. I'm not being critical. I am being realistic. I have seen other missionaries from other regions use the graduates from the seminary to plant churches and serve as pastors. I also wanted to do the same. However, I was determined to see their fruit first. "You are not pastors yet. Open a cell first. Produce some fruit. If you are faithful with little things, God will put you in charge of many things. You will automatically walk the path of a pastor when your ministry begins to bear fruit. Your diploma does not make you a functional minister," I insisted. After a few years, I was able to see with my own eyes lives of true Christians fostering vital ministries that bore much fruit. The motto of our church has become, "If anyone wants to be a pastor, he must personally show forth fruit."

The church must construct a system to form cell groups. Such training and a nurturing system must be divided into four stages. The first stage is the Win stage, where an unbeliever becomes a believer. The second stage is

Connect, helping believers to remain in faith. The third stage is Training, where the believer is made into a disciple. The fourth stage is Send, where all believers are sent into their own ministries where they themselves Win, Connect, Train and Send. Through these four stages, everyone must be given opportunities to serve. The person who has gone through all four stages and opens a cell group can become a true disciple. This is an important principle of PRINCIPLE OF 12.

Fifth, everyone must save souls and develop the hidden leader within them. If unbelievers do not come into the church through evangelism, leaders cannot be made. If leaders aren't being made, the church cannot grow. The ultimate goal of church is to save souls. However, too many churches concentrate solely on saving souls. Some churches strive to save souls but do not make disciples. Some churches have discipleship but do not evangelize. Both churches are crippled. They cannot become healthy in the long run. There must be a program to make disciples out of newly born Christians. We ask all our church members to pray for three unbelievers at all times. People don't pray when they are told to just pray for unbelievers. People don't pray when you ask them to pray for too many people. So we started the Prayer of Three movement. We started to pray for 3 unbelievers at all times and at every gathering. I like the word "movement" because if something does not become a movement or a lifestyle, people don't seem to persevere through it. There is no benefit in general programs. Even the smallest things can bear fruit if it can become a movement or part of your lifestyle.

That is why we always pray for 3 unbelievers at our church. The key here is not just to pray that they would be saved but to pray that they'd become your disciples. There is a major difference in simply praying for someone's salvation versus praying to make someone into your disciple. When we simply pray for salvation, we feel relieved to see them sitting in the church pews. We stop the prayer for them thinking that our job is done. However, if they face trials and tribulations before their faith is Connectd or have become disciples, they fall away. It is because they have not yet become disciples. This is why I ask you not to let your guard down until the three people have become your disciples; they join a cell group and start their own ministry. Why? When they open a cell group, they will have a teacher. To have a teacher means that a relationship has been established. To have an established relationship means that the teacher will not give up on the disciple. This person will become the focus of the teacher's interest and training. This is why only those who open a cell can become a disciple. The teacher and disciple relationship is established the moment a cell group is opened.

Sixth, cells are best planted through homogenous grouping. These cells can be described as homogenous and/or same gender groups. Men gather with men and women gather with women or people with the same vocation gather together. For example, if a doctor of a large hospital receives a calling from God to make disciples of all the doctors in the hospital, then he can proceed with a vision to make disciples of the doctors within the homogenous group of doctors. Grace church is not actively pursuing cell groups of the same vocation at the moment. However, we have four basic ministry groups consisting of male, female, youth, and children. We call it Network; Men's-Network; Women's-Network; Youth-Network; Children-Network. The visible effects of gathering together within the same age group or same gender through these four Networks are excellent. If male and female coexist, either the male will hide behind the females or vice versa. In the Asian culture, there is a tendency for women to hide behind men. However, in central Asia, it is exactly the opposite. Women's power is very strong. It is because many men were killed during the era of Stalin and more men died during the Afghan war. Further more, most men are either alcoholics or drug addicts. There is a vacuum of male leadership. As a result, women have taken their place of power as principals, businesswomen and bus drivers. Many husbands even complain about spousal abuse. Even with in cell groups, because the women out number the men by the ratio of 8:2 or 9:1, men tend not to participate in specific ministries. Rather, they simply attend services while criticizing the church. These men must be involved in ministries. Last year, we opened one cell for men for the very first time. Now we have about 70 cells for men. As a result, the men begin to resolve in their hearts "We must restore the family. God ordained men as the head of the family but the families have been destroyed because the men failed to play their part. Men must take on the responsibility of the society." This is the direct effect of Homogenous group. In a mixed group, both genders find it difficult to be transparent. Cell groups can grow at a fast rate when the genders are separated.

The seventh basic principle is that your twelve disciples will become your supporters, becoming one ministry team. The reason people experience difficulty in team ministry is because of the lack of devoted relationships and ministry without respected mentors. The result is disappointment. The team ministry Jesus had in mind was a ministry of twelve disciples with Jesus as the central figure. It was not a team ministry without the involvement of Jesus, nor one in which the disciples had specialized tasks such as preaching, administration, etc. That kind of ministry would lead to failure. The biblical principle is for a group to have one primary leader. God led his people out of Egypt through one leader; Moses. God governed his people through one leader; David. God used one apostle named Paul to evangelize the Gentiles. Even today, God's great dream and vision are accomplished through a team of twelve disciples and one anointed leader with a vision. Yet, one leader cannot do all things. The one who casts the vision is the leader. Thus, a leader must become a man of vision. The church becomes healthy and the team ministry grows stronger when the twelve disciples become the hands and feet which help achieve that vision of the leader.

These days there is much talk about about mentoring. In Western society, there is a tendency to misunderstand mentorship. When Jesus was mentoring his twelve disciples, he was not a counselor who helped them with their problems via a telephone call every once in a while. There was consistent relationship. They shared their lives together. Jesus knew the characters and hidden motives of the disciples. He also knew what their goals were. That is why he was able to transform their lives. A true mentor is someone who can share life. Only then can true disciples be made in the PRINCIPLE OF 12 ministry. I pray you can find such mentors. Everyone must have a mentor. However, today's generation hates mentors. Yet, without mentors, your lives will not be transformed. Without transformation of your lives, God's anointing will never flow. Even if the anointing comes, it will not last long. It is because there is no umbrella to cover you and there is no true mentor to correctly guide you. It is because there is no father like teachers. Apostle Paul wrote in 1 Corinthians, "Even though you have ten thousand guardians in Christ, you do not have many fathers." We are experiencing the same phenomenon today. Everyone must have a spiritual teacher, a father like teacher. Also, everyone must have their own disciples who are like spiritual children. Only then can the outpouring of the gifting and calling of God be maximized.

Part 2:
Biblical Background of PRINCIPLE OF 12 Church

Chapter 2:
Government Order of the Kingdom of God
(Matt. 9: 35-10: 8)

Introduction

We must learn the vision, strategy and purpose of Jesus. We must follow the ministry model of Jesus who ministered to multitudes. We desire to see the works of Jesus again. In John 14th through 16th, as he was speaking about the Holy Spirit, Jesus said, "He will do even greater things than these, because I am going to the Father." Jesus promised that when the Holy Spirit comes upon us, we will receive power and we would be able to do the works of Jesus, even greater works than Jesus would. Therefore, we have confidence that we can do the same and even greater works of the apostles. As long as the Holy Spirit exists (which is of course, eternally), this ministry must continue. It must be restored through us. This model is depicted in the following verses:

> *Jesus went through all the towns and villages, teaching in their synagogues, preaching the good news of the kingdom and healing every disease and sickness. When he saw the crowds, he had compassion on them, because they were harassed and helpless, like sheep without a shepherd. Then he*

said to his disciples. "The harvest is plentiful but the workers are few. Ask the Lord of the harvest, therefore, to send out workers into his harvest field." He called his twelve disciples to him and gave them authority to drive out evil spirits and to heal every disease and sickness. These are the names of the twelve apostles: first, Simon (who is called Peter) and his brother Andrew; James son of Zebedee, and his brother John; Philip and Bartholomew; Thomas and Matthew the tax collector; James son of Alphaeus, and Thaddaeus; Simon the Zealot and Judas Iscariot, who betrayed him. These twelve Jesus sent out with the following instructions: "Do not go among the Gentiles or enter any town of the Samaritans. Go rather to the lost sheep of Israel. As you go, preach this message 'The kingdom of heaven[6] is near.' Heal the sick, raise the dead, cleanse those who have leprosy, drive out demons. Freely you have received, freely give. (Matthew 9:35-10:8)

A God given Vision

The ministry of God must have clear vision and strategy. Vision points to a direction and a strategy. A person without vision is like the blind walking without anyone to guide him. God is the one who gives us vision.6 Chapters 14 - 16 of John and Acts 1:8 present the ministry of the Holy Spirit. The scriptures teach us who the Holy Spirit is. In Acts 2:17-18,

---

[6] See Dr. DeKoven's book, *That's the Kingdom of God,* Vision Publishing.

the Bible tells us, "In the last days, God says, I will pour out my Spirit on all people," and "Even on my servants, both men and women, I will pour out my Spirit in those days." Why does God want us to be filled with the Holy Spirit? For what purpose is God pouring out the Holy Spirit? It is to prophecy, to dream and to see visions. If this is true, what kinds of prophecies, visions and dreams should we expect to experience? It is the vision of expanding the kingdom of God[7] during the last days. It is a vision to see all cities come under the Lordship of Christ. It is a vision to see a whole nation come to serve the Lord. Amazingly, this vision is given especially to newly born-again believers. Everyone is to receive this vision, without exception. It states, "In the last days, God says, I will pour out my Spirit on all people. Your sons and daughters will prophesy, your young men will see visions, your old men will dream dreams." What do these visions and dreams speak of? They speak of the future. They speak of direction. With vision, a person begins to find direction and purpose. If you can cry out, "God, you have given me this vision. What must I do? With what purpose must I go out?" God will grant you vision and a strategy to accomplish his will. At times, God uses our talents to fulfill the vision. In the Bible, God presents an incredible strategy.

Preparation for More

I was led to do a fast in 1995. Shortly before the fast,

---

[7] For more on Vision, see Dr. DeKoven's book, *Catch the Vision: Getting a Vision for Life and Ministry,* Vision Publishing.

our church was able to acquire a kindergarten building for a grand sum of $450,000. I was filled with such gratitude. I prayed to God saying, "God, what do you want me to do? I came here with empty hands yet you fill me with so many blessings. Just tell me what to do and I will obey." I was quite weary then, but God asked me to fast for a season. The following week I started a fast for 40 days at a prayer mountain in Korea. During the fast, God spoke to me, "Transform the consciousness of the people of Kazhastan and the people of central Asia within the Silk road."

As I heard God's voice, I responded by saying, "Thank you," in my prayer. I did not fully understand what that command or vision meant.

However, after returning to my mission field in 1995, I began to cast this vision through the Sunday sermons and at every gathering. The congregation did not seem to comprehend the message, which was no surprise; I did not understand it either. It was as if I was throwing eggs at a rock. However, I had faith that if you throw eggs at a rock a million times over, the rock will break. In order for God to work, one needs determination and faith that will not waver. At this point, the Enemy tried desperately to render God's vision powerless. Unless we go forward with unwavering faith, Satan will try to bring disappointment and discouragement. After striking the rock with eggs countless times, the rock began to break. The wall behind our church is 42 meters long. Two years ago, we drew a map of the Silk Road. After every Sunday service, each member of our church would go to the back of the church to pray for the Silk Road. I would say, "This is our land. God has given this region to us. Every member of this church must visit Turkey in your lifetime. Go there and intercede for Turkey. If you have resources, give your resources for Turkey. I cannot stop until I see the salvation of the nation of Turkey. The fact that only 2000 people out of 70 million people are believers is truly heartbreaking. We must reclaim the land lost to Satan." With that, the rock began to break. A countless number of people started to dedicate themselves to this vision.

The average salary of the people is about $100 a month. As a divine response, five of my members brought $1000 and $5000, asking to use it for Turkey. A woman brought $100 in an envelope. She was not well dressed and she obviously was not rich. She was living paycheck to paycheck. Yet, she brought $100 in an envelope. "What money is this?" I asked. "Pastor, didn't you ask us to give towards missions? As I was praying, the Holy Spirit put it on my heart to give. I want to have my treasure in heaven," she said. "Thank you," I replied and I tearfully prayed for her. This is vision. Vision has the power to move people. Vision gives faith to people. People without vision are people without faith.

The Bible talks about two kinds of faith. First is the faith in Jesus Christ, which leads to salvation. One needs this type of faith to be saved. If you pray to Jesus after receiving such faith that leads to salvation, the Holy Spirit will give you dreams and visions. The vision gives birth to second faith. A passion arises in one's heart to continue God's great works and to accomplish his purposes. We can do new and dynamic work through such passionate faith. If you do not have a vision, you do not have faith. Further, faith without purpose is dead. If one has a sense of purpose, he begins to have faith to accomplish this purpose. He does not back peddle. He does not mind giving of his resources. He runs forward, even when weary. He has faith to make his vision a reality, even if it means giving up his life.

Vision and Strategy

Vision gives birth to faith. However, with vision alone, it is easy to fail. You must seek a strategy from the Lord. You must understand the strategy that God is showing you. The strategy of Jesus was and is to build a team. The strategy of Jesus is to deliver his anointing and his vision through the generations. The vision of Jesus is to make disciples of all nations. It is not simply evangelism, but rather the making disciples of every nation as he commanded in Matthew 28:19-20. Such desperate passion was in the heart of Jesus. Jesus shared that passion with the multitudes but, he knew that they were not able to receive it. That is why he chose the twelve disciples. Matthew 9:35 reads, "Jesus went through all the towns and villages, teaching in their synagogues, preaching the good news of the kingdom and healing every disease and sickness." His ministry was to look after the people. He healed multitudes. He healed their diseases and proclaimed the gospel. The ministry of Jesus is of the utmost importance and must be continued.

Motive of Ministry

"He saw the crowds; he had compassion on them, because they were harassed and helpless, like sheep without a shepherd." (Matthew 9:36)

After seeing the crowds, he had compassion on them. Compassion alone is not enough; however, the vision of Jesus starts with compassion. Vision begins by looking after the needs of the people. The Father's heart began to touch Jesus' heart. At first, he saw their outer appearance. Then he looked at them the second time and saw their spiritual condition; he saw something else.

"Because they were harassed and helpless, like sheep without a shepherd."

He did not just see the crowd, but He saw that they were lost and wandering. We must have such compassion. Compassion came to Jesus the moment he saw the crowds. He saw that they were lost. We must also have a heart of compassion and pity. Yet, we cannot stop there. We must go to a deeper level. When Jesus saw them, He did not simply note the fact that they were lost, but he noticed that they were without a shepherd. Why are they harassed and helpless? They are wandering because they are without a shepherd.

During the days of Jesus there were many religious leaders including Sadducees, Pharisees, and members of the Sanhedrin council. However, in Jesus' eyes, they were not shepherds. In other words, there were leaders and teachers but no fathers. That is the reason the sheep were harassed and helpless. Jesus saw the need for shepherds, not leaders, not proclaimers of the Word, or even healers. They needed shepherds. Then what is the vision of Jesus? His vision is to prepare shepherds. He wants to raise up compassionate shepherds who will not leave harassed and helpless sheep alone.

Shepherd Training

How shall we train shepherds? Should we train them through seminary or through simple Bible studies? Through what process are we to train them? This is the question of strategy. The Church needs strategies. It cannot be accomplished merely through ministry or making disciples. It must be through the strategic making of disciples. The vision of Jesus was not simply to see the nations come to the teacher but to see the nations come to the Father.

> In Malachi 4:6, it is written,
> "He will turn the hearts of the fathers to their children, and the hearts of the children to their fathers; or else I will come and strike the land with a curse."

The important thing is to restore the fathers.[8] There must be father like teachers. A true teacher is someone who will shed tears for God's people, be responsible for their lives, and be sufficiently dedicated and willing to lay down their life for them. A true teacher does not rebuke and reject the relationship at the slightest mistake but rather someone who can nurture and care to the point of mature servant leadership. What parent disowns a child for disobedience? No one acts this way. Jesus saw the need to have compassionate and dedicated shepherds. This was the vision of Jesus. Even though he healed and gave bread to the multitudes, it was not enough. Jesus knew that there was a need for father like shepherds, shepherds who could empathize with the people and minister to them. This is why he chose the twelve disciples. Jesus' answer to the need came through choosing the twelve disciples. His ministry had a focus. He ministered to communicate through the generations. He did not simply preach to the crowds, but concentrated on the twelve. Two-thirds of three and a half years of Jesus' public life were consumed with healings, deliverance and miracles. The rest of the time was spent with his disciples, except for His times of prayer. The crowds were not with Jesus. Jesus was dedicated to the twelve. He was committed, giving His life to them. He was determined to transform their lives by spending time with them.

---

[8] See I Want to Be Like You, Dad: Breaking Generational Patterns, Restoring the Father's Heart, S. DeKoven, Vision Publishing.

His goal was to impart the anointing and vision of Jesus through the generations. The vision cannot be imparted any other way, or He would have ended up with people who only seek ministry. Many churches select associate pastors and interns from people who graduate from seminary. Regardless of this, co-ministers should be people who have the same vision and heart of the senior pastor, because of personal mentorship. This is the only way God's true vision can be imparted through the generations. This is the reason why God's ministry was able to grow explosively, more than twelve times through the twelve disciples. If we were to select 12 disciples and train them starting today we could possibly do the same ministry that Jesus did.

Strategy of Jesus

Why did Jesus choose 12? It is because the impartation of life takes place in small groups. There is no impartation of life among crowds. God's power is able to be imparted and external fruit can be had. However, true transformation of character, personality, motivation and purpose of life will not take place within the context of multitudes. If it does take place, it is extremely rare. Transformation and impartation of life takes place within small groups.

Some leaders may lack skills in key areas. Among my twelve, I have some like that. One is named Alok. He was fired as a chef from a hotel and was in danger of being deported. Our church was able to provide a visa for him and I made him one of my disciples. I did that when I felt that the door to missions in India might open. However, Alok had a very strong personality. He had a strong loyalty to the senior pastor and a passionate love for God; but he rebuked others too often. He tried to change people through harsh rebuke to the point of being legalistic. Therefore, I wondered if he would be able to lead a cell group. I advised him, "Alok, people don't necessarily change through rebuke. You need to be able to discern and look for the right opportunity to speak to them." It was his personality to be somewhat strict and harsh. After seven months, through passion and dedication, his cell multiplied to 24 cells. A common testimony of Alok's disciples was that they all wanted to quit because of Alok's harsh rebukes, but they all came to realize how much Alok loved and prayed for them. They realized that no one had ever loved them as much as Alok, and therefore, decided to stay with him. As a result, they were able to open up cells of their own. We do not have to be perfect. As long as we have passion for God, an umbrella can be formed within the church, and our lives will surely be transformed under that umbrella. If it was not for the twelve-discipleship system, Alok would not have received an impartation of the anointing and he would not have been able to impart his anointing to his disciples. However, under the umbrella of Grace Church, the umbrella of Pastor Sam Seong Kim, and under the umbrella of anointing, Alok was able to raise up 23 cell group leaders, overcoming his weaknesses and shortcomings.

Reason for Selection

Why did Jesus choose 12 disciples? First, life impartation was a key. Second, because there is a predetermined number in scripture. If you were to continually choose people to become disciples, without a predetermined number, you would not be able to share your life with them. The sheer size of your group would prohibit this. A large group would inhibit shared life, thus the disciples would have no sense of purpose and no group to belong to. Once Jesus chose his twelve disciples, he spent his entire life with them. Later, the 70 were added, but they never took the place of the twelve as centrail to Jesus life and mission. A person's transformation comes through prolonged time spent learning with the leader. Therefore, it is not easy to make even twelve disciples. You must be able to develop your own style among different cultures and nationalities.

After 6 months, my disciples asked me, "Pastor, am I your disciple or not?" I answered, "Follow me, believing that you are. There will come a day when I will choose the twelve. I believe that quality produces quantity. When your ministry produces fruit, I will choose my 12 from among them. Even if you are not included among the twelve, do not be discouraged. It may be more beneficial for you to be under the care of one of my disciples than under my care."

If you fear man or try to please everyone, you cannot do God's work. The reason King Saul failed was that he was trying to please the people. Once the twelve are chosen, expect a dynamic encounter to take place. Once the twelve positions are filled, accountability can begin. Without choosing the 12 disciples there is no true dedication or responsibility. Without the selection of the twelve, there is no clarity in relationship or purpose. That is why it is very important to choose the twelve.

The Secret of 12

The foundational priniciple for the establishment of God's government is embodied in the number 12. The church has been founded on the apostles and prophets, Christ being the Chief Cornerstone. But many ask the question, "What does the letter "G" in the G-12 (of course, we use "P" for PRINCIPLE OF 12, but G-12 was the original name) signify? Many people think that it means, "Group of 12". It is true. Some teach that the true meaning is "Government of 12". It means that God's government is accomplished through the 12. When they taught this in Bogotá, Columbia, I had my doubts. I thought to myself, "Why must it be 12? Why not five? In the Bible, there are many important numbers like 4, 70, and many others... but why do they insist on 12?" I began to search the Bible, and found the following principles.

I concluded that the number 12 is very important. God led his nation through 12 tribes during the Old Testament times. In the New Testament, when the New Jerusalem comes down, 12 pillars will support it. Pillars hold up a house. The twelve pillars held up God's Kingdom, called the "New Jerusalem". The fact that Jesus did not choose 3, 4, or 70, but 12 from the multitudes is significant. If you meditate on this, you will realize the significance. During the early church, after Judas Iscariot committed suicide, Matthias filled his place. Why did they insist on filling that twelfth spot? The eleven apostles knew the order of God well. They followed the pattern of Jesus.

God wants to bless this world. His blessings flow through leaders implementing biblical principles within a local context. God blessed Abraham. He gave four amazing blessings: "I will bless you. I will make you into a great nation. I will make your name great. All peoples on earth will be blessed through you." This right to God's blessing was imparted to Isaac. Isaac then passed it on to his son Jacob via the laying on of hands. God gave twelve sons to Jacob and Jacob imparted blessings on them according to their talents and calling. From then on, the Israelites were led by the organization of twelve tribes. This means that God led, reigned, and governed His kingdom through the twelve tribes. During their time in the wilderness, they lacked power to subdue Canaan due to lack of organization. They lacked team ministry. There was no anointing on them. In the wilderness, God reorganized his people through the organization of the army (Numbers 1) because it was impossible to take possession of Canaan without the twelve. Even when they were organized into twelve tribes, they were not able to drive all the people in the land due to lack of vision. (Judges 1) Lack of vision caused destruction of even God's twelve tribes.

Therefore, without God's reigning order, we will not experience the work of God. This is the reason why Jesus shows us his strategy. Possession of Canaan was made possible through military organization. The successful achievement of God's vision is possible when the Kingdom of God is in to order.

The Evangelism Strategy of Jesus

The twelve disciples were Jesus' global evangelism strategy. Many people witnessed the ascension of Jesus in the "Jesus" movie, based on the book of Luke. However, according to Matthew 28: 16-20, only the eleven disciples were present when Jesus was lifted up into heaven. Jesus gave his "Great Commission" to his eleven disciples. Who received Jesus' command to "go and make disciples of all nations"? It was not the crowd, it was not the 70 disciples, it was not 120 followers, but it was the eleven disciples. It is for this very vision Jesus prepared them for three and a half years. Jesus knew that they were to become the channel by which his vision would be imparted. He chose his twelve disciples for this truth, knowing that, once empowered by the Holy Spirit would turn the world upside down for Christ.

In Matthew 16:13-20, Jesus asked His disciples at Caesarea Philippi, "Who do people say the Son of Man is?" The disciples replied, "Some say John the Baptist; others say Elijah; and still others, Jeremiah or one of the prophets." Then Jesus asked his disciples, "Who do you say I am?" In essence, Jesus was asking; "What confession of faith do my disciples have?" He so passionately desired God's Church to have a clear confession of faith. Remember, Jesus concentrated his efforts on the twelve disciples. When Peter answered him confessing, "You are the Christ, the Son of the living God." Jesus replied, "Blessed are you, Simon son of Jonah, for this was not revealed to you by man, but by my Father in heaven." Why did God show this truth to him? It is because Peter walked with Jesus. As he walked with him, he realized the truth about the mystery of God's church in the midst of God's anointing and presence. True confession of faith was birthed in the relationship between Jesus and his twelve disciples. If Jesus only healed and ministered to the crowd, would there have been a clear and accurate confession of faith? How many people are going to church for the sole purpose of healing, or to pray for their children's college entrance exam? This type of faith is very dangerous. For this reason, Jesus chose the twelve disciples so that he could teach them the true meaning of faith and through the twelve, evangelism and discipleship would explode.

Relationship of Jesus' Strategy

PRINCIPLE OF 12 ministry is not a mechanical method for growth. It is not a formula where 12 beget 12 and 12 begets 12 again. Twelve actually becomes 144 disciples, and 144 disciples become 1728, leading to over twenty thousand disciples in the next generation. The purpose of this effort is the formation of Christ's character through relationship. It works because within the context of a small group, all hidden motives are revealed through intense interaction. Hidden motives will never be revealed without nearly constant contact. Life Impartation is impossible without continuous meetings. Someone who truly wants to learn will desire to remain a disciple. Many people do not want others to interfere with their lives. This generation faces many dangers. Many people seem to think that they can do it all; I just need to acquire knowledge and it is all about me. More and more we are witnessing the dehumanization of society. People found it difficult to mention divorce when I left Korea 19 years ago. Nowadays, it seems people find it easy to divorce, period. There is even a trend to stay single. It seems like society is filled with an apathetic and dangerous avoidance of healthy relationships. The Bible presents the principle and need for both natural and spiritual families. Leaders are being called upon to impart true Christian lifestyle and spiritual DNA to their disciples.

The Reason for Grace Church's decision for choosing the PRINCIPLE OF 12 Strategy

There is a reason why our church chose PRINCIPLE OF 12. As I was wondering what specific changes took place in the lives of our church members through PRINCIPLE OF 12, I found two identical testimonies. First, they were able to experience true-life transformation through the PRINCIPLE OF 12 ministry. Secondly, they found their PRINCIPLE OF 12 small group to be the true family that they have always longed for. Many people have said, "I lived a lonely life, even though I had a so called family, but as I became part of a PRINCIPLE OF 12 small group, I found a spiritual family. They care about me, pray for me and keep me accountable. I am now happy and no longer fearful." How wonderful!

We lead unbelievers to church through the Alpha program, teaching them the dynamics of a small group in Christian Life through Alpha's small groups. Through eleven weeks of Alpha, people learn about what it means to live a true Christian life. They discover the true meaning of the gospel as they learn to serve, love and care for each other. They also learn about group dynamics and intimate fellowship. Towards the end of the Alpha program, the leaders and helpers open up new cells with them. We start this way from the beginning. This helps them to transition naturally into a cell as they have already been exposed to small group dynamics through Alpha. Through PRINCIPLE OF 12's small group relationships, people become dedicated disciples. They experience the fullness of joy deep down in their hearts as they experience the transformation of their lives and personal encounter with Jesus. This is PRINCIPLE OF 12 ministry.

Why did Jesus choose and the PRINCIPLE OF 12 strategy? It is because there is something we need within this ministry. Why did Jesus choose twelve disciples? Why do we need this strategy in today's church? First, it is because we need a team ministry. People need a team where they can be truly open and dedicated. They need a dedicated team that meets as a family and not out of need. The twelve disciples became one team. A team ministry that can keep each other accountable begins to form.

Secondly, we need father like leaders. This society is isolated. All relationships have broken down. Individualism overflows. People are living in a society where they do not feel safe to open up. People have possessions but their hearts are empty. There is no way to open up and feel safe. It is because there is no father like leaders. There is no friend you can visit on a whim. That is why PRINCIPLE OF 12 is needed. Everyone needs a spiritual teacher.

Thirdly, life must have a vision and establish clear goals. Twelve disciples and a teacher: this team of thirteen is a team of vision. They can set goals and move forward because they have a vision. Let men gather as men and behave as such. Let us become fatherly men. Visions such as, "We grew up fatherless. We grew up loveless. Let us be the ones to restore the function of fathers. This society must be lead for God's vision to be completed by the hand of men. We must save the men of this generation." This generation needs vision and strategy. We have a sleeping generation, sleeping church, sleeping family, sleeping men, and sleeping women. We have discovered many souls falling away without discovering their God ordained role or the meaning of life.

Fourth, the vision must be imparted to teams. In other

words, in order for the vision to be imparted to a team, we must have generational teams. As Jesus had twelve disciples, there must be yet another twelve disciples under them. This is when apostolic anointing and the vision of Jesus is imparted. Some have said, "Jesus made twelve disciples, but none of the disciples made their own twelve disciples." One can interpret it that way, but I would like to interpret it this way. If the disciples correctly understood what he meant when he gave them the Great Commission to "go and make disciples of all nations," in Matthew 28, then the disciples would have spent three and a half years choosing and training their own disciples, and imparting the anointing to them. This would have led to generational impartation of the Apostolic Anointing. However, as time passed, Christianity began to deteriorate, especially after 500 AD. This was due to the failure to impart the apostolic anointing among teams. What is important is that vision is imparted specifically and continuously in one's life through a team ministry, rooting God's principles deeply in the believer's life.

    Fifth, the most important purpose of PRINCIPLE OF 12 is the continuous infilling of the Holy Spirit. The fire of the Holy Spirit enables the PRINCIPLE OF 12 meetings to be alive and dynamic. Being filled with the Holy Spirit causes the vision to be set ablaze. We must pray without ceasing. Strategic prayer and spiritual warfare are all needed. Intercessory prayer, prayers to bind the evil spirits, and prayers to become an apostolic church are all important. Prayers in the emotional dimension are powerful prayers.

This is the reason why the Korean style of prayer is excellent. It is a prayer that pushes through like a train. From my experience of ministering in a Muslim region, I realize that without a powerful prayer ministry, no amount of knowledge or strategy will do. When the twelve disciples gathered to pray for the infilling of the Holy Spirit, the vision was set ablaze. Each one of them felt the fire burning in their souls. That is when they began to move. They did not move when they had head knowledge but they moved when their hearts became hot. It is a simple principle. I learned that we need the fire of the Holy Spirit.

Sixth, we realized that there must be transformation of character. From the PRINCIPLE OF 12 meetings, I realized six important strategies given by Jesus. The were;

1. The transformation of character
2. The filling by the Holy Spirit
3. Vision that is imparted to the team
4. Vision and establishment of goals, which must be present within the team,
5. Father like leadership and
6. Team ministry must be established.

I came to realize the importance of these strategies to make the ministry successful. If these essential factors are present in your ministry, your ministry will be successful as well. Let me expand on these strategies.

First, we saw the vision of Jesus and His strategy in

Matthew 10:1. The Bible says that Jesus called the twelve disciples. He saw something. After looking and looking, he observed that the people had no shepherds. Why were they without shepherds? There were too many intellectual, self-gratifying shepherds. Thus, Jesus sought to impart his vision through small group, through the twelve disciples. That is why he chose the twelve. This is the strategy of Jesus.

What is the ministry or goal of Jesus? Jesus not only imparted his vision and strategy, but he had a goal. His goal was to commission his disciples into ministry. The ultimate goal of church ministry is to enable every member of the church to serve as ministers. We must go beyond the ministry of church itself and have a goal of commissioning every member to go into his ministry. Everyone can and must have his own ministry, whether it is on a mission field or on a job site. This is the most meaningful thing we can do with our lives. When I first selected my twelve disciples, I chose 12 young men. I asked them about their hopes and dreams. One young man was a chef. He wanted to become the best chef in Kazakhstan. He wanted to testify that Jesus enabled him to become the best. It was a good dream. Another disciple, a man in his thirties, worked at an insurance company. He became a manager and was paid well. With the crumbling of communism, young people were rising up taking key positions in society. His vision was to become a successful businessman, using the money to help the church. That is also a good vision. They all had good dreams. I told them, "None of you have a vision that is useful, however. It is because the vision of Jesus is not within you. When Jesus gives you dreams and visions, he gives a vision that goes beyond becoming a great businessman or a great chef. That vision is the vision of making disciples. You must have a vision to make dedicated disciples by transforming lives. My vision is for all twelve of you to become full-time ministers. I want you to be able to quit your jobs and follow Jesus with joy." By God's grace, I will make it happen. I continue to proclaim it. By this, I am not saying tha every believer should become a 5 fold minister or pastor. But I am saying that everyone must become a minister, as servant of Christ, using the gifts God has given for the betterment of the world.

A person can make a lot of money. However, that is not their number one priority. The number one priority is to make disciples. Without this focus, God's vision begins to crumble. Even my disciples will slowly fall away unlesss they realize this truth. But finally, they have to come to this conclusion, not out of fear, but with joy. I asked them, "How many disciples do you want to have under you?" Some say, "As of now, 144." "Then what about 10 years from now?" I asked. They answer that they want to have at least ten thousand disciples. "Fine," I said, "but if you are going to have ten thousand disciples under you, how can you effectively have this ministry, while still holding on to your job and salary?" There was no answer. "Should you quit your job? How can you take care of ten thousand disciples? Are you certain about your vision? You should pray again," I challenged. It may seem a little over the top, but I believe I am right.

The ultimate goal of Jesus was to make disciples and to have all of them minister. The church of God must produce ministers. Jesus showed us three important ministries, found in the New Testament; Jesus did three ministries. His ministres were healing, deliverance, and finally preaching/teaching the Gospel of the Kingdom ("Repent, for the kingdom of Heaven is near!"). He did not concentrate his efforts on preaching solely. These three important ministries must be spread out to all nations through disciples. Leaders are to prepare the disciples and commission them into ministry. This is the goal of Jesus.

There is a young woman among my wife's disciples. She had 16 cells, but within 6 months they grew to 72 cells. What was her secret? She had a burning passion to see every soul become a minister of God. One of her disciples gave this testimony, "I lived my life without realizing the purpose of my life. I grew up in an orphanage because my parents left me after getting divorced. I was filled with hatred and unbelief. I had a difficult time opening my heart even when my cell group leader was sharing God's love with me. However, while attending the Alpha program, I came home to pray after the sixth week. As I was praying, the Holy Spirit showed me how much he loved me. After the Alpha program, I became part of my leader's cell. He began to tell me about life's vision, endlessly. My first vision was to be paid $500 a month. After six months, my life's vision changed drastically. Now my goal is to see the lives of young people of the Silk

Road region transformed, just like the vision Pastor Samsong Kim received from God."

She testified that God helped her to realize this vision as she was praying. Because of this vision, she went into a university, even though she was older. Without this vision, she would not have gone. However, because of the vision she received from her leader, she went into a university and now is preparing to open a youth center. As she prayed for college students, God gave her the inspiration to make disciples by feeding poor and hungry college students. Because Muslims do not come to church, she started to hold Alpha programs at a restaurant. She has finished her third Alpha program. Through this program, she now has seven disciples. This is the result of a God size vision!

God will not leave a person with a vision alone. However, you must clearly realize the vision; then commission them into ministry as Jesus did. The proven results will be transformed lives leading to devoted disciples for the cause of Christ and His church. This is the goal of ministry God has given us.

In sum, we need to focus on the following principles: Have the vision of ministry Jesus had, understand and implement the Principle and Stategy of 12, and have the goal of Jesus, to make disciples of all people groups, as God gives strength.

Chapter 3: Holy Vision
Holy Vision enables church to be church!

It is truly amazing how one man, David, with a true vision from God, was able to prepare so many people and transform an entire people for God. Also, we will see how David's vision enabled many people to follow him, in spite of his shortcomings. David was not perfect by any means: adultery, deception, and murder. Even though he committed such grevious sin, he was still God's man, a man after God's own heart.

> 12:23 These are the numbers of the men armed for battle who came to David at Hebron to turn Saul's kingdom over to him, as the LORD had said: 24 men of Judah, carrying shield and spear-6,800 armed for battle; 25 men of Simeon, warriors ready for battle-7,100; 26 men of Levi-4,600, 27 including Jehoiada, leader of the family of Aaron, with 3,700 men, 28 and Zadok, a brave young warrior, with 22 officers from his family; 29 men of Benjamin, Saul's kinsmen-3,000, most of whom had remained loyal to Saul's house until then; 30 men of Ephraim, brave warriors, famous in their own clans-20,800; 31 men of half the tribe of Manasseh, designated by name to come and make David king-18,000; 32 men of Issachar, who understood the times and knew what Israel, should do—200 chiefs, with all their relatives under their command; 33 men of Zebulun, experienced soldiers prepared for battle with

every type of weapon, to help David with undivided loyalty-50,000; ³⁴ men of Naphtali-1,000 officers, together with 37,000 men carrying shields and spears; ³⁵ men of Dan, ready for battle-28,600; ³⁶ men of Asher, experienced soldiers prepared for battle-40,000; ³⁷ and from east of the Jordan, men of Reuben, Gad and the half-tribe of Manasseh, armed with every type of weapon-120,000. ³⁸ All these were fighting men who volunteered to serve in the ranks. They came to Hebron fully determined to make David king over all Israel. All the rest of the Israelites were also of one mind to make David king. ³⁹ The men spent three days there with David, eating and drinking, for their families had supplied provisions for them. ⁴⁰ Also, their neighbors from as far away as Issachar, Zebulun and Naphtali came bringing food on donkeys, camels, mules and oxen. There were plentiful supplies of flour, fig cakes, raisin cakes, wine, oil, cattle and sheep, for there was joy in Israel. ¹³:¹ David conferred with each of his officers, the commanders of thousands and commanders of hundreds. ² He then said to the whole assembly of Israel, "If it seems good to you and if it is the will of the LORD our God, let us send word far and wide to the rest of our brothers throughout the territories of Israel, and also to the priests and Levites who are with them in their towns and pasturelands, to come and join us. ³ Let us bring the ark of our God back to us, for we did not inquire of it during the reign of Saul." ⁴ The whole assembly agreed to do this, because it seemed right to all the people. ⁵ So David assembled all the Israelites, from the Shihor River in Egypt to Lebo Hamath, to bring the ark of God from Kiriath Jearim. ⁶ David and all the Israelites with him went to Baalah of Judah (Kiriath Jearim) to bring up from there the ark of God the LORD, who is enthroned between the cherubim—the ark that is called by the Name. ⁷ They moved the ark of God from Abinadab's house on a new cart, with Uzzah and Ahio guiding it. ⁸ David and all the Israelites were celebrating with all their might before God, with songs and with harps, lyres, tambourines, cymbals and trumpets. (1 Ch 12:23 – 13:8)

We must become a church made up of true spiritual soldiers. A life of vision is very important. What enabled the men of David to be united? What caused so many warriors to follow David? It was vision. Because of that one vision, people who drew near to David were able to become a family-like army or army-like family. We must gather under a vision. Of course, the vision must be pure and clean. In order to accomplish great things, there must be a leader with pure motives. This is an important biblical principle. God works through leaders. People talk about team ministry all the time. However, even teams must be led by a leader. A ministry led by a team of leaders can be very daunting. The Bible does not support such a model. Team ministry is formed through the vision of an anointed leader, who is ultimately responsible for the completion the vision received from God. If that vision is from God, there will be unending joy and unity, no matter how difficult the task. For example, there was joy among the Israelites. They had an abundance of flour, fig cakes, raisin cakes, wine oil, cattle and sheep; true prosperity. Anythin g is possible when you are joyful.

It is helpful to examine the warriors of David who formed God's Army. There are many points of interest we can see through the life of David. It is true that David's warriors formed God's army. But what kind of people were they in the beginning? In 1 Samuel 22:1-2, we read about the time David hid in the Adullam cave from Saul:

> [1] David left Gath and escaped to the cave of Adullam. When his brothers and his father's household heard about it, they went down to him there. [2] All those who were in distress or in debt or discontented gathered around him, and he became their leader. About four hundred men were with him.

David willingly became a mentor to people who were in distress, in debt or discontented. Compared to God's magnificent vision, they were pathetic people.

When I first started the church and surveyed the members and their commitment level; I felt so discouraged. My beginning was similar to that of David's. David was being trained by God in the wilderness, pursued by Saul, but in the midst of his trial God sends people who are in the same predicament as David, in order to complete the preparation to accomplish his vision.

We should not be disappointed. Hardships will come our way. However, the biblical principle dictates that God blesses the people who have gone through the wilderness. In Deuteronomy 8, the Bible tells us that the reason why God brings us through so many hardships is because God wants to test us to see if we will live by the word of God instead of living by bread alone, even during difficult times. God wants to test us to see if we are prepared to give up our lives for the vision. He wants to test us to see if we truly do believe that the vision is from the Lord and if we would be completely dependent on him. Only those who can pass the time of testing and trials can enter into the land of Canaan.

Saul's officers could have followed David because David was already a well known figure when he was being pursued by Saul. God had other plans. When things come too easy, they perish easily as well. This is a basic principle. This is why God sent the defeated to David. True success in ministry is to succeed with genuinely broken people. This is God's desire. God makes the impossible possible. God wants to receive glory from us as he enables us to do the impossible. The principle is the same. That is why God sent those people to him. The exact same thing will happen in our ministry. If God wants us to accomplish his vision, he will use the same principle to do it. Just as Moses' 40 years in the wilderness and Paul's 10 years in Arabia were preparatory for God's work, God is teaching us that tribulations such as life in the wilderness and David's flight are essential for all great servants of God. We must learn to rejoice during our time in the wilderness. We must throw away our complaints. We must learn the lessons of the Israelites. Hebrews records that God allowed people to hear his voice. However, in the Old Testament, we do not find a single incident of this. What does that mean? Even in the wilderness, God continuously spoke to them either through Moses or by touching their heart. It is the same for us. God definitely speaks even when we are in the middle of difficulties. God speaks to us even when we despair in the midst of trial. There is no need to be discouraged by seemingly unimpressive people God sends our way. As long as the voice of God is with us, they can be transformed and we can do great things together. Please remember that this is how God lays down the foundation so many generals and warriors can arise from it.

Our task is to mentor the people God has placed in our lives at the present and to cause them to become servants of God. We must not lose sight of the fact that they will one day become part of God's army, accomplished through the seeds planted. Everyone God brings to you will be transformed because of the hope that is in you. May you receive such blessings.

Driving force behind Unity: Fulfillment of God's Word

How did such unity take place? The driving force behind unity was the word of God. In verse 23, it says, "These are the numbers of the men armed for battle who came to

David at Hebron to turn Saul's kingdom over to him, as the LORD had said."

God had already spoken. David knew that God made a promise when God anointed him through Samuel. The vision had already come. The vision was to save the Israelites and to turn them back to God. This vision was in David's heart. However, David did not use man's means. He had a high respect for the Lord's anointed, to the point of feeling guilty for cutting off a corner of Saul's garment when he had an opportunity to kill Saul. God took delight in David because David respected His ways. God's word is true. We make mistakes because our faith is weak. If we live by faith, believing that the word of God does come true, we can surely overcome tribulations. If Holy Spirit has spoken to you and has given you a vision, if you have received a confirmation from the Lord, you must hold on to your vision to the end, in faith without wavering. God completes his work through faith. The greatness of David is the fact that he relied on God. When he slew Goliath, David had nothing. He only had a sling. However, he relied on the Lord of Hosts, the God of War. David was able to declare,

> "You come against me with sword and spear and javelin, but I come against you in the name of the LORD Almighty, the God of the armies of Israel, whom you have defied".

He knew that God was with him. We are living in a time where we must rely on God more than ever. Perhaps now, more than any other period in history, the hunger to give glory to God must arise strongly within us in order for the Holy Spirit to give us vision and to work through us.

God has always chosen a leader in order to complete his will, especially during times of great peril. The time of Elijah was a time of danger. The nation was in danger of collapse. They were corrupt and all the prophets fled. Elijah complained that he was the only one left. Yet, it is during this moment of crisis when God chooses someone. Even though Elijah was just one man, he was able to cut down 450 prophets of Baal and 450 prophets of Ashtoreth single handedly by relying on the power of God. God chooses his servant during times of crisis. When a family is facing a crisis, he chooses a member from the family to bring salvation to the family. When a nation is facing grave danger, God chooses a leader in order to save the nation. When a church is facing a critical situation, God raises up his leader to save his church and his people. In fact, it is God who starts a new movement. David was a man who started a movement. He started a movement to turn people's heart back to God. This movement stirred the heart of God. It also stirred the hearts of the people as well. It is a simple truth, but it has a fundamental power to give life. Revival and growth doesn't come naturally. We must believe that God's blessing is a byproduct; it cannot be our goal. The Bible promises that when we are one with God's heart, will and spirit, all these things will be added unto us. I pray that you hold onto these basic principles.

Characteristics of David's Warriors

There is a need for us to inspect closely the characteristics of David's warriors. What type of men were they? When we do our PRINCIPLE OF 12 ministry, what type of men do we need? In order to accomplish God's holy vision here on earth, what type of men should make up the team? What should be the mindset of the vision team? What should be the spirit of the ministry team? Who should share their lives with us? Who did David prepare? What ever became of the people whom David prepared? The Bible has clear answers for these questions.

To win a war, it takes a people prepared for battle; people with resolve for the vision. Verses 24-37 present the characteristics of David's warriors. These can also be the characteristics of the disciples of Jesus Christ.

Which disciples should be a part of a ministry team? God wants conquerors, like the conquerors of Canaan. Lead by Joshua, they were able to conquer a barren land. Today we need men and women who are committed to refor, whether it be the corrupted churches of East or West, ones to re-evangelize a nation, ones to bring new revival. So, what type of believers should we become? What type of believers havew been prepared by the Senior Pastor? Herein lays our keys to success. It is the same for business as for people who do ministry in the Lord's church. It is the same for people who lead their families. We must ask ourselves, what kind of family am I building? What kind of team am I building? We must give serious thought to these questions.

When I read this passage of scripture, I was deeply comforted and I found my direction. This is where my church members ought to head towards. The vision that God gives us is enormous. God gives his vision to people who are so small, they cannot possibly accomplish His vision on their own. His dreams are truly dreamlike. However, we can build a team like David so that God's work can surely take place.

People who are adept in battle

Let us look deeper into verse 24. David's warriors were preparing for battle. They had a clear goal to defeat the enemy. They knew that their vision came from God. Thus, they would not back down under any circumstance. Verse 24 tells us that they were armed for battle. Verse 25 tells us that they were warriors ready for battle. Verse 33 tells us they were men of Zebulon, experienced soldiers prepared for battle with every type of weapon. These weren't simply men who were courageous but they were effective in combat. They were trained for battle. These are men who can lead the Alpha Course seminar. These are men who can minister at Encounter retreats. These are people who can pray effectively. These are people who can reach people's hearts with God's word. We need disciples who are prepared for such tasks. We are in need of not just one leader but an army of God who are prepared to minister in this way. This is the only way a church can be the church. This is the only way a church can transform society. Twelve disciples cannot be disciples in name only. They must be people who are adept at every facet of ministry to Win, Connect, Train, and Send. They must be trained to the highest degree regarding these areas. They must be prepared to receive such rigorous training and experience actual ministry. They must have experience in leading someone to Jesus Christ. They must have experience in leading their own God-given cell. With each encounter, they must have spiritual strength to challenge their souls.

Spiritually strong people do not fall. They are not influenced by the environment. David had such warriors around him. I pray that countless numbers of such warriors would rise up in your church. You must prepare them. Without such warriors, we cannot help but fall when Satan comes against us. If there is no intercessory prayer, no strongman at home, none even at church, then we will surely fall. A countless number of spiritual attacks await us. Therefore, we must be prepared. As the end draws near, the evil ones will attack more vigorously. There will be attacks by society, numerous divisions within the church, and bickering due to doctrine. Where should we stand? What exactly is God's vision? Are there people prepared to complete the vision? Is there someone to protect me? Is there someone who will draw the water from Hebron to quench my thirst? Is there a warrior who is willing to risk his life for me? It is God's great challenge for us. We must prepare. We must prepare for a great war. We need such warriors in order to cultivate a barren land. Canaan was a land promised to us, but we've lost it. We must remember that there is still countless numbers in the nations who aren't believers. For example, of 47 million Koreans, there are slightly over 10 million believers. It is estimated that less than 20% actually attend church. We must bring transformation. There must be true soldiers. If there are true disciples, we can have a powerful voice in society. This is our calling. If we can be prepared, we can be world class warriors. Without preparation, we will merely be a mob. In actuality, the world is watching the Korean church. Everywhere you go in the world, you will run into a Korean missionary. They respect you once they find out that you are a pastor from Korea. All the biggest churches of every denomination are in Korea. Everyone knows it. Yet, we are in need of warriors. We must begin a new chapter in a new generation. It is possible.

People who would make David King (v. 31)

Third, these are people who would make David king. That was their purpose. It means that they knew clearly that the man with the vision was from God. They weren't trying to lift up a mere man. Their attitude was to acknowledge God's chosen as their spiritual leader. Whenever I visit small Korean churches in the US, I notice that the congregation members do not recognize their pastors as pastors. If this unfortunate trend continues, they will never be blessed. This is a great mistake. It is good to serve the pastor as they would God. It is an absolute necessity. It is very important. Why did Joshua become Moses' successor? In Joshua 1:1, God describes Joshua as "Moses' aide." Joshua was not God's servant but Moses' aide. He was an aide who washed Moses' feet. Joshua served

Moses as he would God, because he knew that God had sent Moses. This is why God poured out Moses' spirit on Joshua. It is exactly the same principle. The warriors sought to make David King because they knew that David was from God. This is why the warriors were able to become part of David's vision team, the dream team. Every church must have such warriors. God's will cannot be accomplished if there is a culture of criticism and slander towards the senior pastor. God's work will not take place. There can be no grace. It will spread like cancer and destroy a church's spiritual atmosphere. Senior pastors can make mistakes. However, it is my understanding that God personally deals with the leaders Himself. He deals with them in a strict manner, but he never discards them. Do not worry about such matters; just concentrate on your duties. Instead, intercede on his behalf. Pray for your pastor with passion and God will work. There was a desire to make David king. They knew that it was God's will to make David king after Saul. Maybe they knew through Samuel. Maybe they knew that only David was fit to be king without Samuel saying one word. They all wanted to make David king. No one was opposed to it. There is power in that.

People who understood the times. (v. 32)

The fourth characteristic of David's warriors is that they understood the times. Verse 32 tells us that they were men "who understood the times and knew what Israel should do—200 chiefs, with all their relatives under their command."

Chiefs help to create a certain tone or mood. It is because they understood the times. There must be people who understand where the churche stands and what must be done as a result. This group began to influence others. They weren't simply good in battle but they were able to grasp the situation with the help of the Holy Spirit. We are in need of people who understand the times in order to follow through with the strategy. I pray that these people will rise up. People who understand God's time and recognize what Israel must do, what churches must do, what elders must do, what deacon boards must do, and what pastors must do - they must start a new movement by creating the right atmosphere. Then, we will have hope and others will naturally follow. When you do the right thing, people will follow.

People with undivided loyalty.

Verse 33 tells us that they were men who were "experienced soldiers prepared for battle with every type of weapon, to help David with undivided loyalty-50,000." David's warriors were not double minded. They didn't follow to see what they could get out of the situation. We must not be double minded. Once we let our roots down, we must stay until we bear some fruit. It is God's principle.

For six years I was studied in Germany. Honestly, the pastors were very conservative; it was very difficult. Once, my wife said, "Let's leave. Let's leave this place. I can't stand it here. The environment is too legalistic and critical. I can't stand it." So I answered, "No. We cannot leave here until the

Lord moves us. We must leave after we see the flowers bloom." That's the commitment I made. Even if it was harmful to me at the time, I knew that I should stay. Even if it is difficult and painful, you must pray without ceasing for the church's revival and transformation. Do not allow your heart to be shaken. Once it is shaken, your heart will be shaken forever. You will continue to go back and forth, and because there is no resolution, your faith will not grow. Therefore, you must stay in one place and bear fruit. Big churches, small churches, good churches, bad churches- they are all God's churches. God pours out his love to good and bad children alike, desiring a change in his churches. Be devoted to the church with all that you have. Be faithful. God will see and will surely repay you. His is the only way churches can be changed. If you leave easily because of disagreements in vision, then all kinds of people could leave and wander, never finding a group who share the same vision. I read 2 Timothy 4:3 as a stern warning. It tells us, "For the time will come when men will not put up with sound doctrine. Instead, to suit their own desires, they will gather around them a great number of teachers to say what their itching ears want to hear."

"To suit their own desires, they will gather around them a great number of teachers," means that they will stay only to hear words that are pleasing and then leave at a moment's notice if they don't like what they hear. They are willing to leave their teacher and pastor at anytime. They will begin to lend their ears to the stories of the world, flesh pleasing stories. That is truly dangerous. We must seek truth. We must stay to bring change. How do you know if God wouldn't change your church through you? Perhaps God will change your church through your silent prayers and fasting. If you leave, who would change your church? I pray for you to be steadfast. Do not be double minded.

People with determination and resolution

Verse 38 tells us that they were "fighting men who volunteered to serve in the ranks. They came to Hebron fully determined to make David king over all Israel. All the rest of the Israelites were also of one mind to make David king." They were determined and resolute. Their hearts were unwavering toward David. Today's churches desperately need such people. I pray that all of you can be such disciples. When that happens, the world's churches will be transformed and Christianity will expand at a rapid pace. Time will come quickly when a countless number of people will confess that they want to know Jesus.

Joy in Israel

Why did so many people gather? It was because of God's word. It was to fulfill the word. How was the word fulfilled? Who was David that such work of God took place?

Originally, the bible was not separated into chapters and verses. All the verses were interconnected with the same content. Through the description of the warriors, God is showing us the heart of David. Chapter 13: 1-8 reads,

¹ David conferred with each of his officers, the commanders of thousands and commanders of hundreds. ² He then said to the whole assembly of Israel, "If it seems good to you and if it is the will of the LORD our God, let us send word far and wide to the rest of our brothers throughout the territories of Israel, and also to the priests and Levites who are with them in their towns and pasturelands, to come and join us. ³ Let us bring the ark of our God back to us, for we did not inquire of it during the reign of Saul."⁴ The whole assembly agreed to do this, because it seemed right to all the people. ⁵ So David assembled all the Israelites, from the Shihor River in Egypt to Lebo Hamath, to bring the ark of God from Kiriath Jearim. ⁶ David and all the Israelites with him went to Baalah of Judah (Kiriath Jearim) to bring up from there the ark of God the LORD, who is enthroned between the cherubim—the ark that is called by the Name. ⁷ They moved the ark of God from Abinadab's house on a new cart, with Uzzah and Ahio guiding it. ⁸ David and all the Israelites were celebrating with all their might before God, with songs and with harps, lyres, tambourines, cymbals and trumpets.

David had a desire to gather God's people together. He called them to restore their relationship with God. In a similar fashion, let us bring back the ark of our God. God has a heart to bring God's ark back in the midst of Israel. Why? During Saul's reign, they did not inquire of God. This was the reason for their failure. David had one clear purpose and vision. It was God's will for him to be king. But what was in the heart of David whom God had chosen to be king? It was to bring people back to God by bringing back the ark of God. The ark needed to be returned to its rightful place. Just as the Israelites lives were centered on the ark, and just as the twelve tribes were divided into three tribes each and moved with the ark in the middle, Israel must once again go through spiritual renewal. In order to do so, the very first step was:

"Bring back the ark of our God. Place it in the midst of the people. Gather the priests of God. Gather the Levites. Let us serve God. Let us start a new movement to serve God."

These were David's new slogans. Why wouldn't God be pleased! Why wouldn't God gather these people? Is there any ulterior motive? Absolutely not. Is it because of man's wisdom? No. It is because of a pure heart that God is most pleased. Let us bring back the ark of our God. They did not inquire of the Lord during the reign of Saul but because David did not have hidden agendas, he was able to help his people restore their relationship with the Lord. Thus, we must have a desire to return our disciples back to God, and make them into people of God. I'm not saying that you can't make them into your people. I'm saying that you shouldn't try to hold on to them through personal relationships. Leaders need to inspire them to hold on to God even more passionately through our dedicated relationship with them. Make enough disciples to ensure that even after you die, they will be able to carry on through the generations. Make it so that people with God's heart and God's vision can rise up. Why wouldn't God help David? Why wouldn't God make David into king? It would be a loss to God… Thus, God raised up David. That is why the people followed David. Look at David's pure heart. When they were bringing the ark back home, he was so happy. He was leaping and dancing with all his might. His heart was so pure! There was no political agenda, only pure motives. People were able to see that. Even Saul's daughter saw it and despised him for it. So, God closed her womb. When you despise God's pure servant, the curse of God will come upon you. Therefore, leaders need not fear men. Just stand firmly before the Lord and run endlessly with a pure heart to restore people back to God. You can make mistakes and you can be lacking. However, if your motives are pure, God will definitely bless you.

We can all become leaders; some to a lesser, some to a greater degree. But we must become a leader like David. A gathering with such leaders will lead to much joy. Verse 38-40 tells us,

> [38] All these were fighting men who volunteered to serve in the ranks. They came to Hebron fully determined to make David king over all Israel. All the rest of the Israelites were also of one mind to make David king. [39] The men spent three days there with David, eating and drinking, for their families had supplied provisions for them. [40] Also, their neighbors from as far away as Issachar, Zebulon and Naphtali

came bringing food on donkeys, camels, mules and oxen. There were plentiful supplies of flour, fig cakes, raisin cakes, wine, oil, cattle and sheep, for there was joy in Israel.

Where there is a true leader and true vision from God, there is an abundance of joy. It will be abundant and nothing will be lacking. God will fill the need at all times and He will accomplish his will. This is what today's church needs. Think about what your vision must be.

God's Vision to Pastor Sam Seong Kim-A Continued Testimony

God gave me a vision. I would like to tell you about it. God gave me a vision of the Silk Road. In the beginning, just like my wife said, our desire was to save just one soul in Almaty, Kazakhstan. We didn't know how God would use people who didn't have any ministry experience like this. We went to Almaty with the desire to save just one soul. However, when we served with all our heart and might, God caused the church to grow to over 1000 members within 3 to 4 years. Then he gave us a vision for all of Kazakhstan. Sometime after that, he gave us the inspiration to reach the entire Silk Road region. This took place after 1997. I just held it in my heart and didn't tell anyone else. However, the vision began to grow in me so I continued to pray to God. I prayed without ceasing after fasting and then I told the Lord, "God, I am just a pastor of a local church. My personality is not that strong." Other local pastors have a tough mindset. They are uninhibited. I feel intimidated when I meet them, even if their churches are small. "How can a feeble person like me bring a vision to transform them? How can I place a vision of God's dynamic church in the midst of every people group?" God responded and spoke to my heart, "I will tell you once more. Did I not tell you that you will see the Glory of God if you believe?" God's word became such an encouragement to me. I continued to pray. Incidentally, I received a phone call on November of year 2000. It was from Gil Ro Lee, a missionary from Korea. (I believe he is a worship pastor at Onnuri Church now.)

He called me, "Are you Pastor Sam Seong Kim?"

I said, "Yes I am." "Do you have some time?"

"Yes, I have some time. You can speak with me over the phone."

"Beginning in the summer of 1997 we started an intercessory prayer journey from Turkey, following the Silk Road, going through all the 'tan' nations, ending up in Mongolia in four separate jeeps. In the midst of our journey, God spoke powerfully to all sixteen of us, promising us, 'There will be a great revival in this land. I will send a great revival on this land, greater than any revival in history.'"

I responded, "Yes, and?"

He answered, "As we were praying, God told us to have an enormous prayer meeting to intercede for this land."

"What kind of meeting is this?"

They were told to hold an enormous prayer meeting

of 10,000 people at a city chosen from among the Silk Road region of central Asia. I was so overwhelmed, I cried. In 1991, all the Grace churches in Russia had a festival for the very first time in Almaty with about 3000 people. In 1992, the second festival was held in St. Petersburg for 4 days and 3 nights with about 7000 people from all over Russia attending. In 1993, the third festival was held in Moscow with 10,000 people in attendance. There was a significant spiritual transformation that took place. In the former Soviet Union, Protestants were considered as heretics. However, through this gathering, they learned that Protestants are the biggest denomination in the world. Many people received their vision there. From that point on, all the Grace churches in the former Soviet Union region began to experience revival. People who attended the festival could not forget the healing that took place.

    Coming back to Almaty, I had such a strong desire, I prayed, "God, please help us to gather all the cell church model churches in central Asia and gather about 10,000 people. Help us to transform central Asia." As I was praying without ceasing, I received a phone call. God is a God who prepares all things and leads us in perfection. Holy Spirit speaks to us in his time without error. The problem is whether we are prepared. I told him, "Come to Almaty quickly. I want to hear everything in detail." A few days later, he came. After hearing him, I realized how important this was, as I also had a sense of revival for central Asia. Since God started it, he must finish it. "How should we do it, then?" "We can do it as an Intercorp sponsored event or my church sponsored event. However, I don't think that is a good idea. We must call all the pastors and missionaries in the region of Almaty and Kazakhstan to have discussions." So we invited Korean missionaries, native pastors, and English speaking missionaries on separate occasions and shared our vision. This is God's vision. We must launch an attack to bring revival to the Silk Road region here at Almaty. Unfortunately, there was much opposition. If you hold such an event in a Muslim nation, not only will the government not give Visas, but there will be many persecutions. However, the natives welcomed the idea with passion. They believed that such work must take place. We said, "Let's accomplish it; we don't care if we die. We need the revival." Ultimately, all the English speaking missionaries, Korean missionaries, and Russian and Kazakhstan pastors agreed to join in together. An amazing, yet impossible coalition took place. A mammoth choir was formed. A hundred plus members met for months to practice day and night for this all important event, and my wife helped to prepare the worship teams.

    The permit for this historic event was granted three days before the event. Kazakhstan's national soccer stadium is a political venue. So, it is never granted to religious organizations; but we continued to pray in faith. We kept pushing through, even 3 days prior to the event. One thousand intercessors from Seoul flew in on three chartered flights. Although the planes were previously reserved, at the last minute, they raised the fare by tens of thousands of dollars. Incredible difficulties and obstacles kept coming our way. However, we refused to let it deter us. We pushed on. Three days before the event, miraculously, the President's personally written permit was granted. Everyone was so anxious, but we realized that this is truly ordained by God. God will instruct us if we keep pushing through even though there is much danger. Much persecution, visa problems, and many other problems came up. We, ourselves, made many mistakes. We lacked so many things. Some people from Korea had to sleep in the streets because the hotels would not give us rooms even though they were already reserved. At times, previously arranged transportation didn't show up. Although there was much opposition, God did an amazing work. Before the event, people tried to predict the number of people who would attend. 3000? 5000? A combined total of Christians in the city of Almaty is less than 20,000. The maximum number of people who can show up would be 20,000. How many would come? Once the doors to the soccer stadium were opened, it was completely packed. 15,000 people packed the stadium. After the doors were closed, thousands were turned away. The police covered every section of the stadium because they were afraid of dangerous insurrections. Then we began to pray blessings for the police. We blessed the President and the nation and repented for all our sins, even the sins of Christians. The representatives from each nation, along with missionaries came forward to bless their nations, youth and families. When these prayers were prayed, there was an amazing turn around among the police officers. With tears streaming down their faces, they pledged full cooperation. We experienced tremendous spiritual transformation. That was the Silk Road Festival of the Year 2000. It took place on July of 2000. God enabled us to do unimaginable things. After the festival was over, a few pastors had gathered and asked, "God, how do you want to continue this project? Will it be a one time program or do you want this project to continue?" God spoke, "Continue it." "How do you want us to continue it?" He helped us to remember the preparation of young people through the amazing summer camps of CCC in Korea, so I made a proposal. Every year, for the next ten years, let us gather the young people and equip them. They are the ones who are going to possess this land and the people in the name of Jesus Christ. So we decided to start a ministry to prepare people with the words of Christ, beginning in 2001 for the next ten years. There were no resources or sponsors. Intercorp was an indigent mission organization. Our church was in the mission field without any sponsorship from America or Korea. However, we had confidence in the Lord that he would finish what he has started.

In 2001, we had the first festival for Young Adults, held at my church. The main sanctuary holds only 2200. However, because it was so hot and we didn't have any air conditioning, we only accepted 1800. Many applicants didn't actually have money because they were young. It cost an enormous amount of money to bring them in from Central Asia, Turkey, China and various other regions; about $100,000.

Again, we prayed with faith. We sought the Lord and money started to come in from USA, Canada, and Korea. God filled our need precisely. We were able to complete the first event successfully. We were satisfied with simply meeting together the first time. However, amazing things happened when these young people gathered. Christians from Turkey, Azerbaijan, and China came and left with a vision to build churches, host similar events and pray for revival at their churches. That is when the prayer movement started. We held the second event in July of 2002. It cost about $140,000. We needed about $70,000 by the middle of the event. All the money was raised by Wednesday, which was the midpoint of the event. I give all the glory to God. Ultimately, who is responsible? It was my responsibility. What if we were short? Then I would be rebuked. However, God provided all the finances at the last moment. As a result, many regions of Turkey started a morning prayer movement. People who came to Almaty to attend the Encounter Retreat, went back home with passion to pray for revival in Turkey. Some congregation members of a church planted by a Korean missionary from Istanbul came and made a commitment. They said they would not die until five million people in Turkey were saved. They would pray endlessly. Two young ladies, who were 16 and 17 years of age started a prayer movement with such resolve. People from Azerbaijan were quite surprised. After attending the Encounter Retreat, they asked me to come to their church to lead them through the Encounter Retreat and PRINCIPLE OF 12 Seminar. This is how God's amazing work started to take place in Turkey, Azerbaijan, Uzbekistan and all of China last year. God told me to bring organization into everything that was going on. I wanted to hold a festival for the young people on the second week of every July. I said that if there were any churches who were interested in coming, to prepare in advance - Monday through Saturday of the second week of July, every year from 7 am until 10 pm. It is a gathering of young people who will pray and sweat for the Silk Road. The 2nd week of every February will be set aside to raise up leaders from them to train them through Alpha and PRINCIPLE OF 12.

The Vision of Silk Road is the vision to take over the Silk Road. The strategy is to arm ourselves with Alpha courses and PRINCIPLE OF 12, to make warriors like David. The Silk Road will be conquered. Our goal is to help plant 1000 churches on the Silk Road by year 2010. Other nations must bear the financial burden. Central Asia is a treasure chest of missions. There has never been a time when the gospel was accurately shared. There has never been a revival in history. However, because God desires to bring revival to this place, He raised up someone like me and has given me many co-workers. God wants us to do great things. I am confident that the vision that God has given to us will be finished by the year two thousand ten.

Unique Korean's

I always insist that Koreans have two spiritual DNA's. First, there is DNA for prayer. We have the authority through prayer to destroy the powers of darkness. Not many people pray with the same intensity. Muslim areas are heavily oppressed. You cannot do anything without prayer. People get oppressed. People get sick. People get depressed. As a result, the ministry becomes insignificant. There is not much you can do without prayer in Muslim areas.

The second DNA God gave to Koreans is church planting. Koreans plant churches everywhere they go, like the Chinese build restaurants wherever they go. These days, Chinese people are also planting churches. There are about 300 Korean Missionaries in the Central Asia region and most of them have planted churches. There are about 300 western missionaries as well, but most of them have not planted churches. It is an amazing comparison. This is the reality. What am I getting at? To us, church planting is a natural part of us. We plant churches whether the member is one, ten, or thirty. This is the gift God has given to us. Central Asia is a place where Turks have gathered. From Turkey to Azerbaijan, all the "tan" nations and Shin Jang Sung of China are all Turkish people and the spoken language is Turkish as well. It is difficult for a Korean missionary to preach in Russian even after living in Russia for ten years. However, all the nations on the Silk Road pretty much speak the same Turkish language. The words are very similar. The most important thing is to preach after studying their language for about 6 months. Their grammar structure is the same as Korean. We only need to learn the words. This is why God has chosen the Korean people for the Silk Road. We must do global mission work. I pray because I am in the Silk Road. Many Western missionaries cannot work here due to cultural and linguistic differences. People in the Muslim and Arab region have much hostility towards Americans and Europeans. However, Koreans are well received ever since the Seoul Olympics. Now, they are respected and loved. They treat us as a superior people wherever we go. This helps in strategically positioning ourselves for missions in this area.

Honestly, I want to start a movement to reach the Silk Road in Korea and beyond. I want to start a PRINCIPLE OF 12 and Silk Road explosion of the Gospel. My prayer is to be able to do mission work with all our might. How do we know of God's plans to bring revival to the entire region of the Silk Road? It is because the Silk Road region is the passage to return the gospel back from Asia to Jerusalem.

I was invited to China last year and it was my very first time. I heard something truly amazing from one of the leaders of the underground church of China. He told me that there was a common vision among all the church leaders of China since 1930.

"What is that?" I asked.

"It is a 60 year old vision," he replied.

"What is that vision?"

"It is the vision of going back to Jerusalem."

"What do you mean?" I asked.

"We received the vision to return to Jerusalem via the Silk Road just as we have received the gospel from Jerusalem."

As a result, all of the underground churches and even the government run churches are carefully unfolding a plan to prepare 100,000 missionaries. They want to send them to Jerusalem through the Silk Road. There are three routes. One route passes through southern Viet Nam, Thai, Myanmar, and India. The other route goes through Tibet and Northern India. The third route goes through the Silk Road, through the Central Asian countries, through Turkey to Jerusalem. And this is the route they have chosen. To the Chinese people, the West North region of Shin Jang Sung is a tremendous mission region because it is a Muslim area. Initially, they plan to commission a very large number of Chinese missionaries to the Shin Jang Sung area. From there, they are going to teach them the Turkish language and then send them into Jerusalem as an attack force, going through the Silk Road, sharing the Gospel. They call themselves the "West North Spiritual Attack Force." They are starting a tremendous ministry to spiritually attack the West North region.

When I heard their story, I realized that it was God's plan. We didn't know about China. We only had a conviction about the revival within the Silk Road region. But now we realize that the revival of the Silk Road is not only for the Silk Road but it is to open the passage to "Back to Jerusalem." Thus, we have named our vision, "The Vision of Silk Road: Back to Jerusalem." We must spread the gospel all the way back to Jerusalem. Now our focus is not only on the Silk Road, but it also includes evangelizing Arabs. Every time we go to Turkey, we ask the Turkish leaders to "be responsible for

Arabs." God is doing something amazing and it requires our prayers, our commitment, and our finances. This is why I want Western and Eastern Churches to take on the task of planting and building 1000 churches. I ask you to pray about it. God will do his work. I am confident that he will pour out incredible blessings. Come to Almaty. Come to the Silk Road. Let us do Alpha and PRINCIPLE OF 12 together. Let's share this vision with every country in Central Asia and instill this strategy and train the soldiers together. I pray that you will be able to accomplish the will of Jesus. Our God is a great God. He will do great works through you.

Vision and Strategy

Vision is only attainable when coupled with a strategy. It is not possible to fulfill it without a strategy. We need the vision and strategy together. This is why God has given us the vision of PRINCIPLE OF 12 now, to those of us who are living in the last days.

I received an urgent call last December. I was leading an Encounter Retreat and a PRINCIPLE OF 12 Conference in Uzbekistan, where 4000 people from 23 churches were gathered. The call came from China. There are about 100 million Christians in China, with 70 million belonging to underground house churches. These 70 million Christians are being governed by 5 networks. In other words, there are 5 denominations. The call came from one of the five denominations, which includes about 8 to 10 million members. They wanted to learn about PRINCIPLE OF 12. They wanted me to come and teach. I said, "OK! When do you need me?" They needed me in two days. I didn't even have a visa. "Yes, I will be there," I answered. I flew to Almaty, arriving in the morning. After getting the Visa, I flew to China that evening. I flew to in China. After touching down, I rode the taxi to a remote part of China. It was minus 10 degrees and the taxi itself felt frozen. There were about 50 people gathered in an underground bunker type of building. These 50 men were the leaders of 10 million Christians. Their eyes were alive. All of them were in their 40's. They were committed warriors. I shared PRINCIPLE OF 12 with them. They were doing better than our church. They weren't aware of God's governing order but their mentorship was stronger than ours. They were like a sponge. They wanted to incorporate PRINCIPLE OF 12 with all their 10 million members. They gave me a special room to sleep in because I am a missionary. It would have been better if I'd slept with them in the same room because the room was freezing. The cement floor was so cold and the blanket was so thin. I was shivering all night. When I woke up in the morning, I was coughing. I was frozen by that time; I still cough from time to time. It was still a wonderful experience. I was so deeply moved. What would happen if 10 million people are transformed by PRINCIPLE OF 12?

    I heard from them again about a month after returning from China. It was from the leader of Shin Jang Sung, who is directly under the leader of the 10 million. He asked, "Please lead the Encounter retreat for us. Please do a PRINCIPLE OF 12 Conference for us." When I went back, there were 50 core leaders who were in charge of Shin Jang Sung. They were 16 to 17 years old. Their eyes were filled with determination, literally willing to die for the gospel. Most of them were girls, yet their hearts were on fire. For the next four days, I led them through the Encounter retreat and the PRINCIPLE OF 12 conference. I realized God's awesome plan of ushering in China's incredible passion for missions and evangelism through the Silk Road, bringing revival not only to the Silk Road Area but also into the Arab region. Thus, ultimately spreading the gospel to Jerusalem. I am so thankful that I am Korean. Why? It is because I received two spiritual inheritances. I received the DNA for prayer and the DNA for church planting. I feel like these are all we can do. Yet these are the most important things. Please begin to pray for the Silk Road starting today. Please pray that by the year 2010, 1000 churches will be planted and 1000 church buildings will be constructed.

  I went to Turkey, in July of 2004. 150 people were gathered, out of 2000 total Christians in Turkey. We completely rented out a three-star hotel. Many members from our church went with me, with offerings given by financially challenged people. Satan's attack was intense. During the Encounter Retreat, on the second day, 50 people were stricken and bedridden with diarrhea. 3-4 people had to be taken to the hospital. I told them, "If you are going to die, die at the Encounter site. Satan is attacking us because he knows that God is about to bless us tremendously. Even if you are about to pass out, come out of your beds and serve." We completed the 3 nights and 4 day retreat with sick bodies. My wife led the young men of Turkey in prayer. They prayed out loud for Turkey on their knees. This was the first time they prayed for their nation.

I led the second Encounter Retreat in February of 2005. I want to see the biggest church of Turkey convert 100% to the PRINCIPLE OF 12 system and become a model church. Please help transform Turkey. I plan to go into Turkey on a monthly basis, leading Encounter Retreats and PRINCIPLE OF 12 Conferences. We are going to need enormous finances. You must join us. You need to arm yourselves with Alpha and PRINCIPLE OF 12. The next time I go in, I am going to call on you. I will call on every church. I will call on you to join in on Encounter. I will ask you to give sermons and the intercessory prayer team must come as well. Finances must come along to build churches. Please prepare in advance. However, prepare on this land first. Prepare your church, first of all. I pray that you will be able to start an amazing movement of God within the Churches around the world.

Part 3: Spirituality and Anointing of a PRINCIPLE OF 12 Church

Chapter 4: PRINCIPLE OF 12 Spirituality

PRINCIPLE OF 12 spirituality is a very important part of the PRINCIPLE OF 12 ministry. It can be considered as the core of PRINCIPLE OF 12. The spiritual principles are developed from the Acts 2.

> ^{42}They devoted themselves to the apostles' teaching and to the fellowship, to the breaking of bread and to prayer. ^{43}Everyone was filled with awe, and many wonders and miraculous signs were done by the apostles.^{44}All the believers were together and had everything in common. ^{45}Selling their possessions and goods, they gave to anyone as he had need. ^{46}Every day they continued to meet together in the temple courts. They broke bread in their homes and ate together with glad and sincere hearts, ^{47}praising God and enjoying the favor of all the people. And the Lord added to their number daily those who were being saved. (Acts 2:42-47)

A Leaders Prayer

Father God, we sincerely thank you. We thank you for the revelation of your wonderful vision and strategy in the last days and moving our hearts to join you in what you want to do. Holy Spirit, it is our hope and our prayer that you completely reign over our lives, use our lives and work through our lives. We desire to see spiritual transformation in each church. Help the church of this generation to accomplish what you wish to accomplish. Help the members of your church to become genuine soldiers and disciples of Jesus Christ. Allow them to have a ministry that brings light and transformation to the dark and depraved world. We desire to see the spirituality of disciples in today's PRINCIPLE OF 12 church. Speak to us and transform us. We pray in Jesus Name. Amen.

All churches base their growth on their own spirituality. All growing churches have a unique spirituality. No system or program causes church growth. Only God's special anointing causes a church to grow. Anointing and spirituality forms the environment of the church. Even without any particular teaching, a new believer naturally conforms and assimilates themselves to the church's spiritual climate. That is why the environment of the church is very important. God accomplishes his will through such spirituality.

A PRINCIPLE OF 12 church requires absolute devotion. A PRINCIPLE OF 12 church requires absolute commitment to spirituality. It is not about different methods, seminars or programs. The key is whether the church has the spirituality of a church belonging to God. Is the senior pastor, the elders and the members prepared to be totally committed to following the unction of the Holy Spirit? When we are committed to God's purposes, God uses us. Therefore, our commitment is very important.

Within the PRINCIPLE OF 12 church, commitment is required between the mentor and the disciple. Beyond programs and tithing, it comes down to the commitment to people. I believe that if you can be faithful to God and then to the people, all the other issues tend to take care of themselves. One of the problems is that we are not committed to other people. In other words, because we lack faith in God and in man, we are not able to care for others to that degree. In PRINCIPLE OF 12, it is also necessary for the disciples themselves to be committed to one another, not just the mentor. This is to ensure a successful team ministry. What is this team ministry for? This is a team ministry formed with the purpose of saving souls. If the disciples aren't committed to each other, if the disciples and the mentor are not committed to each other, or if individuals are not completely committed to God, God's work will not take place. More than anything, commitment unto the vision is important. The vision from God has the power to bring people together. There are bad visionaries as well, such as Hitler. However, because Hitler had a vision, he was able to bring the Germans together. God's servants must learn to receive the vision of God. When people know that the vision is actually from God, they can be committed to it and extend the commitment to the leader who first received the vision.

Role of the Senior Pastor

The role of the senior pastor is vital to the success of

PRINCIPLE OF 12. I contend that 100% of the church is dependent on the senior pastor. It is because he is the one who stands at the pulpit. He casts vision from the pulpit. So, if you realize that the vision is from the Lord, you must become an advocate by supporting the senior pastor as best you can. God makes history through leaders. For example, when God led the Israelites out of Egypt, he used Moses. When Moses captured God's vision, two to three million people were set free from Egypt. It was through one man's obedience. God did not raise up many leaders because often times that allows for more dissension and division.

God also raised up David, and He raised Solomon. God considers one person very precious. He knows that when he gives a vision to one man, that vision has the power to lead a nation. Today, we need God's vision more than any other time in history. God gives his vision to leaders. Thus, the role of the senior pastor is enormous, as he is the communicator of the vision.

He must be able to discern the voice of God when he speaks to us concerning the church, the city, the nation, and the future generation through prayer. We must fall on our face and pray until we receive such vision. Once the vision comes, we must pray for the strategy to accomplish the vision. Once God gives you the strategy, we must pray for a team to help realize this vision. Then we must accomplish the work of God by setting a direction. The senior pastor's role is important because he is the communicator of faith. The word that is preached from the pulpit has the power to change the course of a believer's life. The word must be willed with faith. Every word must be loaded with faith because of the conviction that the word brings. When the word of God is preached with conviction, believers can be transformed into warriors of faith.

He must also act as the bridge of the Holy Spirit. He must be able to hear the voice of the Holy Spirit anytime, anywhere. He must be a pathway to communicate the unction of the Holy Spirit purely, without any compromise to anyone or any circumstance. The senior pastor must also maintain the atmosphere of devotion. He must help the entire church follow through with their passion for the Lord. "I used to be devoted…" will not do. It is not about "restoring the first love." We must not try to restore the first love but pour all efforts into maintaining the first love.

Moreover, the church must maintain the passion through worship. The senior pastor must make sure that all the aspects of worship are led by the presence of the Holy Spirit, not based on formality or rituals. If the senior pastor feels that the worship has become too ritualistic, he must do everything in his power to return to spirit filled worship, whether through prayer or fasting. The senior pastor must seek God's grace. This is so important. The type of spirituality that is communicated is the key to the church's well-being. Programs are secondary. When spirituality is there, any program can be effective. Any program can be a blessing because the church's spirituality is already formed. The reason for the failure of many programs comes from a lack of dependence on the Holy Spirit.

I believe that Acts 2: 42-47 clearly illustrates the PRINCIPLE OF 12 spirituality. I would like to explain it as 5 Powers and 2 Totals. To follow are the specifics as we study the scripture more closely.

First of 5 Powers is the Power of Prayer

There must be power in prayer. The spiritual atmosphere of prayer must be maintained. In Acts 2: 42 it is written, "They devoted themselves to the apostles' teaching and to the fellowship, to the breaking of bread and to prayer." Prayer was so important; God had the apostles devoted to prayer and the ministry of the word.

There was a time when I repented deeply for my lack of prayer. When the church was growing, I found myself constantly working. There were more administrative duties, just generally more to do. So, instead of spending time in prayer, I found myself just doing. I began to notice that my prayer time had decreased. Through it all, God consistently spoke to me. It was so basic: "My son, devote yourself to prayer and ministry of the Word, as it says in the Bible." God impressed that in my heart. My wife also spoke to me concerning the matter.

Meanwhile, the church was operating smoothly and was growing. We were leading seminars, having received the vision of the Silk Road. All the members of the church had captured the PRINCIPLE OF 12 vision and everything was running smoothly. However, I was beginning to be pulled into working more and more. Subsequently, my prayer life suffered. I felt God's admonishment: "Devoting yourself to prayer and ministry of the Word is your priority as a leader. There may be all kinds of work but do not busy yourself with those. When your spirituality falters, when you can no longer hear my voice due to physical fatigue, stop everything. Restore your relationship with me." The voice of God is not only for me but for all the believers.

The early church devoted themselves to prayer. Jesus prayed through the night. I personally believe that Jesus prayed throughout the night because at times, he didn't know what tomorrow would bring. So he probably prayed for direction and for his Father's clear will. Or, he must have prayed all night in order to replenish his weary body and his spirit from the toils of ministry. The point is that Jesus never lost sight of his relationship with the Father. The greatest danger to pastors and lay people alike is the loss of a vital relationship with God due to repeated, meaningless rituals or even the daily activities of running a church. Although, it is a simple truth, we often need to be reminded.

Dr. C. Peter Wagner researched on the amount of time people prayed daily among American and Korean Pastors. American Pastors, it turns out, pray less than 10 minutes on the average. Korean Pastors on the average, pray about 20 minutes. How unbelievable is this? This research shows how little we pray as a whole. Then, what about the rest of the time? I know the answer to this, since I am also a pastor. I also surfed the internet, listening to other pastors' sermons and time really seemed to fly by... three hours.... four hours.... five hours. It would go by so fast. At times, I would even just copy their sermons. However, there was no inspiration. The congregation obviously knows when a message is truly inspired by God. Even if the preaching is not eloquent, or imprecise, if I can share what I've experienced, what I received from the Lord as "RHEMA" through prayer, that is far more effective than rotely preaching someone else's sermon. When we pray, God gives you a message to preach. If you fail to pray, then the message is dead. This is when we start to fall.

The early church was a praying church. The reason their message had power was because of prayer. They devoted themselves to prayer; therefore, there was power in worship, there was power in evangelism and there was power in the teachings of the apostles. In other words, there was an apostolic anointing because of prayer. Often today's messages are sophisticated, smooth, tender and logical, but how much of the sermons are given according to the apostolic anointing which flows from our hearts? This applies to many areas of our ministry and Christian lives in general. For example, when we try to witness to someone, do we really pray with sincere passion to win that soul? If we truly prayed, every word we utter should be felt. Our emotions will be felt. Our love will be felt. He will feel that love and will be deeply moved to tears by a simple honest testimony. This is the power of prayer. Prayer is crucial. That is why we must pray before we witness, before we preach, and before we worship. We must prepare for all things in prayer. This is the spirituality of Korean Churches. No one else can come close to the spirituality of Korean Churches. Some say, "Korean Churches are just loud but have no content." I respond to this criticism by saying, "Without crying out, there is no spirituality or content." A couple of logical and theologically correct prayers just does not seem to convey the heart and longing for God's intervention in our lives. However, a passionate prayer is often indicative of a person's honest and humble dependence on the Lord.

Korean churches, in particular, have been known for their prayer. They experienced revival through such fervency. Korean churches heard the voice of God through all night prayer meetings. In the early days of revival in Korea, they did not have countless numbers of Biblical commentaries. They did not have the internet. They did not have books of sermons or exegesis. Korea's fathers of faith heard the voice of God personally through continuous prayer and fasting. Then they preached the gospel in obedience to the will of God. The early church was the same way. I believe that Korean Churches must restore the spirituality of prayer. We must make praying for three unbelievers into a lifestyle and that lifestyle must become a movement.[9] Until it becomes a movement, we must proclaim it on the pulpit. Such efforts

---

[9] Of course, this would greatly benefit Western Churches as well, as God is no respector of persons.

may seem futile like throwing eggs at a rock.

When I proclaimed, "Let's pray for three unbelievers," I felt that no one paid any attention to it. I asked, "If you throw an egg at a rock, which will break - the egg or the rock?" The congregation answered, "The egg of course." Then I responded, "But if you throw a million eggs, the rock will break." What am I talking about? I'm talking about perseverance. If the vision of the Lord is certain, then we must press on. God will definitely work. That is a fact. Often times, we simply lack faith. We lack clear discernment to decide whether it is right or wrong before God. This generation lacks certainty because they are confused about what they have received from the Lord. Such people can do nothing. I pray that you believe that prayer opens the way for the power of God.

With Fasting

I'm starting a fasting movement at my church. The purpose is to maintain our spiritual fervor. Last year, I told the entire congregation to fast one day during the month of January. I gave them topics for prayer as well. In February, I fasted for three days with the entire congregation. During the months of March and April, I had them fast for a whole week. When they fast for a week or longer, I allow them to eat dinner. I believe that doing it as a collective body is more important than arguing about whether to eat or not to eat a certain meal. There are also sick and frail people so we make adjustments for that as well. The point is to create an atmosphere of participation. It was followed by a two week fast, then a three week fast. Thirty days of fasting followed and forty days was done during the 30 day fasting period of Ramadan. We fasted and prayed for 40 days, 10 days longer than the Muslims. This fast was proclaimed to all the members of the church. Obviously, only the people who were willing followed through. About a third of our congregation participated. I asked them, "Isn't it difficult?" They answered, "No, it is actually easier because we are doing it together." Even my thirteen year old son completed the 40 days of fasting while going to school.

    Because we are fleshly beings, our souls will continuously become secularized if we do not draw near to the Lord in fasting and prayer. After last year, I realized that many of the congregation members were not able to fast for an extended period of time. So, we made a proclamation to fast bi-monthly. Now, the entire congregation of our church fasts for a week every two months. We fast breakfast and lunch, eating only dinner. There is no better way to draw closer to God than fasting. This is why I train even the newest believers to fast. They don't die. It is not that difficult when you fast corporately. And the result of fasting and praying for a week is simply amazing. Even the things they were not able to pray for in their everyday life get answered, resulting in some amazing testimonies. Why wouldn't they fast? Why wouldn't they do it when they are experiencing transformation and anointing in their lives?

    We must fast in order to maintain our passion and

power to pray. It is necessary. It must be done. We know the importance of prayer. Sometimes, when I am on the pulpit to preach, I feel a sudden loss of words or thoughts. It is the attack from the evil spirit. No, I am not being super mystical. The attack is real. No matter how much you pray and prepare the Word of God, the enemy can attack. That is why we need intercessors. Our Sunday services last about two hours to two and a half hours. During that time, my twelve disciples take their disciples and they take turns interceding for the 1st, 2nd, and 3rd worship services. They do nothing but intercede during the whole service. They pray against the powers of evil. They pray for the powerful anointing of the Holy Spirit. We pray because we believe in the power of prayer. Do you believe in the power of prayer? When you pray, there will be an answer. God doesn't work because you do not pray. You do not hear the fresh voice of God because you do not pray. You cannot discern the will of God because you do not pray. You do not have certainty in the will of God because you do not pray. However, when you do pray, you can be certain in the things of God. As you pray, God begins to reveal his will clearly. You are able to stand firm in your conviction no matter what difficulties you face. Whether you are a lay member or a pastor, you all need prayer. If your life is filled with prayer, you will experience an amazing transformation in your life.

Everything that happened in the early church was the result of prayer. If this is true, we must restore prayer. The sound of prayer must never cease. This is why we developed the Kazakhstan Prayer Center. It is a hall that seats about 300 people. It is set apart only for prayer and nothing else. It is always open. Church members can come even in the middle of the night to pray. My twelve disciples and my wife's twelve disciples take turns attending the prayer center. We do it because God commanded the fire of the altar to never go out. Even in the Old Testament times, the priests made sure the fire of the altar would not go out. I believe this is our function. Thus, our church members come to pray everyday. It is open 24 hours. We ask people to come and cry out especially for personal problems during the hours of 5 to 7 PM. As a result, many more people come during that time period to pray and cry out to the Lord. We are continuing on with Morning Prayer as well. Our morning prayers are a little later than the usual Korean morning prayer meetings due to the fact that not many people have personal transportation. We meet and pray holding hands with our own network or cell group from 7 to 8 AM, and then we go directly to work immediately following the prayer meeting. In addition, we fast breakfast when we pray. As a result, I have witnessed God's vision and ministry flourish before my very own eyes.

I learned much about prayer from my wife. I believe that women pray well. They pray with such persistence. When we were living in Germany, during the difficult seasons, she would pray five, seven, twelve hours a day. She is an awesome prayer warrior who prays hours at a time. Because of her prayer life, God prepared us spiritually for prayer. Even when we arrived on the mission field, the very first thing she did was to establish an atmosphere of continuous prayer. Even when we were choosing our disciples, we did not choose them based on their education, background, or preaching potential. We just prayed and we chose those who would pray. It is because we know that prayer is our first priority.

Because the early church emphasized prayer, we have tried to maintain a strong spiritual climate of prayer. We also understand the spiritual DNA of Korean people to pray. This is the only way to restoration. When you pray, God reveals the hidden things. There is no way to learn of such things otherwise. Some people worry without ceasing instead of praying without ceasing. They worry instead of closing their eyes and praying. This must be transformed completely. We must cry out to the Lord. And at times, we must listen to his voice in silence.

This is my 13th year in Almaty. I used to have the most difficult time preparing to preach a message. Now, in all honesty, when I sit down in our prayer center, complete Sunday messages come to me in about 10 to 15 minutes. I am so thankful for this. We don't prepare for the message according to our own knowledge. We rely on God for all our ministry needs. To rely on God is the truest form of prayer. You can be restored when you pray. This is why we need a powerful prayer life. We must nurture and foster this type of atmosphere. I pray that you will be able to establish an atmosphere of prayer before starting anything. Perhaps no one will join as you start to diligently pray. You and your wife may be the only ones in the beginning. If you are a lay person, it may be just you alone. However, as you continue on, people will gather. It will become a prayer movement. The whole church will be transformed. This is of utmost importance.

The Second Power is Power of the Word

The early churches received the teaching from the apostles. The apostles' teachings were from people who had seen Jesus with their own eyes, people who had directly experienced Jesus' words, and people who have had directly from God. Thus, their teachings had explosive power. The reason 3000 people were saved from Apostle Peter's sermon was because of the anointing of God. So where did their teachings come from? I am confident that their teaching came from prayer. The question is whether such apostolic anointing is continuing on in our preaching and teaching. When Apostle Paul was preaching the gospel in different areas and teaching at The School of Tyrannus, he must have taught the word through an apostolic anointing. He did not teach the Bible according to his knowledge or logic but he taught according to the apostolic anointing and teaching. He did not insist on transferring his own knowledge. What is important is that we truly must be sensitive to the Holy Spirit. The word must have relevance. The word must be able to give life at that moment. God gives such word during our times of prayer.

I say that the most important aspect of discipleship is mentoring. So where do you find the messages to be able to mentor someone? People ask, "Pastor, what message do we share during our cell group meetings?" I say, "Within your cell group meetings, briefly share what God spoke to you through the Sunday message. Then pray and have a time of ministry. Take time to hear their stories and to pray for them." They ask, "Then what do we do during PRINCIPLE OF 12 meetings? Is there a manual?" I tell them, "There is no manual. Holy Spirit is the manual. You must pray to Him." My disciples must hear the voice of God on their own. That is the only way they can be stirred up for God, revealing their hidden agendas and becoming transformed in the Lord through his power. This is the power of the Word. Christians must restore the power in God's Word. It cannot be mere teaching or transference of knowledge. We must hear the "Rhema" of God from countless "Logos" in the Bible. We must be able to find exactly what our people must hear at this critical juncture in their lives among thousands of different words that are found in the Bible. As they strike a core in the vein, we must strike the vein of the Word to awaken the souls of believers. This is apostolic teaching. This is more than possible. Then the church will grow, no matter what type of system they facilitate. The church can grow through a pastor or under a cell church system or a PRINCIPLE OF 12 system, if the message is overflowing with God's anointing. We must restore this.

If we can prepare the disciples with the same spirituality through PRINCIPLE OF 12 by the same word, that church can experience growth that is exponential. For this reason, when we have an Encounter Retreat or Alpha Course Conference, I don't do everything by myself; my disciples take turns speaking. I delegate to them saying, "I want you to give the first of ten lectures at the Encounter Retreat." However, I make sure to check up on them. Sometimes, when we are pressed for time, we meet during Morning Prayer time. "For this week, all of you (disciples) need to meet with me during Morning Prayer time. The congregation will meet and pray on their own." I call all of the twelve disciples together. "You are to give the second lecture of the Encounter Retreat next week. Give us that lecture right now." So he gives the lecture right then and there. Then I critique it thoroughly. "This is the problem with the sermon. Your logic is not clear. Your focus is not clear. Your testimony is too vague. You were supposed to share this testimony but you shared something that was completely irrelevant. Your message has too much baggage. Your pitch is high but it is not from your soul. Your pitch is too high and it is not a moving message." I give them all sorts of advice that sounds like criticism. There is no need to beat around the bush. This is the place of discipleship. Sometimes, I speak quite directly: "You are lacking in prayer. So don't do the lecture at this time." How embarrassing is that? However, because we are a family, we can share directly. In response to that, that disciple fasts: "Pastor, please let me do the lecture this time. I will do my best," and I say, "You may try again." I praise them when they do well. I believe that the powerful word of God must be imparted through the generations and the disciples. The key is not about transference of knowledge but whether we can find the word of God as we strike a vein in their core. How can we communicate the message to others? Is the message truly relevant to the listener? Such training is very necessary. According to Acts 5:42, the early church never stopped teaching and proclaiming the good news that Jesus is the Christ. They didn't just proclaim any word of God but they thoroughly proclaimed the Lordship of Jesus Christ.

The Third Power is the Power of Worship

In Acts 2:47, it says that they praised God and they enjoyed the favor of all people. As a result, the Lord added to their number daily those who were being saved. Where there is an overflowing of praise, there will be the presence of God. Where there is the presence of God, people will gather. Therefore, there must be genuine worship in our churches. It cannot be ritualistic praise. It cannot be praise that is just added onto the service. Even if praise is an afterthought, that praise must be given to God in all sincerity and lifted up to God in unison.

Worship takes different shapes and forms from generation to generation, almost as if it wears new clothes from season to season. There are so many worship movements throughout the world. The older generation cannot understand the praise and worship of younger people. The younger generation cannot understand the worship of older people. Therefore, we must help them to worship God in their own way according to each generation. My church has 3 worship groups. One of the worship groups has a big choir. For our last Easter service, about 200 members of the choir sang Handel's "Messiah." Another team is a passionate worship group that ministers to an age group of young people from 17 to 25. There are so many wonderful worship movements everywhere around the world. Even in Korea, many wonderful praise songs are being developed by many different worship ministries. Interestingly, my teenage son wouldn't listen to the praise music of the young adult group (age of 17 to 25) because, according to him, they are too old. This is how fast this generation changes. Young people jump up and down from beginning to end. They don't know the reason why or what it signifies. They wave their hands, kick… they do all sorts of weird things. What is important, however, is that if they are not allowed to express themselves, they end up leaving the church. So what can we do? We must jump with them. So I jump with them, sweating profusely.

There are a variety of styles of praise and worship songs everywhere. There is a worship ministry called Hillsongs from Australia. Their songs are sweeping the world. These songs, by nature, evoke genuine confessions of faith. Young people are completely in love with them. God is churning out so many wonderful praise songs all over the world. We must learn. We must be receptive because the world is becoming smaller and smaller. Furthermore, younger generations are becoming one across the board, over race and culture, especially when it comes to praise and worship. Do you want to activate your church's young adult ministry? Try singing new praise music continuously. They will gather.

Obviously, the most important part is for the worship leader to become a true worshiper. The worship leader must be a worshiper himself. He cannot be a mere musician. He cannot be a mere singer. He must encompass technique, musical talent and spirituality. How effectively God uses the worship leader is dependent on whether he can worship God with his entire being with all sincerity. Because Satan fell when he became prideful as the worship leader, the humility of the worship leader must be thoroughly held in check. It is because he stands before other people. We must take care of their spirituality. If we can help the church members go into the very presence of God, all other prayers seem to be answered naturally. If prayer opens the doors of heaven, worship brings heaven to earth. Worship is to tangibly feel the presence of the Holy Spirit of God by bringing his presence down to earth. There is a need to develop new ways of worship. There is a need to research different worship styles for various groups of people. No matter what style of worship, we must seek to experience the presence of God.

The Fourth is Power of Evangelism

Mark 16:19-20 reads, "After the Lord Jesus had spoken to them, he was taken up into heaven and he sat at the right hand of God. Then the disciples went out and preached everywhere, and the Lord worked with them and confirmed his word by the signs that accompanied it." When Jesus first came and led the multitudes, he did not lead them by his words but by many signs, wonders and healing. Today's generation only believes when they see the direct presence of the Holy Spirit with their own eyes. It seems to be a generation that will not come to God without first being shocked by signs and wonders. Therefore, we need to pray and live out the gospel in order for us to be effective evangelists. I believe that God can work powerfully if we ourselves believe in the power of the Holy Spirit.

When I first went into the mission field, many healings occurred, even the healing of cancer. As I shared before, after an epileptic person was healed by prayer, numerous sick people started to come. It was to the point where I could not tell if it was a general hospital or a church. They would bring honey in a little bottle or other small gifts, wanting to be prayed for. It took a long time to transform them into disciples of Jesus Christ. The important truth, however, was simple: "God is still alive today, Jesus paid for our sins on the cross, God forgives us of our sins when we pray in Jesus' name and he heals us." These are very basic words of truth. Then I would say, "Let's pray." And we would pray until God heals. That is all.

I only have one gift and that is the gift of faith. That's what I use to push ahead. No matter what gift God gives you, you must use it to the fullest extent. This is what I tell people: "Do you know the secret of being strong in God? Don't try to learn to use a gift you don't have but if you continue to use the gift that God has given you, you will naturally learn to develop other gifts as well. What is the gift that God has given you? Be faithful to that gift. If you can maximize that gift for the Lord, then God's work will take place in your life."

The power of evangelism must take root in church. In the beginning of my ministry, all the church members focused on me. However, after converting to the cell church mode, the Holy Spirit told me to "raise up every member as a minister like you." So, I poured all my energy into training the cell group leaders to do the same ministry that I was doing. I began to speak faith into their hearts so that they would begin to believe that the miraculous work of God would take place even through a simple prayer. When I did that, incredible things actually began to take place. People began to gather as they saw miracles in the cell groups. They gathered in homes. Then they gathered together in church. We were able to become the site of God's power ministry. Today's society needs God's manifestation. This is a generation that needs the presence of the Holy Spirit. Signs and wonders must come about through the hands of ordinary people who confess Jesus Christ as their Lord and Savior. It can happen. Then the world will confess Christ as their Lord. This is the purpose of our life.

The Fifth Power of PRINCIPLE OF 12 Spirituality is the Power of Cell

God demonstrated great works in every house. The

text tells us, "Every day they continued to meet together in the temple courts. They broke bread in their homes and ate together with glad and sincere hearts." They met at the temple courts and they met in their homes. Do you think they did that because they had extra time left over? Do you think they had their own cars? There was a certain power that drew their spirit. Why? Because every time they gathered in their homes, there was the presence of God. "Where two or three come together in my name, there am I with them." The word of God began to manifest in power. People continued to gather in homes as God's will was taking place within cells. Even unbelievers attended and that home became a church. Amazing discipleship began to take place within this context. Therefore, the early church was a church that experienced the ministry of God through small home gatherings. When you study the Pauline letters, you will find greetings that says, "I greet the church in so and so's house," or "Greet so and so in so and so's house." Yes, they did live during a time where churches weren't able to have their own facility, but it was truly God's great providence. We must be able to see God's great work in every individual home. My wish is to see house churches established on every corner of Almaty, Kazakhstan, and the Silk Road region. I want to see God's cell group established in every business, every office. It is my wish to see the work of God spread out into every facet of society through the hands of God's trained, anointed people. It is the desire of the Lord. This is the spirituality of PRINCIPLE OF 12.

Please remember these five powers: Word Power. Prayer Power. Worship Power. Evangelism Power. Cell Power.

When you do these ministries, God will work in powerful ways.

In PRINCIPLE OF 12 ministries, there needs to be two "totals" along with five powers. These are things that are given to Jesus in absolute "total"ity.

First is Total Holiness.

After God established his church, he was deeply concerned. He wanted his church to be pure. He wanted the church to be the body that obeyed the word of God. We know very well what happened to Ananias and Saphira. Why did God kill Ananias and Saphira when they sold their possession and gave it to the Lord, keeping only a small portion to themselves? There is only one reason. God did not want his very first church to lose holiness. He wanted his first church to set an example of serving God with total holiness and purity. That is why he took such extreme measures.

These days, we tolerate everything even when we know it is clearly sin. It creates a spiritual atmosphere that says that it is "okay" to sin, limiting the work of the Holy Spirit. How can Holy Spirit work in the midst of sin? God's church must restore holiness. Then and only then, will the Holy Spirit work and the Lord will draw near. David prayed this way, "Take not thy Holy Spirit from me." When he sinned, when he moved away from holiness, the very first thing he felt was the departure of the presence of God. When the church sins, when believers sin, we all suffer as a result of the things that are done in darkness. Therefore, the psalmist tells us to take time to seek the Lord. There is a need to come before the Lord to repent and to restore the presence of God. God's church must always maintain holiness. It must not compromise. Never, ever! The church members must be able to recognize it. We must set the spiritual tone. We must never allow a glimpse of compromising with the world. We cannot give the impression that we condone sin. While we can have a culture of forgiving the repentant, we cannot forgive those who are unrepentant. There must be absolute holiness in the church - total holiness.

Second is Total Commitment.

Is Jesus truly your Lord? Are we his servants? Does your life depend completely on Him? Then you must be absolutely devoted to him. Don't be committed 10% of your time. Don't be committed 50% of your time. The Bible commands us to completely deny ourselves. When Jesus was preparing his disciples, he told them that they couldn't follow him or be his disciple unless they were willing to deny their most precious possessions, their family, riches, parents and everything else. He spoke of total commitment.

How many theological Ph.D.'s do you have? How vast is your biblical knowledge? What type of training do you have? These are not important to Jesus. Jesus can simply give you these things. Jesus gives you the power to minister. The important question is, "How committed are you to me?"

One person, as he was turning away, said, "I will follow after burying my parents." Jesus said, "Let the dead bury their own dead, but you go and proclaim the kingdom of God." He is calling on us to make a commitment. He's telling us not to hesitate. The Lord is telling us to make the commitment today and not tomorrow. If a leader can live according to this full allegiance, I am positive that the members of his church can also live by the leader's example. When that happens, then the Lord will use us as a perfect channel. The problem is that there is often a lack of commitment. There is a problem with our holiness. We are still lacking the power to deny ourselves. I am the same way. This is my personal struggle. It must become a struggle for all of us. "Lord, I am still unclean. I am a man with unclean lips, unclean heart. I lack patience. I lack complete commitment before you. Lord, please help me." The Lord will lead us when we can confess such prayers.

Let's bring this image into the church. What was the image of the early church? "All the believers were together and had everything in common.

[45]Selling their possessions and goods, they gave to anyone as he had need."

This is the picture of commitment. I train my church to be committed. As I've shared before, the average monthly salary of the church members is about $100. However, only a few receive their paycheck on time. The company delays payment noting lack of funds. Sometimes they aren't paid, period. A certain company hasn't paid its workers in three years. Yet they still work for this company. I thought these people were so interesting. When you see their real need, the compassion overtakes you. You want to continue to help them. I wanted to bring in aid from Korea and from America to have a ministry to meet their needs. When I prayed concerning this matter, God said, "No. Teach them about commitment. Raise up people like the widow of Zarephath. Then I can bless them abundantly. Get your people to be committed." Do you know the reason for the failure in missions to South America in the beginning? It is because the Catholic Church only did relief ministry. They did not plant faith in their hearts nor train them to give. They simply kept on giving and aiding again and again. One of the reasons for the Korean Church's revival is that the missionaries did not build the church with their own money but they taught the Koreans to build their church with their own money. In other words, they taught them about commitment. We must be committed. Because I have been away from Korea for over twenty years, I am not familiar with Korean Church practices. For example, I asked a pastor, "How do you get your church people to go to a seminar like this PRINCIPLE OF 12 seminar?" "It costs about $70 but no one would go if they had to pay for the entire cost. When we offer to subsidize $30 or $50 of the cost, then they start to reconsider." This is a big problem. Truly, there are too many problems. This is my honest expression. There is no hunger when they ought to be hungry. We must restore the hunger.

We must recreate the atmosphere of commitment. There are only 15 Christian churches in all of Azerbaijan. 13 of those churches wanted to learn about the PRINCIPLE OF 12 ministry in a united conference. About 250 people were willing to come. We needed to get permission from the government. My wife's name and my name were turned in to the president for a permit. We needed about $12,000 to hold the conference at a conference center. This is an enormous amount of money for the mission field. How much money can I expect my church members to give when their average monthly income is only $100? As I was praying to God about the needed $12,000, God gave me an impression, "Get your members to give their offering." I had an impression to make an announcement to recruit 5 people who would give $1000 each. "That's right. Some people can give little and some can give a lot. But they will commit according to what they have." On the following Sunday morning, I made the announcement. "As I was praying for the $12000 that was needed for the conference in Azerbaijan, the Holy Spirit is leading me to recruit 5 people who can give an offering of $1000. I need your prayer and offering. If you are able to give, please bring your offering to me." A similar event took place in Turkey as well. And then I waited. I made the announcement in 1st and 2nd service. I told them to bring it by 3rd service. I too am very stubborn; banks aren't even open on Sundays. Amazingly, by the end of the 3rd service, 6 people brought $1000 each. One of the ladies looked quite poor. She looked as if she'd even have a difficult time giving an offering of $100 or $10 dollars, let alone $1000. So I asked her, "How are you able to give such a large sum of money?" She answered, "Since about a year ago, God told me to save up $1000 dollars so that I can give it when Pastor Kim asks for an offering of $1000." So she did and brought her savings of $1000. I was so deeply moved... I was so thankful... One person was a businessman of a small company from Egypt, who was deported for sharing the gospel. So he came to Kazakhstan (Egypt is also a Muslim country) looking for opportunities. He had attended the 2nd service. Since Azerbaijan is also a Muslim country, he wanted to give towards evangelism. Following the service, he went to his company immediately to gather what money he had, it turned out to be exactly $1000. He brought the money to 3rd service without delay. It was even more incredible because it was only his first time at our church. Another lady came up to me and asked, "Pastor, how about $500? Can I give $500?" "Holy Spirit hasn't spoken to me about $500 yet," I told her.

Although we are a mission field, we are a mission field that helps other mission fields. I'm truly thankful for that. We became autonomous about 7 - 8 years ago. God has blessed us by allowing us to plant 23 branch churches. All the branch churches are operated by our own resources. There are people who send special offerings of $10,000, $20,000, and $50,000 for church building projects. In such cases we do buy the branch churches their own buildings. However, in general, all the expenses and pastors' salaries are paid by our church. This is possible on the mission field. Why? How is it possible?

Simply put, it is commitment. My church members know that we are able to do such things by God's help. Even though we didn't have money, when we were building our church facility, we bought a 3 acre lot with two buildings in the middle of downtown for about $450,000 to use as a church and a mission center. This is an amazing work accomplished by the grace of God. If I were to share, there'd be no end to such testimonies. It is God's miraculous work. I asked the church members, "Let's build the church with our own strength." So, some people sold their homes. I said, "If you have two apartment units, sell one. Let's store our treasures in heaven." I didn't ask those with one unit to sell. I simply said, "Let us give to the Lord with passion and devotion. Your next generation will enjoy the blessings. Do you believe this? Where are you going to invest your money? Are you just going to store it? Are you planning to give after you save up a little more? By then, it'll probably be too late. You must do it when the Lord is asking you." We have spent about 3 million dollars so far in constructing the church that houses about 2500 people. About a third of the money is purely from our church member's offerings. Mission fields are poor. Yet one time, for two consecutive weeks, an envelope containing $5000 and $6000 was given. I made an announcement, "I don't know who you are but I thank you. God will truly bless you greatly."

We must teach commitment. You must be committed. When you are committed, your children will be committed. When you are committed, your children will enjoy the blessings. Why aren't we familiar with this spiritual order? We must allow this mindset of Total Commitment to take root at our churches and God will do his work. Because Kazakhstan and Silk Road is Muslim areas, you cannot have a ministry without your own building. I have led three PRINCIPLE OF 12 conferences in Turkey so far. The biggest church in Turkey made a transition into a PRINCIPLE OF 12 church. When I visited them, altogether they were less than 200. They had already reverted back to a traditional church. I was so frustrated... They were not committed. I am in the process of getting them to be committed. They can no longer gather to pray. When they pray out loud, they are arrested by the police. What can they do? You make the commitment for them. The churches of the Silk Road region needs church buildings. With the money to build one beautiful building here, you can build many churches over there. There are buildings that you can buy for a mere $15,000 to $20,000. Some buildings are in the $50,000 to $70,000 range and bigger buildings cost $100,000 to $200,000. It's a lot of money. But compared to building projects in Korea and America, this is such a small amount. Because they lack so much, they are not able to maintain their church.

There is an area where a building became available for $60,000 to $70,000. This would enable 500 people to gather to worship. This building can be bought for $60,000 but they can't buy it because they don't have the money. They are still waiting and fasting. They have no means. Churches in many areas simply don't know what else to do. I boldly share this with you without shame. I bless you to be able to make a commitment for the kingdom of God. I bless you in the Lord's name that your children will enjoy God's blessings for thousands of generations.

There are two spiritual basics of PRINCIPLE OF 12. Based on my ministry experience, there are two important factors for maintaining one's spirituality. The first is being sensitive to the voice of the Holy Spirit, every minute, every hour. We must always remain in the state of openness to be able to discern which direction He wants us to go, to what He wants to say, and how He wants us to minister. Holy Spirit comes and goes like the wind. He passes by after softly whispering to you. We want to be able to hear that whisper. Every moment, there is a voice to be heard and a command to obey. Sometimes, his soft rebuke goes unnoticed as well. If you are not sensitive, you will miss it. If you miss it, it will take even longer to find it the next time. It becomes difficult unless you experience even a bigger presence in deeper prayer. This is the Holy Spirit's presence in the present sense. In order to make a disciple, with a compassionate soul, you need to see the person in the same light that Jesus sees him. He may be lacking, impure, dishonest, and so forth but you need to have an eye to see what the Lord sees. You need to be able to hear the voice of the Lord, the voice of the Holy Spirit. If you are able to hear that voice and relay that voice, that person will experience an awesome spiritual transformation. Acknowledge the character of the Holy Spirit. The one who is speaking to you now is God who will also speak tomorrow, speak wherever you are, and speak to whomever you have a relationship with. If you are sensitive to the voice of God, you can have all these spiritualities.

The second basic truth is that of the cross and the faith in the resurrection. We must know the grace of the cross of our Lord. We must realize how big of a sinner we are in order to powerfully and tangibly experience the grace of his redemption. When I was studying theology in Germany, I had many conflicts with my wife. "Why did I struggle with my wife even as a pastoral intern? Why can't I understand even one woman?" I was in such turmoil and despair. "Why do you bother to feed yourself? Are you a man? Are you the man of the house?" Such questions and rebukes entered my mind. One early morning, as I was praying and crying before the Lord in the woods, out of pure frustration, I realized I was in the wrong. Yet I couldn't change myself even though I wanted to. I began to confess, "God, I am a sinner. I can't do anything. I can't preach. I am not even a pastoral intern. I am a sinner." I was weeping before the Lord when the Holy Spirit spoke. "Now do you understand?" He was asking if I realized that I was a sinner. After asking me if I realized that I am a sinner, he told me, "I love you." That meant everything to me. I cried so much that morning. "Lord, I am a sinner. But I thank you. I thank you for cleansing me with the blood of Jesus Christ. From now on, I will live only for you. I will deny myself even more." When you realize who you are, forgiving your wife becomes easier. We misbehave because of pride. We stick to our views, passing out judgments left and right.

We try to judge with our righteous eyes but we fail to act according to the Lord's grace. I came to realize why the faith of the cross is so important. "When I die to myself, God resurrects me by giving my spirit the life from heaven. But when I try to live and win, the life of Christ dies within me." I came to realize this truth. How wonderful is the cross of the Lord? I pray that such grace can be with all of us. The church of the Lord will experience awesome power as a result.

Chapter 5: Anointing for Explosive Growth

The work of God begins when the Lord's word comes to us in faith. There are so many words and promises of God recorded in the Bible but not all of them come to me with conviction. God works by giving us his word personally according to his time. The impossible becomes possible in one's mind when the voice of God is heard clearly like a revelation, deep in one's soul and the conviction of "this is it" sets in. Afterwards, then our hands and feet can begin to move. We develop perseverance and persistence which will overcome any and all obstacles. We may at times fall or be discouraged but because of the conviction given by the Holy Spirit, we bear fruit in the ministry. Because of this truth, we must be sensitive to the voice of the Holy Spirit as we pray. Many people ignore this truth. Some say, "It'll be okay. I'll just pray." Even though there is truth in the voice of God, they ignore it. Actually, to pray means to receive the affirmation from the Holy Spirit. We must pray until we receive and we must pray with the conviction we have received, until what we have received becomes a reality in our lives. When such things take place, when we can enter before the Lord and give true thanksgiving, true joy will spring from our spirits. God will take delight and will give us new tasks in response. This process must continue. We cannot stop after a single success but the process must continue as a life of blessing. In that sense, the relationship between the Lord and us is an important progression which must be continued forever. The core factors that we must focus on are our intimate relationship with the Holy Spirit and listening to the voice of God from deep within. Many people ask. "How can I receive God's vision? How can I dwell in God's vision?" There is no secret. We must enter into his presence through deep, continued and prolonged times of prayer. We must hear the voice of the Lord through our prayers. When that happens, we will experience new works in our lives.

The Vision of Habakkuk

In Habakkuk 2:1, it is written, "I will stand at my watch and station myself on the ramparts; I will look to see what he will say to me, and what answer I am to give to this complaint." As Habakkuk was watching the circumstances and situations of the world, the society and the people, he was consumed by the essential question, "What is the God of righteousness doing?" We must ask essential questions, rather than trivial questions. Most people gloss over in imprudence saying, "Such things happen as you live or do ministry. They will take care of themselves with time." However, Habakkuk went before the Lord with his question. He went into his prayer room. He went into the presence of the Holy Spirit to get answers. When you receive the answers to essential questions, you can have vital ministry. When the ministry becomes essential, people who are interested in essentials will begin to gather. At this point, true commitment will begin to emerge. This is why Habakkuk waited on the

Lord to hear God's voice and answer. When you hear from God and receive answers to your questions, a vision is birthed from that moment on. Most questions are the same. It is because we all live in the same society. We all face the same difficulty. We all live with the same hurts. The problem is people cannot get answers if they are not certain. Once the answer appears, the vision is given. The answer will appear in our lives as a vision. Once you hold on to the vision, followers will appear. When the vision is clear, faith arises from the corporate body. When faith arises because of vision, it can transform the spiritual atmosphere of the church and people will begin to move. People will come in agreement saying, "This is a proper vision. He is a servant loved by God." At such moments, true revival and true work of God begins. Habakkuk 2:1 tells us that we must enter deep into his presence to receive such vision.

When it says, "I will stand at my watch," it means to stand between God and his people. He stood in the place of the intercessor and longed to hear the voice of God as he watched over the circumstances of the people, as he understood the powers of the evil one. Furthermore when he says, "Station myself on the ramparts; I will look to see what he will say to me," speaks of desperation. It also speaks about his expectation that God would answer. The reason we stop praying is due to lack of faith and expectation that God will answer. It is due to a lack of passion to partake in God's holy work, willing to do what God desires in spite of difficulties. It is due to a lack of motivation from within. Habakkuk decided, "I want some answers. I will wait and watch what God will say as a person who stands before God and before the people." It shows us that his spirit was in a struggle. He continues, "I will look to see... what answer I am to give to this complaint. I will see. I will not give up without answers. Lord, please speak to me." To get up and move before the answer is given is to begin a ministry without goals. It is an ephemeral life. We cannot allow our lives and our ministry to be dragged around by others' programs, only to fall and die when we run out of energy. Even if we have to wait a long time, we must start God's work, flying high as an eagle, after discovering what God's voice is and what God's vision is. Without fail, many followers will gather around this particular eagle.

In verse 2, it is written, "Then the LORD replied: 'Write down the revelation and make it plain on tablets so that a herald may run with it.'" God's voice is finally heard. He commanded us to make clear goals. God does not want us to take his vision lightly. He wants us to give our lives for it. We cannot be lazy about God's revelation. Revelation passes by. It is gone in a moment. That is why we must be sensitive. Someone who is sensitive to the Holy Spirit does not miss the voice of God. If we do not miss the voice of God, we can obey. When we miss the voice of God, we follow the methods of the flesh. When that happens, there will be no fruit no matter how much you struggle or work. We can fly like an eagle if there is confidence that we are doing the will of God. We will not die because of the vision. We can survive even if we are weary.

However, without vision, you will die due to weariness. With a vision in mind, you can overcome weariness and ultimately win. This is the difference between people with vision and people who lack vision.

In verse 3, it is written, "For the revelation awaits an appointed time; it speaks of the end and will not prove false. Though it linger, wait for it; it will certainly come and will not delay." If God's vision is given, if you heard his voice deep inside, if you are certain that it is from God, then, you must not wait. We must go forward even if it feels as slow as a tortoise. Go forward even if success cannot be seen. Why? If you have the conviction, if you have seen God's revelation and heard God's voice, do not be shaken. There will be followers around you. There has to be followers of God. Two million, three million people followed Moses because he met God in front of the burning bush and heard his voice and revelation. Moses was ultimately to lead the Israelites into the promise land of Canaan, even though there were oppositions from numerous multitudes, such Nadab and Abihu who set unauthorized fires, and Aaron and Miriam who spoke against Moses. It is the same way with your church. I am confident that if you can go forward with the correct vision, clear conviction, precise direction and goal setting, your ministry will be fruitful. This is why the most important thing in our life is for the leader to receive a vision and to set direction. God's work begins the moment you hear the voice of God. Please do not move in carelessness before you hear God's voice, however.

I received a revelation as I was starting the PRINCIPLE OF 12 ministry. A conviction came and because of the conviction that came, the church grew incredibly. It experienced explosive growth. It is so simple; why didn't I know this? It is because we lived a careless life of transferring knowledge rather than treating revelation as revelation and welcoming revelation into our lives. This is why our hearts were not moved. This is why we were not motivated. We would nod our heads but would not move our hands and feet. However, when revelation comes to the core of our being, we begin to move. When the revelation of God comes upon us, we are inspired and we are led to move. Our rigid bodies begin to loosen.

God's will in Genesis

Genesis 1:28 is an amazing revelation that God has given to me. I believe it is one of the wonderful revelations people, who are involved in PRINCIPLE OF 12, have received. I live by it as my motto. Genesis 1:27-28 reads:

> [27] So God created man in his own image, in the image of God he created him; male and female he created them. [28] God blessed them and said to them, "Be fruitful and increase in number; fill the earth and subdue it. Rule over the fish of the sea and the birds of the air and over every living creature that moves on the ground."

Testimony of Pastor Sam Seong Kim

I graduated from Dae-Gwang High School. I sang in the school's choir and other choirs of big churches in Korea, such as Youngnak. I even attended Bible study during high school but did not believe in Jesus. I went to Wednesday services but I could not believe in Jesus. Then I began to question the meaning of life. I was attending law school but because of the questions I had about life, I volunteered to go to the army. I grappled with my questions for 3 years.

It was a very serious matter to me. Without a purpose, whether a man lives rich or poor, life can be meaningless. What is the difference if I die now or a hundred years from now? These questions haunted me for 10 years. Upon my discharge from the army, I re-enrolled in school as a junior. Yet I still did not have answers. I did not know where I came from and where I was going. I read philosophy books. I once wrote to a philosophy professor. He wrote back saying, "Like adolescence, such struggles will pass with time. In time, you will forget about such questions. That's how we are meant to live." The philosophy professor was a deacon at church. Why didn't he introduce me to Jesus? My hunger for God did not dissipate. It is because he designed me to seek him forever. Nevertheless, at the time I did not find any answers. In order to know God, I shared my struggles with my roommate. He had been a Christian all his life and apparently he prayed for me day and night. I became born again because of him. After, I would scour the bookstores to study the Bible: "Secrets to Bible Study," "Secrets to Bible Memorization". I wrote out 150 verses on construction paper. I cut them out and began to memorize three verses a day. I did it according to my friend's suggestion. I am foolish that way. I memorized the 150 verses as I would memorize vocabulary words. I memorized 3 verses a day, 27 verses a week. Then I would start all over from the beginning the following week. I still did not understand. I asked my friend, "I really want to know God. What should I do?" Therefore, he responded, "Let's go fast." I went to fast for a week. I fasted but I just became hungry. God did not show himself to me. Yet I had a good time reading the book of Job. I read it three times. Interestingly, the book of Job was of great help to me. It helped me to understand God more deeply and to understand the sufferings in life. Upon returning, my friend gave me a 10 tape sermon series called "Man Must Be Born Again in Spirit." As I was listening to the tape, I learned that I must be born again through the Holy Spirit. I have such a particular personality. As I was listening to the tape, I had to make sure, if the pastor was quoting the Bible correctly and whether he was taking the passage out of context or not. I could only understand it if the sermon was extremely logical. It took me a long time to listen to the sermons completely. After days of listening, I was able to get to only 5 to 6 tapes. On the sixth or seventh tape, I heard that man had to be born again in the spirit. The pastor began to expound on John 14, 15, 16 and then Acts 2. He spoke about the Samaritan woman's conversion and the Holy Spirit's encounter with the church of Ephesus. He talked about the need to be born again by the Holy Spirit. "Ah ha, this is the key. God's word is not effective to me because I have not been born again by the Holy Spirit and have not been filled with the presence of the Holy Spirit. I began to confess my sins but it was difficult without the conviction of the Holy Spirit. Yet I wrote down all my sins on a piece of paper. I began by writing down the sin of taking tuition from my parents even though I had received a scholarship. I wrote it all down and then I began to repent. As I was repenting, my roommate came back from the library and saw that I was serious about my struggles. He put his hands on me and began to pray for me. He opened the Bible to show me the passage that read, "When two or more are gathered in my name, I'll be there," and he encouraged me to pray with him. He told me that he just received Christ just a week ago, even though he had been going to church all his life. He began to pray for me saying, "Let's ask for the Holy Spirit to come today." Then the Holy Spirit of Acts 2 came to me. I was on fire. I prayed for about three to four hours, sweating profusely. As I prayed, the fire that came to the upper room on the day of Pentecost came on to me. The 150 verses of the Bible I had memorized began to pierce my heart. I could not stand it. God gave me two very special verses on that day. They were Acts 1:8: "But you will receive power when the Holy Spirit comes on you; and you will be my witnesses in Jerusalem, and in all Judea and Samaria, and to the ends of the earth," and Romans 10:13-15, "for 'everyone who calls on the name of the Lord will be saved'. How, then, can they call on the one they have not believed in? In addition, how can they believe in the one of whom they have not heard? Moreover, how can they hear without someone preaching to them? And how can they preach unless they are sent? As it is written, 'How beautiful are the feet of those who bring good news!'"

Through these words, God helped me to realize what my ministry was to be. My mission was to share the gospel to those who have not heard it. I realized that I was to become a missionary the moment I became saved. A missionary was born that night. The next day, I shared the gospel with a person sitting alone at the school gymnasium. The Bible became so sweet; I read the Bible standing in the subway train and even while walking. I had to go to lectures but I had no desire to. The Holy Spirit just filled me with such excitement that I began to call my friends one by one to a coffee shop, sharing the gospel. I passionately shared with them about why they need to believe in Jesus, what the meaning of life is, and what the most meaningful thing in one's life should be. Every morning, I would wake up at 4::00 AM, to pray for people to be saved by placing my hand on their dorm room doors. Once I even fasted three days for someone. I actually fasted frequently. Yet I was so filled with joy. The Bible was so sweet that I had read the entire New Testament on a daily basis. Everyday. I would tell myself, "I have a test tomorrow. I am only going to read the Bible until midnight and study for the test." I would have to ask my friends to make a cheat sheet for me because sometimes, even after midnight, the Bible was so fascinating, I would give in. I would just think, "I don't know. I'm just going to read the Bible." Then the following morning, I would simply try to memorize the cheat sheet. Interestingly, what I memorized would show up on the exam. God truly helped me. I received scholarships until I graduated. It was truly an amazing work of God. It was because of God's revelation; the revelation that I was called as a missionary helped me to overcome many obstacles, including difficulties in life, difficulties in relationships, difficulties in finances and other numerous struggles.

Importance of God's Revelation

All servants go through a time of adversity. The key to overcoming afflictions is God's revelation. The voice God gave me when he met me becomes more than sufficient and that enables me to overcome any situation. That one experience alone gives me enough passion for Christ and evangelism to last the rest of my life. That encounter enables me to have the courage to be martyred. Our God is great. Among countless words, God has the ability to transform us by his revelations alone. So how important is it that we hear his voice? More than displaying countless knowledge, it is far more important to be able to hear the revelatory voice of the living God. Even if we should only hear the same voice repeatedly, that voice is able to transform any man. I pray that you will be able to hear the voice and conviction of the Lord.

God's Blessing

As I was reading Genesis 1:28, I profoundly realized that God truly wants to bless us. Pastor Yongi Cho said he shouted, "God is so good," hundreds, thousands, ten thousands of times. I also shouted this but I did not feel the deep revelation of how good God really is. I realized that even a simple phrase like that must come to me as "my word." The Bible tells us that God created man in his own image. This is very important. What is the first thing that God did to the man who was created in his own image? This is very crucial. To his creation, those created in his own image, God commanded his blessing: "God commanded blessings to me." "God blessed them and said to them..." God's word has awesome power. He gives us suggestions. God's word gives us the power of suggestion. People are beings who move according to suggestions. Hypnotism has power as well, although it can be the suggestion of the Enemy. Even Satan puts suggestions in our hearts before he begins to move. He places thoughts of negativity, impossibility, and impurity. Once we accept these thoughts, our hands and feet move according to the suggestions. God gives us his suggestions through his words. Why does John 1 tell us that God is the Word? The power to govern us is within the Word of God. The awesome power of the Word governs our thoughts. This is why we must study the Word. However, these words must come to us as revelation in order to have true power. Yet, we see that the very first act of God to his creation was to proclaim his blessings over them. It is God's will to bless. God's plans never go awry, even when people sin and fall. The plan of God stays the same even when you sin. Adam fell and Eve fell. Were they sent out as a punishment for committing a crime? No. The curse came as the result of their sin. They changed into people of scorn who must sweat in order to eat and live. However, God's plan of blessing did not change. Man fell even deeper into sin since Adam. Cain killed Abel. Many other murders were committed and the world fell deep into sin. The Bible tells us that God regretted creating man. Still, God's plan of blessing did not change. This is how God's plan began. What to do? He would wipe away all of humanity but he would choose one man. He chose Noah. The Bible tells us that Noah found favor in the eyes of the Lord. He was not chosen because of his righteousness. Rather, he was able to live his life of righteousness because he found favor in the eyes of the Lord. In other words, he was chosen. His entire family was saved through Noah. The plan of blessing remained unchanged. God chose Noah in order to enable people to enjoy true spiritual blessings and divine blessings in God. In Genesis 9:1, Noah built the altar and sacrificed burnt offerings to God. God smelled the pleasing aroma and promised never to judge men by water, and gave the rainbow as the sign of his promise. One thing that God did after Noah sacrificed burnt offerings to God was to pronounce blessing over Noah: "God blessed Noah and his sons, saying to them 'Be fruitful and increase in number and fill the earth.'" This reiterates the fact that the blessing that was pronounced, the plan of blessing that was set in motion, will never fade away. God's plans for blessing do not change no matter how you have lived your life. Even if you lived your life in sin, if you are living in sin, or under God's discipline, God's plan for blessings does not change. Even discipline turns into God's blessing. Discipline itself is a blessing. Adversity is a blessing. All things work together for good because God is a God of blessing. He is waiting for us to repent. God is waiting for man's response and answer.

Man rebelled against God after Noah by building the tower of Babel. They came against God. While God wanted to bless and his plans do not change, there rose another difficulty. It was the plan of blessing through faith. In Abraham, God's new principle of blessings in faith began.

God's blessings to Abraham

In Genesis 12:1, God chose Abram. He appeared to Abram and told him, "Leave your country, your people and your father's household and go to the land I will show you." Blessings overflow when you obey God in faith and when you obey God's word, promise and command. God promised these blessings. In verses 2 and 3, he said, "I will make you into a great nation." God promised Abraham that he would make him into a great nation. Abraham was not a great nation at the time. He was a nameless father of a family. He lived in Ur of the Chaldeans, which was the land of idols. Yet God chose him. Similarly, you were chosen to become a great nation and to become a source of blessing. An incredible nation will rise. God chose me for the Turkish people of the Silk Road. I am not saying this because of pride but from a very healthy self-respect. I am confident of this and this confidence makes me human. It makes me act like a father. Without such conviction, I would act like a tail, instead of acting like a father. God gave me this conviction. This is how I am able to travel back and forth from Turkey to China as if I am moving about in my own house. It actually feels like home. Everywhere I go, I am happy because I truly believe in the promise that he would make a great nation. I prayed, "God, give me the Turkish people. Give me the Muslims. I want to reach the Arabs through these people. Give them to me. Let me be the father of a nation." I started out as a father of a family, the spiritual father of Almaty, Kazakhstan. Now I want to become the spiritual father of all of Kazakhstan and the Silk Road. We only live once. I want to give the greatest glory to God with my life.

Secondly, God blessed Abraham by telling him, "I will bless you." God wants to bless you. God wants to bless your thoughts. God wants to bless the works of your hands and your feet. God wants to bless everything you are a part of when you are obedient in faith. This is the secret in enjoying God's blessing in faith. Often we run into problems because we are disobedient. Why is disobedience a problem? It is because we have not heard from God. Why didn't we hear from God? It is because we did not go deep into his presence. We keep going in circles, like most people, doing the same things repeatedly. God is telling us to stop that. He truly wants to bless us so we need to hear his voice.

This third blessing was given: "I will make your name great." No one knew the name of Abraham. Now, everyone knows his name. Muslims and Christians alike know his name. Abraham is the father of faith. When I first came to Almaty, no one knew who Sam Seong Kim was. My wife was the only one who knew my name; my kids did not even know my name. The kids really did not know what kind of man their father was. They did not know that I was God's son. They did not know that God chose me. Now, they all know. All my church members know and all of Almaty and Kazakhstan knows. Even the president knows me. All of the Silk Road knows me. It is not that I wanted to make myself known but God made my name known. The reason I am telling you this is that the same thing can happen in your life. Abraham was not the only one chosen. All who are willing to live in obedience to faith have the same blessings promised to them. Are these my words? Am I simply trying to encourage you? No. In Galatians 3:13, it is written, "Christ redeemed us from the curse of the law by becoming a curse for us, for it is written: 'Cursed is everyone who is hung on a tree.' He redeemed us in order that the blessing given to Abraham might come to the Gentiles through Christ Jesus, so that by faith we might receive the promise of the Spirit." What is the blessing Abraham received from God? The blessing comes to us as the curses depart and as we believe in Jesus Christ. This is what is written in Galatians 3:13-14. This is biblical. Such blessings are available for us. He wants to make your name great and God desires to see his people lifted up.

The fourth blessing is that "you will be a source of blessing." God wants people around you and related to you to be blessed through you. It is not about being blessed alone. This is Christian ethics. This is the meaning of Christian blessing. Many people will be able to eat and prosper through you. You will feed people spiritually and physically. You must continue to feed and share. God wants us to be a source of blessing. Even if you pour out, it will not come to an end because you are a source. This is the purpose of God's call and the secret to great faith. When you obey God in faith, you can be blessed in this way. I pray that you will be blessed in such a way. I am confident that Genesis 1:28 is God has promised blessings for us.

Genesis 1:28 is the most basic picture of God's blessing and with it, includes a commandment. God wants to bless us with a strong anointing. I will give you the anointing of blessing to you. What is true blessing? God said, "God blessed them and said to them, 'be fruitful and increase in number; fill the earth and subdue it. Rule over the fish of the sea and the birds of the air and over every living creature that moves on the ground.'" This is the substance of blessing. This is the essential blessing. Continue to subdue, continue to rule, continue to increase, and continue to be fruitful. This is why explosive growth is the will of God. Businesses must increase. This is God's plan and not man's greed. Is it man's greed to want the expansion of the kingdom of God? No, not man's greed - it is holy greed. God's kingdom must be expanded. The world of darkness must be pushed out and God's kingdom of light must expand. We must have holy greed and have a holy vision. This is the vision Jesus had: go to the nations, preach the gospel, make disciples and cause all nations to kneel down before Jesus Christ. "Let your will be done on earth as in heaven." This means that the will of God has not been accomplished yet. Why must we be caught up with such frivolous things? Why must we rob God of his tithe? Why do we disobey when he calls on us to do missions? Why do we do things in name only? He wants us to do it truthfully. If we are going to evangelize, we must do it faithfully. He wants us to enjoy God's blessings and live a life of blessing. This is what the text is saying. There are five verbs in God's blessing. I personally like repetition so I must have preached this text many, many times. This is the revelation. If I realize that a message is from God, I have a tendency to preach the message until the members digest it fully. After preaching this message many times, the revelation of God came. The understanding of the Holy Spirit came. The 5 points are "be fruitful, increase, fill, subdue, and rule." If this is what God commanded us to do, I believe that God has also given us the ability to accomplish his commandments.

Immanent Power of Increase

The command to be fruitful, to increase, and fill means that God has blessed Adam and Eve both. God blessed man as well as woman. We must come together in order to be fruitful, to increase and fill the earth. In other words, God desires growth and expansion. He desires explosive growth. He gave us the blessing to increase. This is why I had four children but I really wanted to have 12. I am not sure if I will have opportunity to have more. Not only does he want us to increase in family size but his church as well. He wants the church to grow both quantitatively and qualitatively. He wants us to invade Satan's territory, conquer it and go into the land of Canaan. Specifically, go in, conquer the land of the seven tribes of Canaan, and return it to the Lord. God is a warrior. God is victorious. This is the content of our blessing. I pray that you will believe it. I pray that you increase. All the PRINCIPLE OF 12 churches firmly believe in God's plans for increase. God has given us the authority to increase. If you are Adam's descendents, you have already received the authority to expand. If your ancestor is Eve, then all you women already have received the blessing to increase through Eve.

Do you believe that it is God's will for your business to expand? Believe it. You will be happy when you believe. You will find yourself smiling, even when you are alone. My church members are growing to be 10,000, 100,000, and 200,000 in number... even having to move to another city because the city may not be big enough. They might possibly be moving to another nation. God's kingdom will continue to expand when people submit to the name of Jesus Christ. How exciting is this? God wants us to continue to increase.

When I assessed my church, I realized that my church really was not growing at the time. For about three years, the cells had stopped at around 300. We adopted the cell church model and for the first 3-4 years the church had grown through the cell churches. It grew to 80, 90, 100, 150, 200, 250, to 300. Once it reached 300, it stopped. What was wrong? If the church is not growing, there is a problem. Something is plugged up. Where is the blockage? What went wrong? I could not figure it out. Then I started the PRINCIPLE OF 12 model. I believed. I began to understand that growth is God's clear plan. I thought I had understood it but in reality, I did not fully comprehend. I had believed but my church members did not. The work of God does not take place until all believe. All must believe. This is what you call a movement. Holy Spirit likes movement because he is like the wind. He is like a wave. We describe the Holy Spirit as the wind and as the wave. A person who can generate it is a visionary. A person who can generate it is God's true leader. If you move by yourself, you will fall. You will get exhausted and die. However, a smart person makes disciples. He creates a movement within them and he makes his disciples move. Then, he simply directs. He commands and directs. In the truest sense, his direction has to have the authority to change the disciples' whole life. Then, the work of God takes place. I did not experience the work of God until January of last year. They had told me that the explosive growth of PRINCIPLE OF 12 does not happen until about 4 years into it. I didn't have the patience to wait four years so for the past 2 years, I'd been teaching my church leaders on what PRINCIPLE OF 12 is, why we must adapt it into the church, what it means, why commitments are needed, why the deep presence of God is needed and why passionate prayers are needed.

We started Encounter at the beginning of January of 2004. Every week, 100, 150 and 200 people attended the Encounter. When I announced it to the church members, they had a difficult time with it saying, "How can we attend the Encounter for $20 when our monthly pay is $100?" Therefore, I continued to challenge them to go. I said, "The church has money but the church will not sponsor you. Do not serve God with such passivity. You will give it meaning when you pay your own way. Even if you do not have money, if you pray to God, God will give you the finances in order to bring you healing and transformation. Do you believe this?" They said amen so easily. Nevertheless, I demanded that they demonstrate their "amen" with action. The offering is quite high at my church. It is enough to boast about for a church in the mission field. Yet, I refuse to pay for my church members. Some must think, "Boy, our pastor is so stingy." I do not mind being stingy. My goal is to mature their faith. I cannot keep giving fish. I must train them to catch their own fish and to be a source of blessing so that they may be blessed. Some are willing to pay enormous amounts of money to see psychiatrists and for medicine but they are not willing to pay $20 for a retreat to be healed by God. I asked them to change their mindset. People did change their mentality. Each week, 100 - 200 people went to Encounter and came back completely changed. The testimonies came pouring in each week: "I met God, I was healed, my husband changed, I changed, we were on the verge of divorce but through Encounter we discovered our problem, the demon was cast out of me, etc."

All kinds of testimonies poured in and changes began to take place. We continued every week for 6 months. Now we hold it twice a month. Every first week is the Men's Encounter. Every second week is the Women's Encounter. The Young Adults and Youth have their own Encounter. Even the children have Encounter during vacation times. Six months had passed but the number of cells remained at 300. I was not satisfied. Natural growth is not explosive growth. I was not satisfied with natural growth. I was not satisfied with horizontal movement. God's kingdom must expand; horizontal movement does not add to the kingdom of God. I began to wrestle with that issue.

As I continued to preach Genesis 1:28, I had a realization. We did have a problem and the problem was me. My role was to communicate the revelation so people can believe, have faith and move on. However, I kept telling them to "do it" in a legalistic sense, which led to difficulty due to a lack of understanding. I realized that I had to convey God's revelation. From that time on, based on the word, I began to convey the revelation night and day. God's plan is for explosive growth. You have seeds of blessing given to Adam, already sown into you. If such blessings were commanded to Adam and Eve, if God has given them the amazing power to increase, you also have the same power within you. Because you have been born as a descendent of Adam, you definitely have the authority of blessing. You will increase. Afterwards, around July, during my conversation with my wife, I heard that the members were having a difficult time. My wife is a strong spiritual woman. I was hesitant because I tend to be too soft. I asked my wife to preach on that Sunday. When she got on the pulpit, she proclaimed, "Why are you not growing? Why can't you change your mindset? You will all experience explosive growth within three months." Then she called her disciples in and told the cell district leaders to make 40, 100, 144 cells within three months. She instructed them firmly. So I called all my disciples, "Associate Pastor, make at least 12 cells within 3 months. No more conversation is necessary. I have taught all I can. You all know how. You have heard enough. Now you must move." I called in some others. "How many cells do you have?" "I have 3." "Make 12 cells. Make 12 disciples. Do you believe in the vision of Jesus' 12 disciples?" "I believe." "Show me your faith." I pushed on. When we met the following week for PRINCIPLE OF 12, I could tell that they did not understand.

You can read a lot from people's faces but I could not be mad at them. It was my fault entirely. It was my inability to convey the vision. I told them yet again and then I gave them an ultimatum. I said, "If you are not able to achieve the goal within three months, you will be excluded from the 12 disciples." It is their dream to be my disciple. By becoming my disciple, they can journey throughout the Silk Road. When I told them that they would be excluded if they cannot come up with their own 12 disciples, it seemed to sink in. They thought, "Pastor Kim is not kidding around…" I said, "You are no exception, associate pastor. Make twelve disciples."

My associate pastor is truly faithful and committed but I did not have faith in him. He is a little bit older and sometimes, as you get older you become more conservative and set in your ways. I was going to cut him some slack but my wife said, "You are not leading spiritually." So I said, "Okay, okay." Three months passed and my associate pastor, who seemed to have the least potential, made 12 cells from zero in a matter of three months. He was so excited: "Pastor, I gathered all the newcomers (although they weren't all newcomers, some of them were people just attending cells). He grabbed alcoholics, drug users, and brand new Christians. I had my doubts but God made it happen. He made 12 cells. A person with three cells made 11-12 cells. One person from India who had one made 21 cells. I extended the deadline from 3 months to 6 months. I gave them a break since it was the first time we did anything like this. A woman deacon with 40 cells made 100 cells. In the beginning, she said she complained, "This is too much. I have to lead the Alpha course, leadership school, Post-Encounter, and Encounter. I do not even have time to see my husband anymore. Now I have to increase my cells. I may as well be dead." However, she began to get excited.

Teams were formed. The church began to move. A single sister who had 60 cells increased her cells to 144 by the year's end. They were celebrating on their own. I told them to set their own goals. One deacon who was able to make 100 cells said he could make 400 cells. He understood that it is possible according to the biblical principle he has been taught.

People who said they could not were transformed. In July of 2004, we had 375 cells. After the proclamation had started, and since the drive to increase the cells in August, our cells have grown to 950. This is our 3rd year and we are experiencing explosive growth. Once the leadership school starts and the school begins to turn out leaders, we will experience growth that is even more explosive. It is because we have started on our concrete preparation of leadership development.

Inherent Power to Conquer

The fourth verb tells us to subdue the earth. The second message of God's blessing for us is to subdue the earth. The church of Jesus is not just a defender but also an invader. We must conquer new lands. We must go into unreached places with the gospel. You must form a team. You have no power without a team. Joshua had twelve tribes as his team and each tribe had soldiers. Joshua commanded them and divided the land between them. This was a command to go and conquer the land. God is a God who conquers. Do not remain where you are. Do not wait. You must go in with full force. You must go into society. You must train soldiers with an urgent determination to plant God's church in every area of society. God is a God of vision. He wants us to continue to conquer by providing visions for us. Please be mindful of the fact that we are called to do just that.

Inherent Power to Lead

Thirdly, he told us to rule. He said, "Rule over the fish of the sea and the birds of the air and over every living creature that moves on the ground." He gave us the authority to rule. Since we have been made in God's image, we have been born with the natural authority to rule. PRINCIPLE OF 12 churches believe that whoever comes before the Lord is a potential leader. Even a new believer is a potential leader. We believe that God will do great things through him.

These three are the contents of blessings God has given to us. The Authority to Increase, the Authority to Conquer and the Authority to Lead has been given to us. I ask that you believe in the authority of the Bible. These are simple words but I believe that these simple words are words of Rhema that have the power to change our lives. Proclaim it without ceasing. In my experience, I learned that when I continue to proclaim the message given by God, it becomes Rhema. I preached on Genesis 1:27-28 several times. Then God showed me. This became my message. I pray that you possess the authority to increase. I ask you to conquer. I bless you to be a great leader in Jesus Christ.

If you want to have discipleship, a ministry with vision, and mission endeavors through the PRINCIPLE OF 12 ministry, then you must continue to hear the word of God. Continue to fight for PRINCIPLE OF 12. I have invested incredible time and money to learn it. I went days without sleep. I kept asking countless questions to God and slowly began to understand. As I began to understand little by little, I experienced enormous blessing coming over my life. It is the same way with the Alpha Course. Even if you attend a conference, you will not understand it completely by hearing it just once. In order to make it yours, you must attend the conference at least 3 times and invest time for at least two years. You must wrestle with it after understanding it to bear fruit. Please remember it. Koreans are very quick tempered and they like to see results immediately. Few things in life bear fruit immediately. However, in comparison, Alpha Courses bear fruit sooner than later. If you attend the conference, you have access to a solid manual, so you simply need to follow the manual. There is no need to add extra agendas. If you follow the instructions and take baby steps, within one year, you will see results. However, PRINCIPLE OF 12 is not that easy because it is more of a holistic ministry. Fruit comes forth after true commitment, deeper research and setting of clear goals.

We need a certain anointing for explosive growth.

Know that the will of God is to be fruitful and increase in number and to fill the earth. We must know his will in Genesis 1:27-28. Secondly, we need to have an inner healing experience. Satan has torn families into shreds. The marriage relationship is broken. Because of it, the children grow up with incredible wounds in their hearts. Even when they grow up, there is a child within them. They must be healed. You cannot become a leader before you are healed. Therefore, the church must risk its life healing souls. When you are healed, you can rise up as a great leader.

This is my experience with Inner Healing. I studied the subject in Germany for six years, but I felt that God wanted me to study theology a little more. I did very well in seminary. In a very short time (within 1 year, I finished studying the German language, within a year and a half, I finished studying the classical languages-Hebrew, Greek, Latin) I was able to read original texts and translate them into German. I passed the national exams as well, with flying colors. In Germany, in order to finish a masters or doctorate degree in theology, one must complete three language and classical language courses. The national exam is so difficult, more than a third of the Germans fail. It is a very stringent exam process. I was able to finish the courses in a year and a half. God even helped me to get started on my doctorate degree. Then the call of God came. So which has higher priority?

I knew very well in my head, but it was not easy to carry it out. But when I put my desires into action, my wife declared her desire to divorce me. So I fasted. Ultimately, God moved my wife's heart and we were able to take our four-year-old daughter and one-year-old son into Almaty via Warsaw and Moscow. Moscow seemed like a post war city to me. The temperature went down to minus 10-20 degrees while it felt like minus 30 degrees. In the midst of such frigid temperature, people were lining up longer than 100 meters to buy a piece of bread. When they ran out of bread, they dispersed without a single complaint. Then there would be another line. When I asked them what was being sold, the person in line did not even know. When my family arrived in Moscow, the missionary who came before us said we were lucky. I asked her why we are so lucky and she told us that she was able to buy a hard piece of bread-about a size of a brick, a little bit of butter, and two eggs for our family. She said she was fortunate. One time I was on a subway and a grandma happened to get on with a cabbage in her basket. Everyone on the train car was glaring at her cabbage. I thought they were going to kill her to take her cabbage. To make things worse, we brought our children into this circumstance.

Then, we flew from Moscow to Almaty. There is an internationally famous ski resort next to the airport. It is merely 30 minutes from where we live but we did not know about it for 10 years. I only found out about it two and a half years ago. As we were getting off the plane, my wife's heart was heavy. She said she felt like she came to Almaty to bury her own kids. It was a communistic, Muslim, foreign land without food. Yet when she was getting off the plane, God told her, "My daughter, this is your home." He comforted her. Therefore, she knew that God was with her and we began to minister together.

When we started the ministry, it was so tiring and overwhelming but I was so filled with joy. I was so moved by the fact that God called me. It did not matter that I lacked mission funds or people did not know who I was. I am going to pour my life into this ministry God. As I began to pour my life into the ministry, my wife suffered. She wanted to talk to me but I had no time for her. I was ministering in Almaty but I did not know any Russian. The translation was not satisfying. The interpreter did not know Korean and I did not know Russian. We both had to learn. I lived with a Korean dictionary made in North Korea in my hands. There were no such words as "Called Righteous" or "redemption." I literally had to discover these words. After struggling for 5 years, the Holy Spirit told me to preach in Russian. I simply started, even though I did not have any formal education.

They were so blessed... they would clap when I was stuck. It felt like family. I struggled that much more because I did not know the language. Furthermore, Almaty was not the only place I ministered. I also planted a church at a place called Karaganda, the capital of Bishkek. It was 250 KM away from Almaty but it took five hours by car. I would go there every week. I was never home. My wife did not know the language. The children were with her and there literally was no food. There was no car and no mission fund. She was trembling in fear and her resentment towards me grew. I have such a one-track mind that my wife was filled with wounds. We could not even communicate well because I was crazy about ministry. Women need to talk to people. All I needed to do was to listen but I could not even do that.

I had my own excuses as well. I have completely committed to the Lord but you lack commitment. No matter how much she tried, I was so committed to ministry; I could not take care of my wife or my family. Therefore, we would quarrel after my return from various places. There was that unseen darkness. My mind could not rest. There just was no rest, so I was miserable, and so was my wife. In the midst of all this, God commanded me to fast in 1995. I fasted for 40 days. I am truly thankful for the fact that while I was fasting in Korea, all my church members, over 1000 of them, prayed and fasted for me for at least a day. They even drew graphs. During my 40 days of fasting, my associate pastor fasted 30 days for me. The district leaders fasted 3 weeks for me. Small group leaders fasted a week for me while the members fasted any where from one to 3 days. 40 days of fast. 10 days before the fast. 20 days after the fast. My church prayed 70 days for me. I was so grateful.

    I really thank God for my staff as well. They truly love and respect me. I have many faults, and I am quick tempered. Sometimes I hurt them and we have had our differences, but they truly love and support me. With such support, 40 days of fasting was not difficult at all. It was so easy. Through all the prayers, I received God's vision. As I was doing my 40 days fast, I could not pray, in all honesty. I would just sit all day. I was so burned out before the fast, I asked God, "Please let me rest for three months. Other people would rest one year after three years of ministry, but I have yet to rest. I have not rested for even one month during the last 13 years. Why is my church so difficult? Won't you give me rest?" When I prayed this prayer, God ordered me to do a

40 days fast. Consequently, I rested for 40 days. I did not eat and I did not work. God, let me read the bible in its entirety during my fast. For forty days, I read through the Bible once. I read it very closely. On the 28th day, I was reading John chapter 11. The word began to speak to me. It spoke to me so deep within. "Did I not tell you that if you believed, you would see the glory of God? What have I required of you? Have I not required faith alone? Did I not give you the gift of faith for that reason? Believe. Believe in me completely. Believe in me when things are difficult. Rely on me even when things are well. When you believe, I will show you what my glory is."

I was so excited; I woke up other people who were also fasting for 40 days. I said, "Wake up. Listen to the voice of God. He said if you believe, he will show his glory to you. It is not for lack of materials you cannot do missions. It is not because you lack something, education, or a sponsoring church. It is because you lack faith in God. You must go forth in faith." After talking to them all night, I began to think. "What should I believe? God, what should I believe? What should I believe in?" Then God answered, "Transform the mindset of the people of Kazakhstan and the Silk Road region with my gospel. Share the gospel to one person as if you are sharing it to millions of people." God gave me such a heart. "Yes, Lord," I replied. The vision started from there. I was so happy; I was not tired from the 28th day on. I was so excited that I wanted to end the fast. I was thinking, "Should I stop the fast now that I have a vision? No, I should finish what I started." I continued to push on. God was not done with me yet.

On the 38th day, my hand was trembling and I was seeing double. My wife had come from Kazakhstan to take care of me after 30 days of fasting. When she was next to me, I was able to sense her spiritual state in the spirit. Her heart was completely closed. She was in deep struggle. I thought to myself, "This is strange. Why is she struggling?" I am not sensitive in that area but God gave me grace. "Look at your wife," he told me. As I saw her, she was in despair. Yet she could not divorce me. She still loved me and loved God so she was simply going to serve without saying anything. She was just going to serve, even if it meant killing herself. She was going to minister with me for the sake of our children. I said to her, "Honey, talk to me." "What do you want to talk about?" she asked. "Open your heart. We must talk. God has shown me that you have some issues in your heart." She replied, "I don't have any issues. I obey you. I pray when told to pray, help with ministry when told to help and raise kids… I don't have any issues." I felt stifled. I knew that she had issues. I kept talking to her more seriously. She told me, "Please don't provoke me. This is enough. I sacrificed as much as I could. I love the Lord and I am willing to die for the gospel. I know that God has called you as a missionary so I do not have a desire to get divorced to find my own life. I am going to obey so do not provoke me. Don't ask me to open my heart."

Nothing is more painful to a man than when his woman does not open her heart to him. It does not matter how good she is to him. The process of gaining her trust is important. It was difficult. My heart truly ached. For the first time, I realized that I had been so wrong to her. "How can I claim to understand others when I can't even understand my wife? Is this what I meant by vital ministry? Is this how I should serve God?" I would question myself with such questions. We kept talking to each other. I would say, "You know how I am. I am sure I have given you much grief because of my personality. But you need to understand that it was the result of God's calling on my life. There is absolutely no change in how much I love you." Women want to see it in action.

Before, I was not able to do that. On the 38th day, I was seeing double. I knelt in front of my wife and said, "Honey, you must forgive me. If you have resentment towards God, you must forgive that as well. Please forgive me with your whole heart. Please forgive me for not being your husband and concentrating only on ministry. I cannot promise you that I will be able to live up to your expectation but I am going to do my best.   Please believe me. If you and I are not restored, I cannot continue with my ministry. I cannot continue with my ministry without resting in you and resting in the Lord together. You know that our children see us. Please forgive me." I begged her. She told me that she began to think these thoughts, "I will never forgive. I will never open my heart." She had already given up on us. However, as I knelt in front of her begging for her forgiveness in all sincerity, the Holy Spirit moved her. She threw herself in my arms, weeping, begging for my forgiveness. God gave us a tremendous time of healing that evening. Our vital ministry began from that point on.

When the pastor's wife is happy, the church is happy. When the pastor's wife is happy, the pastor is happy. We are human. You may think that you can live with ministry alone. We come alive when our souls are restored. Our relationship began to be restored. As our relationship was being restored, the women's ministry began to rise up. If my wife were not healed, the women's ministry would not have grown. I cannot touch the area of women's ministry. Within the limits of a man, I can share the gospel with them and disciple them, but it is impossible for me to go deep into their lives to touch the deep areas of their lives. If the restoration does not occur within the spirit of women, women leaders cannot rise.

After the restoration of our relationship, my family was first to be restored. The children were able to sense it. They said they were happy. They said they were so at peace and happy. Their fears of living in the mission field, coupled with tension between their parents began to dissipate. From then on, the children began to respect the ministry of their father which their mom finally respected. When the pastor's wife begins to complain and is not committed, then the children also follow suit, taking lightly what their mother takes lightly. They do not want to become pastors. Their view on church becomes distorted. Their view on God is warped.

Thankfully, after our relationship was restored, our children were also restored and the whole family is strengthened and rejuvenated. The home becomes a place of peace. I was able to come home and rest. In the past, when I got home, going to sleep as early as possible was important because I was so tired. Now I am able to drink tea, converse and rest. Now I can listen and truly hear my wife. In the past, I only knew what was mine because I was deaf. I was satisfied with an obedient pastor's wife. Now she is my helper. She fills all my shortcomings. The reason some pastors do not change is that their relationship with their wives is broken or damaged. They treat their wives' advice with disdain. However, they must listen.

In my opinion, a Korean pastor's most crucial blind spot is that they have no one to give him or her advice. They are all dictators. This may be true in other cultures as well. When you are that way, you will never change. Everyone knows your faults except you. Wives try but they have given up. Some do not even start because they have been taught that a pastor's wife needs to be silent. This is neither true nor biblical. Pastor's wives must have open communication with their husbands.

A Pastor's wife must be the opposing party in some sense. The party in power must learn to hear the voice of the opposition. Then they begin to change. Their essence begins to change. The church's constitution begins to change. The atmosphere changes. People begin to feel that the church is a family. It cannot work with mere soldiers. It has to be a family of soldiers. They must be soldiers who are bound to family ties. It is then that they will have a willingness to sacrifice their lives.

Now, my church members are blessed just by seeing us. They give my wife an ovation when she simply stands in the pulpit. As I shared with you before, the first service is for men and the second service is for women. Sometimes, after being disappointed during the first service, I would peek into the second service. I had been keeping myself from the second service on purpose but once, when I opened the door, I was so surprised. Twenty five hundred seats were completely filled. It was standing room only. The room was so highly charged with expectation; they were like sponges, soaking in the word of God.

What message, do you think was preached? Do you think the message was about rising up in opposition to the husbands? No. It was about the fact that we need broken hearts. We need forgiveness. We have the need to embrace our husbands and pray. As we nurture a child within us for nine months, we must also hold onto our city and nation and pray. When they were told that they must cry out for revival, the fire fell upon the women. This is true. This is our calling. This is our mission. The atmosphere of the church changed completely. If change did not happen between my wife and me, if true reconciliation and healing did not take place, we would have missed God's incredible treasure. We would have become a crippled church. We would have become a church that only does work but has an icy atmosphere. We would have been dedicated without relationships. We would have been emphasizing relationship without forming relationships. That is all we would have become.

Once, I was waiting for my luggage at an airport in America when a pastor asked for my help. I saw him briefly on the airplane. He was looking for his luggage. He seemed so kind and good. We began to have a good conversation about each other's ministry. I was thinking that he is such a good person. However, when his wife came to say something to him, he barked at her, saying, "Go over there!" I was so shocked. He was so kind and nice to me yet he did not mind barking at his wife. His behavior toward his wife showed me his true nature. I do not mean to criticize the pastor. What I am saying is that he was the picture of our own selves. We cannot hide our true nature. The church members see our every move. How can we speak of true nature? It is not possible. If I am transformed, how was I transformed? Of course, we all change by the Holy Spirit. To me, my wife was the Holy Spirit. We cannot hear the voice of the Holy Spirit because our ears are closed. We are too calloused. Our wives have eyes to see, at least regarding the things that concern their husbands. Sometimes, they may nag. This is women's nature. We must submit to it. When you listen, you will discover that she is telling you some important things. She may be saying it to you in passing but she is telling you things that other people want to tell you. We must listen to our wives. Then, we will experience transformation. The healing must take place. When husbands listen, wives experience healing. We created the church's atmosphere so that healing can take place through the Encounter Weekend.

My third point is that husband and wife have to be a team ministry. I have already shared this with you as I shared my second story. It is very important for the husband and wife to minister together, according to the gifts of each. God blessed Adam and Eve. We must minister together. The wife is a helper. Without a helper, a leader is crippled. He is not whole. In what sense is she a helper? She is not a helper in the sense that she helps with work, but she is a helper in the sense that she helps with character. She helps to make sure the man does not become crippled. There is accountability. She keeps the husband accountable and the husband keeps her accountable. They can talk about the ministry all night long without growing weary. As healing takes place between them and the atmosphere of tolerance and listening forms, the church is also affected. All the couples within the church begin to change in the same way. When the relationship between the pastor and his wife is restored, it flows into the church. It flows from top to bottom.

The best way for the couple to remain accountable to each other is to minister together. It helps to enhance their spirituality. They become genuine comforters to one another. One morning, I was so tired. My wife held my hands and prayed for me; I felt so refreshed. This is what a husband and wife can mean to each other. I always make sure to hold her and to embrace her when we walk together. It is so good. When we first went to America, people from Grace Church made fun of us because we always held hands. I told them, "Don't make fun of us but learn from us." Wives can be true comforters, true coworkers. My wife is very sharp. I am easy going. However, I obey very well the will of God. This is why I need a wife who is sharp. She makes very accurate diagnosis. I would ask, "Honey, what should I do in this situation?" I am not good at making decisions. I trust too easily. I end up losing everything, making many mistakes. But I am always with the best secretary. She is like the chief secretary of the communist party. She is an amazing adviser. She is excellent. I am completely satisfied. I am free. She takes care of all my needs.

When a husband and wife work together, they begin to have a correct understanding of children's ministry also. They understand how important ministry is. They discover that ministry is the purpose of life. If not, the pastor may be giving up his life for the ministry while the wife may be telling the kids, "You need to go to a good college to get a good job." Something is out of focus. The children will set up wrong goals for life. That is a problem. How can you expect to communicate the correct vision? It is the key that helps you set your values. When a husband and wife have a team ministry, they are able to minister through their lives. This is why a husband and wife team in ministry is needed.

Fourth is holiness and purity. Failure and curse of life comes from loss of holiness. Satan can work in your life because there is sin. Rats gather around trash. The core message of Charles Craft's healing and deliverance ministry is that rats gather around trash. The devil works when we have impure motives, thoughts and sin. Evil spirits will work in your life. He will torment you. It is the same principle. We need holiness. In order to transform Abram into Abraham, God told him, "I am God Almighty; walk before me and be blameless." Why does he tell Abraham to be blameless when he knows that it is impossible? God desires to have his holiness continue to grow within us. When we are holy, God's vision becomes stronger. God's vision becomes stronger when it is placed in a holy vessel, a clean vessel. It becomes transparent. Everyone sees it. No matter how good a vision is, if it is placed within an impure vessel, it will seem impure. This is the problem. What a pastor says may be correct but his actions, motives and conversation methods are too political. He tries to handle things in a political manner. Things may be done to a certain extent but because of impurity, impure people will begin to gather. You cannot deceive. The fruit will expose you. You must be holy. You must be holy even if you suffer loss. You must be holy even if you look like a fool. Then the Lord will work in your life. This is the basic cause of explosive growth. If the leaders of PRINCIPLE OF 12 are holy and pure before the Lord, pure and holy people will gather. People who do not love money or fame but who love to accomplish the will of God will gather. Holiness and purity is absolutely needed.

Fifth is a Life of Forgiveness. Do you do a lot of Inner Healing Ministry? You must. Do you do much deliverance ministry? You must. Do you want to know a secret? Do you know where you can find the best power of healing? Continue your healing ministry. The scar of the wounded remains forever. No matter how long you continue with your healing ministry, the scars remain. The memory remains. How can we heal them? We must teach forgiveness. Continued victory and ongoing healing are only possible for those who have learned forgiveness. This is what the Bible teaches. This is why God desires healing through forgiveness rather than simple acts of healing. God desires profound healing through forgiveness rather than humanistic healing or occasional healing. God is aiming for complete healing of body, soul and spirit through forgiveness in Jesus Christ. Forgiveness is needed.We must learn to forgive. Forgiveness enables us to experience complete healing. We must teach the secret of forgiveness in church. We must create an atmosphere to encourage forgiveness.

When I was in Germany, God helped me to realize something very important. He helped me to learn the essence of forgiveness. When we confess with our lips, "I am a sinner," is that true repentance? However, after believing in Jesus for a long time, the true essence of repentance will come about. You must repent after realizing your true nature. "Lord, I am a sinner. Depart from me." Such confession must be ours. Even though I love my wife dearly, we had many quarrels. I feel that I am right and she is wrong. When I explain to her why she is wrong, she would answer, "It's because I don't know. I don't know anything because I grew up in a Buddhist family." However, after giving into my argument for three, 4, 5, 6 years, she began to think that she could not be the one who is wrong all the time. So the arguments would get heated and intense.

As the arguments became more serious, she began to be wounded. I would wonder, "Why can't I understand my wife, even though I love her so much?" I was disappointed in myself. I felt such despair. "How can I call myself a minister when I am so vile?" I would wake up early in the morning to go pray in the forest in Germany. I prayed so that I would not lose my faith. As I was crying out to the Lord that day, a thought popped into my head. It was that of Paul the apostle's confession in Romans 7: "I do not deserve to be forgiven. My old nature wants what I do not want and what I want, it does not want. Oh what a wretched man I am." I could not understand myself. How can a man like me do ministry? I was so disappointed in myself that I could not stand it. I wept, "God, I am a sinner. I do not deserve to be a missionary. Even though you have called me, I am unclean. I am a wretched man. I am a sinner."

For the first time, from the depth of my soul, I confessed, "God, I am a sinner." For the first time in 6 years since I had been in Germany, God spoke to me. "Now do you realize, my son?" God wanted me to know that I am a sinner. He wanted me to know that I have been saved by grace. That is why God sent his son. I began to praise God after that. Then I had a basic desire to deny myself. Before, I thought I was always right. I made a decision then. I will never judge or condemn anyone. Whom can I condemn when

I was the one who was forgiven of my sins? After the Lord told me, "Now do you realize, my son?" the next thing he told me was, "I love you." I cried so much. My eyes were puffy from all the crying. I did not even bother to go to my classes that day. I was so thankful; I felt like I could fly. God, now I can be a missionary. My heart was overflowing with gratitude. I was thinking, "This is the gospel. I must share the gospel with this joy. This is the gospel." I had an impression in my heart. I decided that I would not condemn anyone. My wife and I still fought, but because there was a profound transformation in my heart, I could feel the change taking place in me. It was restoration.

Restoration comes through forgiveness. The desire to forgive comes when we realize how blessed and gracious God's forgiveness truly is. The ability to forgive someone who owes us wells up within us. I pray that you receive this power of forgiveness. This is the type of atmosphere that should be cultivated. This is how growth takes place, not necessarily through works. This is essential.

Sixth is complete commitment. When the church members are not committed, they end up using God for fleshly purposes. They end up praying endlessly for their own agendas. If the prayers are not answered, everything stops. Morning prayers are packed only during college-entrance exam time. There is no desire to live life according to God's will on an everyday basis. They have the intention but they do not have the determination. It is because they are not committed. Because their lives are not committed to live for

Christ, there is no purpose in life or action towards goals. We must help them to realize how important ministry is. We must teach them about the explosive power that comes from vital transformation. Testimonies must become a lifestyle. We must create the atmosphere for the church members to be set free from Satan's bindings through their testimonies. This causes the church members to head towards commitment in joy. My wife once asked me how long I was willing to change my congregation members' diapers. I agreed with her. After much training, they now have ownership. This is commitment. They must be led to make absolute commitment.

Seventh is Faith and Vision. The essential makeup of God's people is the vision of life. Great men and women of God emerge because of faith and vision. Faith does not form without vision. In addition, we must be able to set goals beyond our limitations. We must not settle to give only what I am able to give. We must be willing to do and give beyond our own limitations. This is how we experience the power of God. We should give in such a way and minister in that way as well.

My church has started construction on our property. So far, we have spent about 3 million dollars. Where did the money come from? My church members have given about 1 million dollars. Please remember that the average income is about $100. Some sold their homes. Someone sold his apartment to immigrate to Germany. He gave $2000 for tithe from the money he received from the sale. God will bless people who sacrifice their resources for the sake of vision.

When you live a life of such faith, your children will learn to possess the same type of faith and will be blessed because of that faith. After setting up the entire framework for a sanctuary with the capacity to hold 6000 people, we had to stop for 5 years due to lack of money. I prayed to God, "Lord, where are you going to send us the money from?" God answered, "Do it with your own hands." I responded, "But God, the members have given to the point of exhaustion." He said, "Just do it." However, God gave us a way to do it.

A construction company came and proposed to build the basic, necessary components, with the condition that we make monthly payments. There is no such thing as bank loans in Kazakhstan. A one-year loan has an interest rate of 30%. The construction company proposed that if we can pay them $100,000 up front, we could make monthly payments. Therefore, we did as they asked. We paid off about $200,000 during the last 5 years. They built our building in faith. When we built, the construction went smoothly through God's blessing. I am certain that God has prepared this money already for us. We should be able to get started next month. This is the work of God. We can certainly be independent and be led by God. We will receive the financial blessings to cover the Silk Road region. God will give us the authority to transform Turkey, China, and all the nations in Central Asia. God will accomplish it. Impossible becomes possible through vision. I pray that you receive God's vision.

Eighth is the Current Voice given to us by the Holy Spirit. In Proverbs 1, it tells us that God calls aloud in the street. God's voice can be heard everywhere. We are missing it. We must go deep into his presence. We must know what the Lord desires and we must obey. That is the only way for growth to happen. I pray that you will be victorious in Jesus' name. I pray that every one of you will dwell in such blessing.

Chapter 6: Restoration of Anointing

A believer's life must be led by the Holy Spirit. If one person or leader can minister before the Lord with the anointing, the outlook on the city, church, family or the nation will bright. How can an individual live within the anointing or presence of God? Here in lies our destiny; God uses the anointed, especially in difficult times. In 1 Kings 18:20-46 we read;

> [20] So Ahab sent word throughout all Israel and assembled the prophets on Mount Carmel. [21] Elijah went before the people and said, "How long will you waver between two opinions? If the LORD is God, follow him; but if Baal is God, follow him." But the people said nothing. [22] Then Elijah said to them, "I am the only one of the Lord's prophets left, but Baal has four hundred and fifty prophets. [23] Get two bulls for us. Let them choose one for themselves, and let them cut it into pieces and put it on the wood but not set fire to it. I will prepare the other bull and put it on the wood but not set fire to it. [24] Then you call on the name of your god, and I will call on the name of the LORD. The god who answers by fire—he is God." Then all the people said, "What you say is good." [25] Elijah said to the prophets of Baal, "Choose one of the bulls and prepare it first, since there are so many of you. Call on the name of your god, but do not light the fire." [26] So they took

the bull given them and prepared it. Then they called on the name of Baal from morning till noon. "O Baal, answer us!" they shouted. But there was no response; no one answered. And they danced around the altar they had made. 27 At noon Elijah began to taunt them. "Shout louder!" he said. "Surely he is a god! Perhaps he is deep in thought, or busy, or traveling. Maybe he is sleeping and must be awakened." 28 So they shouted louder and slashed themselves with swords and spears, as was their custom, until their blood flowed. 29 Midday passed, and they continued their frantic prophesying until the time for the evening sacrifice. However, there was no response, no one answered, and no one paid attention. 30 Then Elijah said to all the people, "Come here to me." They came to him, and he repaired the altar of the LORD, which was in ruins. 31 Elijah took twelve stones, one for each of the tribes descended from Jacob, to whom the word of the LORD had come, saying, "Your name shall be Israel." 32 With the stones he built an altar in the name of the LORD, and he dug a trench around it large enough to hold two seahs of seed. 33 He arranged the wood, cut the bull into pieces and laid it on the wood. Then he said to them, "Fill four large jars with water and pour it on the offering and on the wood." 34 "Do it again," he said, and they did it again. "Do it a third time," he ordered, and they did it the third time. 35 The water ran down around the altar and even filled the trench.

³⁶ At the time of sacrifice, the prophet Elijah stepped forward and prayed: "O LORD, God of Abraham, Isaac and Israel, let it be known today that you are God in Israel and that I am your servant and have done all these things at your command. ³⁷ Answer me, O LORD, answer me, so these people will know that you, O LORD, are God, and that you are turning their hearts back again." ³⁸ Then the fire of the LORD fell and burned up the sacrifice, the wood, the stones and the soil, and also licked up the water in the trench. ³⁹ When all the people saw this, they fell prostrate and cried, "The LORD -he is God! The LORD -he is God!" ⁴⁰ Then Elijah commanded them, "Seize the prophets of Baal. Don't let anyone get away!" They seized them, and Elijah had them brought down to the Kishon Valley and slaughtered there. ⁴¹ And Elijah said to Ahab, "Go, eat and drink, for there is the sound of a heavy rain." ⁴² So Ahab went off to eat and drink, but Elijah climbed to the top of Carmel, bent down to the ground and put his face between his knees. ⁴³ "Go and look toward the sea," he told his servant. And he went up and looked. "There is nothing there," he said. Seven times Elijah said, "Go back." ⁴⁴ The seventh time the servant reported, "A cloud as small as a man's hand is rising from the sea." So Elijah said, "Go and tell Ahab, 'Hitch up your chariot and go down before the rain stops you." ⁴⁵ Meanwhile, the sky grew black with clouds, the wind rose, a heavy rain came on and Ahab

rode off to Jezreel. ⁴⁶ The power of the LORD came upon Elijah and, tucking his cloak into his belt, he ran ahead of Ahab all the way to Jezreel.

God moves during crisis times. When leaders can admit, "This is it. There is nothing more we can do. We are filled with despair. We can no longer evangelize. The society is depraved and even the church shows no signs of life. No one listens no matter what we say." God is able to work at this point of crisis.

God remains silent when man thinks he can do something; when we plan things according to our wisdom. God begins to move the moment our strength is exhausted and we confess, "I can't do anything." Therefore, we must know how to listen to God. He will direct us during these times. We have seen countless times in the Bible and through church history how God begins to move when doors are shut and all hope is lost. We must seek God when our nation is in peril, when the church is in danger and when everything is going downhill. Then, I am confident that God will become our way, show us new visions and make history by raising men like Elijah into leadership.

The Israelites were facing a great crisis. God's people were divided into two kingdoms. They fell into a great apostasy. The king of Israel began to worship foreign gods after marrying foreign women. During this time, God used one person; Elijah. This is of great comfort to me because he was just one man. God needs just one person. He does not need many, just one committed person who is after his own heart, who understands God's vision and who makes decisions led by God. You may feel that there is no such person where you are. Even Elijah thought the same. He said that every one else had been killed and that he was the only one left. However, that was not the case. He tells us that he has "reserved seven thousand" to make history for God. We may think that all hope is lost and the church is declining and that there is no one. This is when God will tell us, "No. I have reserved people." This is why you are here today as people reserved by God. We must have a heart to seek God during crisis. One thing we must recognize is that God does not use just anybody, but he uses the people of "Amen." God is looking for people who will say "Amen" to what God has to say, even if what they see and feel may seem critical and overwhelming. God reveals his glory to the man of Amen. Be confident that when God chooses such a man, all the impossible things will become possible through that man. I pray that you believe that God can bring a great revival through one man.

    What kind of person does God use? What kind of person is God looking for during crises? He is looking for a man like Elijah. Who was Elijah? He had a genuine concern to turn the hearts of his people back to God. There is one thing that I've realized during my 13 years of ministry in the mission field. God is not looking for a person who is able, educated, rich, or good. He is looking for a person who understands his heart. We may lack character, even lack strength and experience, but as long as we are determined to follow God's heart, God will honor and use us, as long as we do not waver.

I was truly a nobody. I went into the mission field without experience. I went with limited ability to share the gospel, without knowledge of hermeneutics and without preaching experience. I did have a heart that cried out, "God, even if it is just one person, please use me as a vessel to save him." As long as I guarded my heart, God guided my steps. Whenever I became prideful, the guidance would stop. My biggest fear was that God's presence would depart from me. When God wants to use you, no one can stop you; except you! No one can come in opposition. In verse 21 we see Elijah's heart: "Elijah went before the people and said, 'How long will you waver between two opinions? If the LORD is God, follow him; but if Baal is God, follow him.' But the people said nothing." This means that no one was willing to follow Elijah. Everyone was worshipping Baal, and was unable to make the decision to serve God. Yet Elijah made the commitment to stand with God, to turn the hearts of the Israelites to God even if no one understood. Thought Elijah had his junior prophets, he didn't have a team of twelve. Yet he stood firmly, seeking God, all alone. Why am I telling you this today? You may be all alone. You have made a decision to start a new ministry. You have made a determination to start a ministry in the truest sense. However, that is not enough. Even if you believe that everyone is against you and oo one understands you, you must have the willingness to say, "Lord, this is what missions are all about? This is true discipleship. This is true evangelism. This is true revival. Lord, I want to be committed for this cause."

Do you have a burning passion within your heart to lead your people, your church, and your nation into the discipleship of Jesus Christ? If you can make this commitment and not waver between two opinions, if your thinking doesn't change, if your heart isn't shaken, then God can truly use you. This is the core of the text. I pray that you believe that God uses people like Elijah, who have a heart to turn the people back to God. Elijah had a burning passion to show people the existence of God. Just as Jesus prayed, burning with desire to have his people come to know His Father.

> [22] Then Elijah said to them, "I am the only one of the LORD's prophets left, but Baal has four hundred and fifty prophets. [24] Then you call on the name of your god, and I will call on the name of the LORD. The god who answers by fire—he is God." Then all the people said, "What you say is good."

What is the meaning of this? Elijah wanted to make God known to his people. He wanted to make God known in the truest sense. He did not want his people to seek material prosperity, comfort or a peaceful life. He did not want them to follow idols. Rather, he wanted them to follow God's will, God's desire, and God's vision. He wanted this people to know God. This is why God was pleased with Elijah. The key is in your heart. The question is, "Where is our heart?" This is the core problem. Of course, you may have problems with your children, spouse, job, future, finances, etc. Many problems will entangle your life. However, wouldn't God bless you if you simply seek his kingdom and his righteousness with simple faith? Why wouldn't God use us? I ask that you believe in God's word that says, "Seek first the kingdom of God and his righteousness. And these things will be added unto you." This is still relevant for us today.

This is how God calls us. This is "Calling." This is devotion before the Lord. Elijah's heart did not waver even when faced with many difficulties, and even when the people, the nation, and all Israel deserted God in rebellion. Why did God choose Elijah during the crisis? He did not lose intimacy with God. In addition, he continued in prayer and kept up his personal relationship with the Lord. He was able to receive God's vision, a humanly impossible vision. Elijah fought a major spiritual battle against 450 priests of Baal on Mount Carmel. There may be such a battle in your life. Will you tremble in fear? Will you resign wisely? Will you compromise? If you know clearly what the will of God is, you will move forward. Elijah had determination, so he fought against them. God wants us to become victorious in spiritual warfare. Raise souls like the dry bones in Ezekiel's valley. Hear the voice of prophecy. Proclaim it. Raise them to life. Take them out of their graves and lead them into the land of Israel. Lead them back to the place of devotion to the Lord by reminding them of God's image in them and reminding them of God's "Calling" in their lives. God wants us to be a part of the great revival movement He has begun. This is it. God is looking for such people during times of crisis.

Beyond that, Elijah was able to do more for the future. He prepared a school for prophets. He mentored and trained Elisha. He had the spiritual eye to determine his successor among countless disciples. God will use a person who is able to see the future, who will boldly go into spiritual battle, who will discover the will of God through intimate prayer and who will have passion to turn the hearts of people back to the Lord. God is looking for such people today, regardless of gender or age. PRINCIPLE OF 12 is not the problem or the solution, nor is Alpha ministry the problem. Our hearts are the problem. When our hearts are ready and we are willing to live according to his will, God can show us His strategies. He will give us the most appropriate strategy for our generation. God is the one who gives us the vision and strategy to accomplish the vision.

We must restore the anointing to accomplish all these things. We must restore the anointing of the nation. We must renew the spiritual climate. What can we do in order to restore the anointing? Elijah did not back down from a spiritual confrontation. He took two calves. He took one calf and told the priests of Baal: "Call your god. The god who answers by fire – he is God." They called the name of their god all morning and well into the afternoon. They cried out, "O Baal, answer us." However, there was no answer.

Perhaps he is deep in thought, busy, or traveling. Maybe he is sleeping and must be awakened. Still, there was no answer.

Restore God's Altar

Elijah did something at that moment. There is something that he did in order to restore the anointing of his people, to revive the broken people, and to turn the hearts of his people back to God. What is something we must do in order to restore the anointing? If we can study what Elijah did, we can come to a deeper understanding. Verse 30 reads, [30] "Then Elijah said to all the people, 'come here to me.' They came to him, and he repaired the altar of the LORD, which was in ruins."

What does it mean to repair the altar of the Lord? It means to awaken a sleeping worship. The expectation has gone from the congregation. They are not able to taste the presence of God. They tend to give ritualistic worship. Christianity is in danger of falling into legalism and ritualism. Many sanctuaries are being built. However, are these buildings overflowing with true people of God? How can people's heart be filled with love for God when the anointing is gone from the altar? We must restore worship. We must restore the altar of the Lord. We must restore praise. We must restore the altar of prayer. We must restore the word of God so that it will overflow with apostolic anointing. We must prepare the surroundings so that the presence of the Holy Spirit can be experienced. We must go beyond praying, "God, do it. God do it." We must be able to pray, "God, what must I do?" When the altar of the Lord is repaired, all things will consequently be repaired. Restoration of worship is very important. We must restore Sunday Worship. We must restore cell groups. We must restore praise. We must restart the life and true power of prayer.

You can do this. You start by taking the first step. It starts with your personal life of praise. You must repair the altar that has broken down in your own homes. You must start a movement to lift up your children before the Lord and to worship the Lord in spirit and truth. There must be conversations with them about how much we love God and his will. We have become too secularized. The future of our children has become too secularized. Our concern for our children's future is not about whether they can live for the glory of God, but rather is about prestige and comfort in this world.

The altar of God has broken down. Your mind changes once the altar of the Lord is restored. The meaning of life and our goals will change. A fresh wind begins to blow. This is why Elijah wanted to restore the broken altar of the Lord. I pray that you can repair the altar of the Lord in your lives. "Senior leaders, you must give your selves to a movement of worship. You do not need programs. Get rid of all of them. Concentrate on restoring worship. True worship, worship in Spirit and Truth, will cause the souls of your flock to come alive. Then you can move to the next step." If worship is not restored, if the altar of the Lord is not restored, then everything else becomes mere programs. People will gather unwillingly. Complaints will rise. The number of people gathering will begin to dwindle. What will you do? Worship will enable you to experience the presence of God and such worship must be restored in our lives.

Restore God's Kingdom Rule

Secondly, in order to restore God's anointing, verse 31 reads,

> 31 Elijah took twelve stones, one for each of the tribes descended from Jacob, to whom the word of the LORD had come, saying, "Your name shall be Israel."

This means to restore God's reign. It means that there is no order in God's church. True spiritual vision is not being transferred according to spiritual order. A man of God would rise here and there intermittently to take leadership, but that will not do. We must restore spiritual order by going back to the model of the early church.[10] We must reture to the example of Jesus.

When the Israelites were living as hostages, God used one person, Moses. What did God do through Moses? He restored the order of sovereignty. I pray that you recognize that the restoration of Israel, the restoration of God's church, which is the spiritual Israel, comes from the restoration of God's order of Kingdom rule. Unless you can make true

---

[10] For more, see Dr. DeKoven's book, *Supernatual Architecture*.

disciples of Jesus Christ, the revival will end with your generation. Elijah was a man of great spiritual discernment. He did not just repair the altar of the Lord. He took twelve stones according to the number of twelve tribes descended from Jacob. He knew clearly that restoration comes from the restoration of the twelve tribes. He knew that Israel was governed through twelve tribes. He knew that Israel would be restored if the twelve tribes were functional. I am confident that the restoration of the church can be accomplished in a similar way. This is Jesus Christ's strategy for missions and discipleship. I pray that all of you would have twelve disciples. God's kingdom can be restored when you restore the kingdom order of the twelve disciples.

The New Jerusalem had twelve doors, twelve pillars and twelve foundations that held up the New Jerusalem. This is talking about how God's order is the foundation of the kingdom of God. Why are so many churches struggling to hand over the church to their own sons instead of finding a successor for the next generation? I do not think negatively about handing down a ministry to your children. If the parent was able to impart 100% of his anointing and spirituality to his son, what better person can there be? There is a problem when the transition takes place without the impartation, however. If the senior pastor spent his life pouring out into his twelve disciples there would not be problems with successors. Why would they have to find a successor outside of the church? There is no true successor to the vision because the strategic order was not established. It means that while there may be a successor to the church, there is no successor to the vision. That is why God's vision stops. This is a serious malady. God's Kingdom must be restored. This is the only way the nation and the church of God can live and be prosperous.

Restore the Lordship of Jesus Christ

Thirdly, what must we do to restore the anointing of God? After repairing the altar of the Lord, it reads:

> 32-33 With the stones he built an altar in the name of the LORD, and he dug a trench around it large enough to hold two seahs of seed. He arranged the wood, cut the bull into pieces and laid it on the wood. Then he said to them, "Fill four large jars with water and pour it on the offering and on the wood."

This was during a time of drought. They brought four large jars of water during the 3 ½ years of drought. This took great effort, but it shows that anything can be done. Before the fire of the Lord or the fire of revival can come, we have to do our part. The Bible says to seek and you will find, and knock and the door will be opened to you. Nothing is impossible for Christians.

> 33-34 He arranged the wood, cut the bull into pieces and laid it on the wood. Then he said to them, "Fill four

large jars with water and pour it on the offering and on the wood." "Do it again," he said, and they did it again. "Do it a third time," he ordered, and they did it the third time. 35 The water ran down around the altar and even filled the trench.

The four jars of water signify the number of perfection. Do it a third time. It is repetitious. Wood obviously does not burn when you pour water on it.Elijah did his best to demonstrate the power of God in the presence of foreign gods. There is a great prayer in verse 36.

> 36-39 At the time of sacrifice, the prophet Elijah stepped forward and prayed: "O LORD, God of Abraham, Isaac and Israel, let it be known today that you are God in Israel and that I am your servant and have done all these things at your command. Answer me, O LORD, answer me, so these people will know that you, O LORD, are God, and that you are turning their hearts back again." Then the fire of the LORD fell and burned up the sacrifice, the wood, the stones and the soil, and licked up the water in the trench. When all the people saw this, they fell prostrate and cried, "The LORD -he is God! The LORD -he is God!"

That was a great victory. What kind of prayers did Elijah pray? Why did God answer Elijah's prayer? Whose prayer does God answer? What kind of person are you? What kind of heart must we have as we pray to God? God wants us to restore the Lordship of Jesus Christ. God wants his people to recognize that He is God. Dearly beloved members of the church and dearly beloved leaders: In the midst of your mission in the midst of your vision, family, and individual lives, there are so many people who do not recognize that God is God. When we are faced with daily difficulties and struggles, was there a confession that said, "God, you are indeed my God." This is the problem. Elijah prayed such a prayer. We need to pray such prayers: "God, let our nation know that you are Lord. Let all the churches established in the name of God know that Jesus Christ is our Lord. Help us to proclaim it. Help us to confess that you reign over our lives. Help us to testify it." God wants us to restore the fact that Jesus Christ is Lord.

All Christians must be able to dwell in the undeniable conviction that the resurrected Jesus Christ is truly the Lord of their lives and he is the one who guides them. We must be able to motivate people into the center of such faith. The question is whether we have faith that Jesus Christ is the Lord in the midst of our lives, in the midst of our land, in the midst of churches, in the midst of history, and in the midst of our reality. God moves through such faith. I pray that God would plant such faith in all of you. I pray that you can proclaim boldly and cause the air to be filled with the name of the Lord before all men, declaring that Jesus Christ is your Lord and Savior, according to the confessions of your lips and hearts. God will work powerfully when his name is proclaimed. Our mighty God will work. God will give us great answers to a single prayer.

Make God's Calling Certain – Raise up the Spiritual Order

His second prayer is just as great. It reads, "Let it be known today… that I am your servant." What does this mean? It means to make your calling secure. What is the reason Elijah was able to be Elijah? What was the secret of his boldness when he faced off against 450 priests of Baal on Mount Carmel? It came from the conviction that God called him. What do you think is the main reason that keeps me going forward in spite of many difficulties, trials and temptations during the past 13 years? It is because of God's "Calling" on my life as a missionary. There is nothing else.

When I was in Germany, I studied theology. I finished the language courses faster than anyone else. I passed the classical languages such as Latin, Greek and Hebrew in a very short amount of time, which was a very difficult task for most people. I was so thankful for that. I was able to get started on my Ph.D. program immediately. God had given me such blessings, even though I had many financial difficulties. However, it was at that time God called me as a missionary. I did not know if the Ph.D. degree was that important. I still do not know. He called me as a missionary. God's "Calling" came to me during my Ph.D. studies. The former "Calling" was a call for the future; This "Calling" was the real "Calling." I was so happy I was jumping for joy. I said, "When I go to

Almaty, I want to become the very first missionary to the Soviet Union." Then, I began to drive my car home. As I was driving from Frankfurt,it dawned on me that I had not talked it over with my wife. I was in big trouble. I did not dare tell her. Yet, it was something I had to do, so I told her, "I decided to go as a missionary." She was shocked but she did not say anything. The next day, she wanted to go to Bonn because the Korean Embassy is in Bonn. When I asked her why we have to go to Bonn, she said very calmly, "We need to get a divorce." When I protested, she said, "Does it make sense that as a father of two children, three and one, you made a decision to go to the Soviet Union without even asking me, especially at a time when there isn't even a piece of bread or egg to buy in the stores over there?" She did not understand me. She continued, "When you made the decision without consulting me that means you are willing to go alone even if I am not willing to go. I will grant you the divorce." This time, I was shocked. However, even though I was shocked, because of God's "Calling," I was not shaken. Therefore, I fasted. I fast whenever there is a problem. Nothing is as powerful as fasting. We must have wisdom but when you do not have wisdom, you can at least fast. As I was fasting, my wife came to me on the second day. Basically, she was hurt because I had not asked her before making the decision. However, I knew what she would have said, had I asked her. Yet the "Calling" came to me so clearly. What could I do? I told her, "You know how much I love you. When I made the decision, it means that I want to take you with me, no matter what difficulties I am going to face. I wanted us to struggle together. We are one body. This is what we must do." My wife knew that it was my "Calling" to be a missionary, but she tried so hard to change it.

My wife majored in piano. She graduated from Kyung Hee University's instrumental music department and I graduated from the same university's Law School. From the first time we met, I had told her about my "Calling." "I am a pastor and a missionary," I told her plainly. She told me she could not become a missionary. When I asked her why, she said because she likes wearing red dress shoes, earrings and a diamond ring. Well, I said, "Why is that a problem? Did God say you could not wear a diamond ring? Did he say you could not wear red dress shoes? That's okay." I had a clear conscience because I did not deceive her. Yet, when she opposed my calling in Germany, I felt frustrated. She came to me as I was fasting and told me that she was hurt because I did not discuss it with her. I told her, "Don't be hurt. You know me. If God called us, how awesome is that? I waited for this all my life. I did not wait for my Ph.D. I waited for my 'Calling.'" If I had thought about it logically, I would have chosen the Ph.D. in a heartbeat.

I know how much my wife had supported me. She stopped her studies so I could do mine first. She wanted to get her Ph.D. after I had received mine. She dreamed that we would teach as professors. In an instant, her dreams came crumbling down. She started playing the piano when she was five. All her life, her dream was to become a professor. Her designated professor at the time assured her that when she got her Ph.D., she would have a professorship waiting for her. Her husband had wrecked this dream of hers. Even though I love my wife dearly, I remembered one Bible verse, "If anyone comes to me and does not hate his father and mother, his wife and children, his brothers and sisters—yes, even his own life—he cannot be my disciple." This is not a joke. Before I got married, I read this verse in the gospel of Luke many, many times. Does God really want me to deny my own wife and children? I can understand up to parents and possessions, but even my wife. Should I even marry then? I thought it through carefully. However, when God brings you together, you cannot help yourself. We were both smitten by each other. Still, no matter how I was smitten by her, the "Calling" would never change.

She complained incessantly in the beginning. After 5, 6, and 7 years had passed, she confessed to me, "You made a good decision." I exclaimed "hallelujah" in my heart. She used to blame me every time she encountered any difficulty saying, "You ruined me. You have made my life so miserable." However, to hear her say that I made the right decision was reassuring to me. A "Calling" brings great reconciliation. If you are sure of your calling, you can overcome anything, even when you are surrounded with difficulty.

Have you received your "Calling?" What kind of "Calling" did you receive? Make your calling secure before the Lord.   Pray. Hold on to your calling as you live. God does not make mistakes. He called you. God undoubtedly called Elijah. That is why he was victorious. That is how Elijah prayed, "Let it be known today... that I am your servant." So, first we must restore the "Calling" in our lives. Secondly, we must restore the authority we have as God's servant. We must restore the calling of the man or woman of God. The authority of Christ and Christians has been marginalized in both America and Korea. We must let unbelievers know that we are the servants of God. The world slanders pastors; they mock us, looking down on believers. We must overcome it. We must pray, "Lord, let it be known that I am a servant of God. Cause all the people to fear and respect Christians. Let my family members know that I am your servant. Let my parents acknowledge it. Let my children acknowledge it. Do not allow children to be unbelievers when their parents are Christians. Let it be known that I am your servant." This was the prayer of Elijah. His prayer hits the mark. Each word brings restoration to his people. We must recover the anointing. We must change the spiritual climate. We must transform the spiritual climate of our communities. This is what God desires and this is why God is looking for modern day Elijah's. I pray that you can be an Elijah; filled with passion and power to fulfill the purposes of God.

Have Confidence in God's Promise

Fourth, in verse 36, Elijah prays, "Let it be known today that you are God in Israel and that I am your servant and have done all these things at your command." What is he talking about? God wants us to have confidence that he keeps his promises. Elijah firmly believed that God's promise would be accomplished before the fire fell. He had confidence that 450 priests of Baal would be destroyed. He was confident that he would win the spiritual battle. Why? Because it was something that God had promised. It was God's command. I am confident that the Silk Road will be restored. Why? Because it is something he commanded me to do. I am confident that God will accomplish it because he told me to be devoted to it. The road back to Jerusalem will open from China through the Silk Road. The Bible said that the great road would open from the east. Just as the Bible said, the roads will open everywhere. The day will come when all the people and nations will come before the Lord to give him praise and worship as the doors to the Muslims, Arabs and the road to Jerusalem open. It is my desire to guide you to that place. I am running towards that day. I pray that you will believe in the accomplishment of the promise.

People will follow a man with a vision, whether they are believers or not. Where does such confidence come from? Where does unshakeable conviction come from? It comes from God. It is such simple logic. I am confident that God will accomplish great works through someone who will pray, listen to his voice and give his heart to the conviction of God. I pray that you can accomplish this great task. I pray that your family, your church, your city, and all nations will be transformed through you in Jesus' Name. When such prayers were spoken, God restored Israel. The Fire of God came from heaven. It burned up the sacrifice, the wood, the stones and the soil, and licked up the water in the trench. When all the people saw this, they fell prostrate and cried, "The LORD -he is God! The LORD -he is God! We must continue to fight the spiritual battle until we can hear the confessions of the people. We must pray until the dry bones of Ezekiel's valley come together to be covered with flesh and be filled with breath and form an army. What should we do next when God answers? What should we do next when we see a tiny starting point of revival, and when we see that the fire of the Holy Spirit has broken out?

Destroy the Devil's Stronghold

We must completely destroy Satan's stronghold. We must destroy all idols that bind the church, wound the hearts of Christians, and bind our hands and feet. According to verses 39-40, we must completely annihilate them. You must completely eradicate any remains of idols from your lives. You must destroy anything you love more than God. You must become a person who trusts in God only. The remnants of idols in church, the elements of compromise with the world, things that keep us from being committed, materialism, secularism...all must be cut off from us. God uses people and churches of commitment. We must destroy the strongholds of Satan completely. Then God's great work of revival and restoration will begin to emerge. We must do what we must do. It is wrong to rely only on God, without doing our share.

We must destroy them. Completely rid yourself of all idols. Allow God to completely cleanse you and heal you. Then God's miracle will begin to take place.

Display God's Proof

What do we need in order to restore the anointing? Lord's servants must display God's proof.

> 41 And Elijah said to Ahab, "Go, eat and drink, for there is the sound of a heavy rain." There was no sign that it was going to rain. Elijah is a man of faith and a man of prayer. There is the sound of heavy rain. I can hear it. 42 So Ahab went off to eat and drink, but Elijah climbed to the top of Carmel, bent down to the ground and put his face between his knees. 43 "Go and look toward the sea," he told his servant. And he went up and looked. "There is nothing there," he said. Seven times Elijah said, "Go back." 44 The seventh time the servant reported, "A cloud as small as a man's hand is rising from the sea." So Elijah said, "Go and tell Ahab, 'Hitch up your chariot and go down before the rain stops you." 45 meanwhile, the sky grew black with clouds, the wind rose, a heavy rain came on and Ahab rode off to Jezreel."

Beloved people of God, people who are called by his name, you must be able to demonstrate God's power to the world. The world will not believe in God by mere words or simple acts of kindness. We must show proof to the world.

Proclaim the power of the Lord when no one knows or sees. Receive God's proof in your times of prayer. Proclaim the name of God. Prophesy about God's great works. God will surely accomplish it. Believe that nations will come back to God through such acts. God is looking for people of faith. There is a reason I proclaim such words so boldly. In order for revival to take place, God needs people. God needs people during times of crisis. What is your "Calling?" What did God tell you when he first called you? I am confident that God is still waiting for your answer in order to accomplish His goal. Do not lose your "Calling." Dedicate your life. The day will come when you will see the glory of God. God will not tarry. We must all respond in faith.

By way of reminder, God has given me the vision of Silk Road. I went to Almaty out of simple obedience. In 2000, he gave me a chance to host a mammoth intercessory meeting at the biggest national soccer stadium in Almaty to pray and repent for the nations, along with 20,000 people who came from all over Kazakhstan and Central Asia. I was able to accomplish this work in cooperation with local pastors, missionaries and English speaking missionaries of Almaty. We accomplished this work together. We were so overjoyed. There were less than 20,000 Christians in Almaty at the time. All of them gathered. We gathered over denomination boundaries. We repented for the sins of nations. We repented for the sins of Russia. We repented for the sins of Kazakhstan's people. We repented for sins we committed ourselves before the Lord. On the second day, we blessed the

President of Kazakhstan in the name of our Lord. We had a celebration of blessing as we blessed the young people, families and cities. Spiritual transformation began to take place. The event ended. Because it was a Muslim nation, it was so difficult to obtain permits. 3 days before the event, the president of Kazakhstan granted the permit in his own handwriting. We carried on in faith.

There were complications with the 3-chartered planes from Korea to Almaty, which were filled with intercessors. What would have happened if we were not granted the permit to hold this event? We pushed through because we believed in God's promise. The permit was granted 3 days prior to the event. We jumped with joy. The event was a huge success. After the event was finished, a few pastors and I knelt before the Lord and prayed, "God, do you want this to be a one time event? What is your desire, God? We believe that you desire the restoration of Kazakhstan, Central Asia and Silk Road. What should be our next step?" We sincerely wanted to know. We sincerely wanted to see restoration. God spoke to us as we earnestly sought him. "Prepare the young generation." Then he showed us a clear goal. "Plant 1000 churches in the Silk Road by the year 2010. Glorify my name."

Thus, we decided to hold a festival for young people on the second week of July from 2001 to 2010. About 1800 people came during the first year. We had 2200 people show up last year. We have had thousands of applicants this year as well but due to space limitations (6000 sanctuary is still under construction), we are only going to accept 2500 people. Young people from Turkey Azerbaijan, Turkmenistan, Uzbekistan, Kazakhstan, Kyrgyzstan, Xingjian of China, Mongolia, Tibet, and even Iran –all the people related to the Silk Road will gather on the second week of July. We saw the vision of God. We saw the vision of discipleship. The soldiers who will conquer the Silk Road will be prepared.

I was deeply shocked after visiting China, two years ago. God impressed upon my heart to restore the Silk Road as part of a stage to prepare the road back to Jerusalem. When I visited China, I was surprised by what came out of the mouth of the director of the entire underground churches of Xingjian. There is a Back to Jerusalem movement arising in China and the leaders of China want to send 100,000 missionaries to Jerusalem through the Silk Road. God, how could this be? We never met or discussed the issue but God had already planned the road back to Jerusalem from China to the Silk Road. I was deeply moved by his plan. I bowed down and prayed, "God, what is the vision?" The clear vision is "Back to Jerusalem." Prepare and restore the road back to Jerusalem. Restore Jerusalem. Restore the Silk Road region. I asked, "Lord, what is the strategy, then? How will you restore the land?" As I visited different nations, they have already started planting churches. Most churches have 20 to 30 members. They do not have any idea as how to guide the church or have discipleship at church, let alone a vision for discipleship. God gave me a vision for PRINCIPLE OF 12 at this time. He gave me the strategy of PRINCIPLE OF 12.

When I studied, put into practice and grafted the idea to our church, I realized that this was the great strategy God has given to us during the end times. The vision is Back to Jerusalem. The strategy is to complete the discipleship of Jesus Christ through PRINCIPLE OF 12, save countless souls through Alpha, complete the discipleship through PRINCIPLE OF 12 and plant 1000 churches by year 2010. I run without ceasing because I have a clear goal until 2010. I have two reasons for coming here. First, I wanted to introduce the PRINCIPLE OF 12 strategy to Korea and other key nations. Secondly, I have a desire to take with me those who aspire to become a missionary to the Silk Road region of Central Asia. There are so many mission fields in the world. Why does it have to be the Silk Road? God has shown me many reasons. First, the Korean people are the people of prayer and church planting. Central Asia is a land under the reign of the Muslims. This land cannot be ministered to without prayer. You do not need a lot of knowledge. You do not even need much power. Only those who can win the spiritual warfare through intense prayer can survive. They will plant and raise churches. They will accomplish God's work. This is why God has chosen Korean's, amongst others. We have an excellent inherent ability to plant churches. Chinese people build restaurants wherever they go; Koreans plant churches wherever they go. Muslims will not accept Caucasians in their land. Besides, Caucasians, fear going into such places. As Asians, we can accomplish God's mission because we have the same skin tone, allowing for acceptance and entrance into their land. That is not all. Our language is very similar to the Turkish nations of the Silk Road as well. The word order is the same. If you study the vocabulary, you can preach in their language in 5 months. I was so surprised when I went to Turkey. The missionaries in Turkey are so fluent. I asked, "How long have you been here?" They replied, "Only 3 years." How in the world! Maybe this is the reason why the Korean missionaries in Turkey have excellent ministries.

God wants to use our people. I am confident that God has prepared us for the Silk Road during these last days. I am confident about this, as God has promised. Please prepare yourselves. Even if you cannot go as a missionary, I bless you to be able to support the missionaries, pray, have a heart for the nations, and bow your knees before the Lord to help accomplish God's promised vision. However, I pray foremost for the land of Korea to be healed. I wish you would all have Elijah's heart. I pray that each one of you would have a heart for winning souls and turning nations to Christ as you become a man of prayer, as you fellowship and make decisions before the Lord. Then the will of God can be accomplished on this land quickly.

Part 4:
How to Develop the PRINCIPLE OF 12 Church

Chapter 7: Ladder of Success (John 15:1-8)

In PRINCIPLE OF 12 ministry, there are some key developmental stages of discipleship. Though stages of development may not be the most exciting way to view spiritual growth, these are foundational to successful growth.

The core of PRINCIPLE OF 12 ministry is to be sensitive to the Holy Spirit. The Holy Spirit is still alive today, giving us dreams, visions, preparing our future paths and faultlessly leading us. Without him, there is no significance in life. We can live passionate lives through the visions and dreams that he gives to us. It is the same in the PRINCIPLE OF 12 ministry. What does a teacher do with his disciple? Some people ask, "What is the curriculum?" I respond, "The Holy Spirit is the curriculum." This is why I emphasize the ministry of the Spirit. How can you know what a person's spiritual problem is without praying? How can you understand the pain in the life of your disciple without praying on your knees? Where would the compassion come from? What should you teach your disciples from the vast subjects of the Bible? Will you start by explaining Matthew 1? Will you make clear what the Holy Spirit wants? When did Jesus gather his disciples to lecture? He didn't do it that way. I am not saying it is wrong. Biblical knowledge is needed and knowledge of the church is needed. However, true discipleship through mentoring is discovering and conveying the Word through all night prayer, through an intimate relationship with the Father, and through the leading of the Holy Spirit. This is true mentorship. Man can be changed rapidly through intimate, Christ directed mentorship.

Some people ask, "The life of Christianity is displayed through maturity. How can you produce a disciple in one year?" It is possible.[11] If we are truly sensitive to the voice of the Holy Spirit, a life can be transformed at an extremely high rate through the proclamation of the prophetic word. Fruitful life is born. This is the dynamic power of the Holy Spirit. Today's generation needs to be sensitive to the work of the Holy Spirit more than any other generation in history.

There are four stages of effective discipleship. If you want to raise up disciples to become effective servants of God, fostering must take place in stages; only then can you bear fruit. Let's reviw the words of Christ from John 15:1-8;

> 1 "I am the true vine, and my Father is the gardener. 2 He cuts off every branch in me that bears no fruit, while every branch that does bear fruit he prunes so that it will be even more fruitful. 3 You are already clean because of the word I have spoken to you. 4 Remain in me, and I will remain in you. No branch can bear fruit by itself; it must remain in the vine. Neither can you bear fruit unless you remain in me. 5 "I am the

---

[11] Of course everyone rows at their own pace, but to ground a believer in life long faith and pupse can be accomplished. The Principle of 12 helps facilitate this process, and is the first stage in developing future leaders. For more on our Leadership process, see www.vision.edu.

vine; you are the branches. If a man remains in me and I in him, he will bear much fruit; apart from me you can do nothing. 6 If anyone does not remain in me, he is like a branch that is thrown away and withers; such branches are picked up, thrown into the fire and burned. 7 If you remain in me and my words remain in you, ask whatever you wish, and it will be given you. 8 This is to my Father's glory, that you bear much fruit, showing yourselves to be my disciples.

God is interested in fruit. God cannot stand trees that do not bear fruit. When Jesus was teaching the parable of the vineyard, the owner wanted to cut down the vine because it was not producing fruit, even with effective fertilizing. However, the caretaker begged, "No, please wait one more year. I will dig around it and fertilize it. If it bears fruit next year, fine. If not, then cut it down." Jesus allowed it. The Lord's plan was to cut down the tree if the tree did not bear fruit within 3 years. Why did Jesus speak of such things? A tree that does not bear fruit only sucks up nutrients. Since God is very interested in seeing fruit, He said He would cast away even believers who do not bear fruit, eg. He would spit them out of His mouth. He said we would know them (and each other) by their fruit. That is how interested he is in fruit. Jesus showed much interest in bearing fruit during this ministry on earth.

You can talk about fruit in two ways. One way is to talk about fruit as a personal transformation of character. It is a transformation of quality. It is to bear the fruit of life.

The greatest problem facing Christianity today is lack of individual change from Christian life. Believers around the world know their need for change, yet are not able to make changes of life and character, to be transformed. Many believers know their need to change, but seem to lack the power to change as required by God's word.[12]

It takes such a long time to change, even when you realize how much you lack. It takes even longer if you do not know your shortcomings. In spite of this, God says he would throw us out if there is no change. That is how much God is interested in fruit. How long will God suffer with a ministry if the servant continues to live a life of barrenness? It is God who helps our ministries to stand. A fruitless ministry will not last long. Many people fall for that very reason and many people will continue to fall for the same reason. In that sense, the fruit of our lives is most important.

It is the same way for believers. They come to church and laugh. However, when they go home, their family is filled with conflict and struggle, especially between the spouses. As a result, wives suffer from nervous breakdowns and husbands are filled with complaints. The children grow up watching the dissonance. There is no fruit of life. It becomes impossible to impart the Christian life through the generations. Why? Because, there is no transformation in the lives of people. One can start a cell, but begin to run into

---

[12] For more on Character Transformation, see *40 Days to the Promise: A Way Through the Wilderness* by Stan DeKoven.

intrinsic problems. The more people begin to meet, the more it reeks of sinfulness. As a result, the people begin to leave. This is why leadership training should be about formation and transformation of character. It is character that matters.

Because of this fact, mentorship is vital in the PRINCIPLE OF 12 ministry. It is not external love that simply covers the shortcomings. True parents help their children to realize their limitations and hopefully, transformation occurs through loving discipline. This is true mentorship. However, that is not the only important element. Transformation in quality brings transformation in quantity. The Bible tells us that when you bear the fruit of quality, then you will also bear the fruit of quantity.

Thus, the second fruit is transformation in quantity. Fruit of quantity means the expansion of the kingdom of God through the salvation of souls. God is waiting for the kingdom to be expanded through the disciples. Matthew 28 alone is sufficient for our understanding: "Go and make disciples of all nations." This means that God desires to have the kingdom of God expand throughout the nations. There are many reasons why we cannot bear fruit but I want to focus on one of the reasons. The problem is that the stages in nurturing disciples are not clear. People mature through stages, from childhood to adulthood.[13] Intelligence matures through stages also. Everything is in stages; everything is a

---

[13] For a thorough understanding of the process of Change, see *Journey to Wholeness* by Dr. DeKoven.

process. That is why stages are needed for an unbeliever to come to a church to become a new believer, have his faith established, then to become a disciple to do ministry. Church must focus on training ministers in stages.

We are not going to produce disciples by having constant worship or training all mingled together. Such endeavors can become too regulated. You must consider such issues.

I was born again by the Holy Spirit in 1981, entered seminary and studied theology for 6 years in Germany. I was commissioned as a missionary and have been ministering for 15 years. My Christian life is entering its 24th year. I have attended church services in Germany and Europe. I have also preached in many American and Korean churches in America. I have preached at numerous churches in Korea. I discovered some inconsistencies in my observation of the churches. Clearly, in order for one person to become a disciple and a mature Christian of character, stages to discipleship are needed. Yet many churches were merely having services without training. Some churches have discipleship programs but they confuse Bible Study with education. I, myself, did not know either. Maybe it is because none of us knew. However, as I was exposed to PRINCIPLE OF 12 - actually, as I started the Cell ministry, I urgently realized that we need to train in stages for effectively fostering disciples. I understood clearly through PRINCIPLE OF 12 that David needed to educate his men in stages to shape the once distressed, in debt or discontented people into mighty warriors. Whether it's

America, Korea, or Europe, there are many churches that concentrate on evangelism only. They evangelize day and night. They wear banners. They shout, "Believe in Jesus and go to heaven. If you don't believe, you'll go to hell." All the members focus their efforts on evangelism. The senior pastor of the church boasts how his church is an evangelistic church that obeys the great commission of Jesus Christ.

So, I would ask them, "Have you been successful in evangelizing?" They reply, "Yes, newcomers are streaming in." I respond, "Then your church must have grown significantly." Unfortunately, that is not always the case. The door to enter is wide open but the door to exit is wide open as well. They may enter but they also leave. This is not surprising. The pastor cannot rely on the gift of evangelism only. If you have the gift of evangelism but do not have the ability to nurture the new believers, your ministry will not grow. If that is your weakness, you need to prepare a staff that can help you in that area.

We must make sure that discipleship becomes a fixture in the church through multiple stages. Some churches just lack discipleship. For others, discipleship is a fad; all they do is Bible Study. They start with Genesis on Monday and continue to study the Bible. The faith of the members is strengthened. They become passionate and do not fall even when temptation arises. Yet, the church does not grow. It is because they don't evangelize. In some churches, newcomers do not fully understand the sermon. All the sermons, from Sunday, Wednesday, and other meetings are too lofty. The newcomers cannot endure the learning curve. This church is also doing discipleship but it is not in phases. They only concentrate on a higher level of discipleship. This leads to barrenness. It is a simple sad fact of church life. Therefore, church needs to have systematic discipleship training.

PRINCIPLE OF 12 Ministry Divides Discipleship into 4 stages

First Stage: **Win** – Win people. In other words, lead people to salvation. In order to save people we must evangelize. We call this stage the Evangelism Stage or Salvation Stage. Since we need to leave the door open so that unbelievers can be saved, we need the Salvation Stage. We must evangelize with passion. How can you disciple without evangelizing? Who can you disciple when there are no people? It is the height of boredom if we try to make disciples out of someone who is already a disciple. Only knowledge and criticism expands while the passion to go into society to save souls is not present. That is the problem. We must go through the Win stage. We must evangelize.

Second, after people are saved, we must **Connect** them. That is, we must strengthen their belief or their faith. Believers must be assured that God answers prayer. Believers must be assured that they are saved because they believe in Jesus. They must have an unshakeable faith regarding the Lordship of Jesus Christ. They must have faith that God heals when you pray for the sick. These very basic truths must be instilled in them. This is also called the establishment stage.

Many people exit church when they do not go through this second stage of establishing themselves. They may have attended the church a few times but because their faith has not been established, they leave. This is why many churches have new believer's Bible Study. A new believer's Bible Study functions as the way to draw them in.[14]

Ju-An church, whose senior pastor is Rev. Gyunil Na, has experienced wonderful growth through the 10 stages of a new believer's Bible Study. Many new believers come to his church because his sermons are easy to comprehend. Many stay because the church has a nurturing program for new believers.

Third is **Train.** This is the stage where you make disciples. After their faith has been established, you must require something from them. You can not leave them alone. Your role is not limited to meeting their requests, to fill their needs, to pray for their college entrance exams, to pray for their healing and to help them enjoy lifes blessings. You have to help them to become committed to the Lord by making them disciples. This is where many churches run into problems. Even after going through the establishment stage, pastors fail to have a vision for training. They fail to lead them to a life of commitment. Rather, they are dragged around by the believers' demands. That leads to a diminished level of

---

[14] See *New Beginnings: A Sure Foundation* and *40 Days to the Promise*...tools for Connecting.

commitment and stunted growth. This is why the discipleship stage is vital. The Lord desires committed disciples. The Lord does not want people who try to use the name of the Lord to bring blessings unto themselves, even after their faith has been established. We need a fostering program or management program to make disciples.

The fourth stage is **Send**. This is the stage of ministry. People may feel that "Send" means to send someone out as a missionary. However, "Send" means to send people into ministries. When unbelievers become believers, make them into disciples after their faith has been established. Then, send them out to ministry. For example, if a believer works at a bank, help them have a vision for people within the bank to be saved. Their vision should not be just for the bank but for all the other branches and banks as well. Then, help them to have a vision to evangelize to every worker in the bank. We have to help them to do ministry. Cast visions into their hearts and have them make a team of twelve to do a team ministry. Out of those twelve people, some will become a part of a team to coordinate the entire Encounter Retreat. A variety of team ministries will unfold and an explosive anointing will come upon them. They infiltrate society and begin to build up the ministry. God wants us to break down the church's walls and make an impact on society. Cast your vision by telling them that evangelizing to the entire city is not difficult. The power of vision is tremendous. People who are ready will understand and begin to move. You must carry out the fourth stage with such vision.

Some leaders have five stages of discipleship, and some can do it in three. That is not the problem. The key is to educate them in stages. However, in PRINCIPLE OF 12, we recommend the implementation through the 4 stages in unison. Some places utilize the same curriculum, some develop their own.

Let me illustrated how the PRINCIPLE OF 12 program can work anywhere. For example, let us say a missionary was sent to Africa. If the commissioning church sends a short term mission team to Africa in July, there is not much to do. They end up becoming a burden to the missionaries in that country. The reason is due to a different focus in ministry. The national missionaries will have their ministry, we have ours. Naturally we have different approaches, even agendas. During the months of July and August the missionaries become airport missionaries. All they do is welcome people and send people off at the airport. That is why I send them a training manual 6 months in advance, presenting to them what they need to do, even if the church that is coming does not know what PRINCIPLE OF 12 is. I say, "Please prepare for the Encounter Retreat. We are going to have the Encounter Weekend for 200 young adults. Please prepare $15,000 for the cost. There will be 11 lectures in total.

We will do five and your team should do six. Come and experience it for 2 nights and 3 days." We make requests of certain teams. "Originally, the Alpha courses are to meet once a week for ten weeks. However, because you don't have time as a short term mission team, please lead an Alpha course at our sister church for 10 days from Monday to Friday. Such and such people will be attending. This is the manual. You need to prepare for everything except certain lectures. You will need to bring certain gifts." We send them all the information. Then we are able to have a ministry that fits and operates together for God's glory.

If the church with the same system in America or Korea would go to a mission field, doing exactly that same ministry, then all they need are interpreters. You can do the same ministry effectively and with a different anointing (the anointing is different from here to there). Then, you can learn from each other. As we do that, God's church becomes stronger and we can witness the explosive work of the Lord. We can see how important it is to have the same discipleship system.

Not only that, but the discipleship program should be carried out with consistency and repetition. Because I am a pastor, I understand the psyche of other pastors. Do you know what our temptation is? We want to hear from our congregation that, "Our pastor always gives us something new." However, here in lies grave danger. It may seem refreshing, but if you foster the disciples differently every time, they will not have the same foundation. In other words, the congregation's DNA will not be the same. It will change daily, yearly. Then you will not know what the distinctive characteristic of your church is. If you continue with the same nurturing discipleship, that becomes your church's DNA, it translates into a lifestyle.

Dr. Choi

There are many reasons why Yeido Full Gospel church has experienced such growth. There are two primary reasons. One was Pastor Jashil Choi's tremendous prayer and fasting. When Pastor Choi emphasized intercession and fasting, the church was able to maintain its spirituality. There was such a strong presence of God; unbelievers would be healed just by sitting in the service. Secondly, the members of that church all had full knowledge of the tri-fold gospel. When I was attending seminary, I would visit and evangelize to people at their homes. The church members of Yeido were different. They were different because they all said the same things. They confessed that God is a good God. As soon as they met me, they'd tell me that God is good. That is the first fold of the tri-fold gospel. They would talk endlessly about the filling of the Holy Spirit, and third, that healing is for today. It is such a simple story but they were persistent and repetitious. They talked about the tri-fold gospel for years, approximately 10-20 years. The congregation grew in their confession of faith. If you keep telling your children the same story, they will take on the character of their father. It is the same principle. They followed their spiritual father, Pastor Yonghi Cho. People could tell that they are his disciples.

There is power when the teaching is the same. When you repeat, the anointing becomes even deeper. It becomes clear. Understanding becomes certain. The advantage of clear understanding is that you are able to share it with conviction and clarity. My wife always used to advise me, "Your sermon is too difficult. Maybe it is because you studied theology in Germany but it is too difficult and logical. You have too much content." For ten years I did not understand what she meant. I barely began to understand it 2-3 years ago. I kept preaching difficult sermons when the level of the believers was not that high. I would get excited about my own meditations with the Lord and say to myself, "What a revelation. This word is so deep!" However, when I shared it with the people, their response was not too positive.

Certain deacons said, "Pastor, I was blessed." However, not that many people would make such comments. This is the problem. It was not being generalized. "I have a lot of problems. I really don't know my own flock. Yet here I am leading them as their shepherd," I thought. I truly repented. My wife said, "I told you for 10 years and now you are beginning to understand?" If a man and a woman do not minister together, the man could be deluded forever. Women speak and live in reality but men live by their ideals. A wife tries to bring the husband down to earth but the husband thinks that she is trying to get in the way. Pastors have much to learn from their wives. Pastors have heard from their wives about the sermon style, tone of voice, microphone usage, and even insensitivity. If the wives are not allowed to speak on such things, they fall into depression. This is a very serious problem. My wife was depressed for a very long time. I had to get on my knees to bring her out of it while doing a 40 day fast. With wisdom and sensitivity, the pastor can avoid such a trap.

Four Stages for the Effective Fostering of Disciples

Let's review again the stages of discipleship:

First stage: Win

We must save souls. How do we save them? What kind of strategies do you use to save people? What kind of strategies do you use in PRINCIPLE OF 12?[15] PRINCIPLE OF 12 does not have a specific strategy for the Win Stage. We can use any program to help save people. My church even uses the four spiritual laws. However, I do not tolerate programs such as "4 spiritual laws" or "Evangelism Explosion" to mislead people into thinking that mere intellectual consent is the actual acceptance of the gospel.

As today's society changed, I felt the need to transform the people through relationships. When relationships deepen, people open their hearts. When that happens, an effective and clear presentation of the gospel is needed. That is why we are operating the Alpha Course. I had yet to find an effective program that could efficiently evangelize unbelievers. Thus, my church uses the Alpha Course to specifically present the gospel and teach the dynamics of a small group.

When the Alpha course is nearing completion, a person who is going to open a cell in the Alpha Course joins the

---

[15] See Dr. Tim Dailey's book, *Bringing Heaven to Earth*.

group as a helper. It is strategic. You cannot miss a moment. There may be churches that only hold the Alpha Course. What will you do after the Alpha Course? The Alpha Course is a process that transforms an unbeliever into a believer. You can see it as a nurturing program for new believers. Alpha Course evangelizes unbelievers. If you misunderstand this and try to have a Bible Study with the Alpha Course, you will fail 100%. I have seen many people fail. Nothing is as uninteresting as using the Alpha Course as a Bible Study. We took the Alpha Course into our community because we understood that unbelievers can become believers through the Alpha Course. I recommend that you run your Alpha Course in a neutral place (restaurant, office, kindergarten school building, hospital building, etc.) where other people's gaze is not present. Of course, we have church programs at my church. It is because we have a steady influx of new believers. We open up one Alpha Course a month with just new believers. As a result, we have three Alpha Courses consecutively. For one Alpha course, about 200 people are involved, including unbelievers, new believers, and helpers. At the same time, my recommendation is not to bring any more people into the church, but to take the church into the world and hold Alpha Courses at the colleges, orphanages, senior centers, schools, and markets. At my church, numerous Alpha Courses are functioning in the community. They have an opportunity to proclaim the gospel without hesitation.

In the beginning, it seemed like a social gathering and people attended without any hesitation. There are no demands or sermons. They simply listen to a talk and they can make choices and decisions according to their own opinions. However, the Holy Spirit works during the discussions. It is because we have prepared ourselves with tremendous amounts of prayer. Then, people whose hearts are opened can attend the Holy Spirit Weekend (half day, 1 day, 1 night and 2 days, or 2 nights and 3 days), which is the Alpha weekend. At my church, about 95 % of the people are filled with the Holy Spirit and speak in tongues at the Alpha Weekend and the inner transformation that takes place is amazing. Through the Alpha Course, I can see people's understanding of God and their consciousness of Him literally being transformed just like the vision God has given me (Transform the consciousness of Kazakhstan and the Silk Road with the gospel). Everyone who comes in is transformed. As a result, the team members are so encouraged. The Alpha Course is a very important tool for Winning people to Christ. It is a very important tool for evangelism. Each generation has a tool of the Holy Spirit that God uses. The Alpha Course is one of them.

If you have yet to get started, start the Alpha Conference first and start to apply it. And make sure to attend the original conference. You cannot attend the Alpha Conference just once. You can maintain the original form if you attend the conference at least once a year with your team. However, if you are too smart, you will fail because you try to do it your way. There is a reason why the originator made things the way they are, because he had a certain goal, direction and reason behind everything. Alpha is being upgraded yearly, all over the world. They have an excellent staff that makes necessary adjustments to fit the actual conditions in the world. Their material is excellent. There is no need to add or to subtract. You just need to change the menu a little bit. Change the pizza to steamed rice. Anyhow, at my church, we use the Alpha Course as an important tool for the Win Stage. Just last year, 130 cells were newly opened through the Alpha Course. It is amazing. When you open a cell with mostly Alpha Course graduates, that cell's relationship seems to remain healthy. They become much more committed. The commitment of a person walking with the Lord for 3 months after completing the Alpha course is much deeper than someone who's been going to church for 10 years without the Alpha Course. This is the magnitude of Alpha's impact. The Alpha Course helps to communicate the gospel and the Holy Spirit's direct indwelling presence. I strongly recommend the Alpha Course to you.

We also use the "4 Spiritual Laws". We hand out the "4 Spiritual Laws" tracts to the congregation and they go out and evangelize. We do this to raise the awareness of the need to evangelize. They can also re-establish their assurance of salvation as they read it to the unbelievers. We use the "4 Spiritual Laws" with that purpose in mind. At least in the city of Almaty, we want people to know that Christianity exists and that salvation is available to them, whether the presentation of the gospel is formal or psychological. We rely on the logic that they will turn to us for answers when they run into problems. This is a program. However, lifestyle is much more important than programs.

I like the word "movement." Whatever you start, if it does not become a movement, it will fail. No matter how good something is, if it does not become a movement to run on its own or continue on, then it has already failed. You need not start just programs; start a movement. What kind of movement do we need? Alpha needs to become a movement, no doubt. But I discovered the most important truth. The reason people do not evangelize is because we do not pray.

In PRINCIPLE OF 12, 3 unbelievers become the object of prayer; every meeting, we place an empty chair in the middle of the meeting and pray for unbelievers. The cell leader checks each member, asking, "Who are you praying for?" Only 3 people are to be on the prayer list, and never 4 or more. I have seen that once you go to 4 or 5 people, the depth of prayer diminishes. These 3 people are not just objects of evangelism but they are also people you want to make into disciples. The goal is different. The strength and commitment level of prayer is different. It is not praying for people whenever you remember. It is different because it is a committed prayer to see the transformation of their lives and to make them into disciples.

What is the strategy for drawing people closer? Find out if the person has any problems and pray over the issue. At an opportune time, start building a relationship by saying, "I will pray for you if you have any problems." They may answer, "You don't need to pray. I am praying to Allah."

However, when you say, "When I pray for you, God will bless you," they will respond well because no one hates the word, "bless." Or, you can just tell them, "If you have a problem, call me." Then the following week, you can say, "If you have a problem, call me. I will pray for you. I am actually praying for you already. Do you have any family problems by any chance?" Everyone has one issue or another with his or her family, so this is a great way to get your foot in the door. Also, at one point or another, someone has some kind of illness. Just by engaging people at this level, we know that there are many opportunities to meet people and evangelize. This is how we meet the three unbelievers that we constantly pray for. Ultimately, you pray and nurture them until these 3 people become your disciples. When one person becomes a disciple, you replace that person on your list with three others. You keep doing it until you have your 12 disciples.

On a side note, awareness of goals is very important. People begin to wither away and die when they do not have an understanding of their goals. They say that people age much more rapidly after retiring because they no longer have a sense of purpose in life. It is the same thing. Young people, who have yet to retire, do not have any energy because they do not have a purpose or goal. Even in their speech, they do not have any oomph or conviction.

The most important aspect of evangelism is spiritual warfare prayer. We have to be able to do prophetic ministry, commanding the spirits not to interfere in the process of saving souls. We must go into a deep prayer that can bind the evil spirit's authority with God's authority, Jesus' authority, and set them free.

Need for the Proclamation of the Gospel to Speak the Word of God.

Ezekiel 37 holds important truths. Today's generation is one of despair. There seems to be no hope. In this unbelieving generation, their life as a whole is bogged down in the mire of despair. "I can't do it; I fail everyday." They hear so much negativity at home and experienced such failure in their everyday lives that they cannot seem to find meaning in their lives. What is it that they need? They need to hear the voice of God and breath of life.

In Ezekiel 37, the hand of God took Ezekiel by the Spirit of the Lord and set him in the middle of a valley full of bones. In verse 2, it says, "He led me back and forth among them, and I saw a great many bones on the floor of the valley, bones that were dry." Then God asked him, "Son of man, can these bones live?" "Servant of the Lord, my son. Can this society live, transformed? Can this city be transformed? Can the souls be transformed?" "I said, 'O Sovereign Lord, you alone know.'" That means he did not know. Then he said to me, "Prophesy to these bones and say to them, 'Dry bones, hear the word of the LORD!'" Do you have such boldness? Have you heard the voice of God in your time of prayer? "This is what the Sovereign LORD says to these bones: I will make breath enter you, and you will come to life." What a statement of conviction? Do you have such a conviction from the Lord?

An evangelist revives souls. A prophet revives souls. The person who has received the word can revive the souls from his fellowship with God; he is the one who can evangelize. You have the power of evangelism when you can proclaim the word of God that brings hope to the souls that are in despair. It comes straight from God and not from memorization. God says, "I will attach tendons to you and make flesh come upon you and cover you with skin; I will put breath in you, and you will come to life. Then you will know that I am the LORD." You will come to life. Do you have such confidence? Your family will come to life. You will not get divorced but reconcile. Your spirit will gain new hope. Do you have such conviction?

As a pastor, some people look dead in my eyes. I wonder, maybe our prayers are lacking, maybe we are not very inspiring, or maybe we missed the voice of the Lord altogether. The Bible says that God does not want anyone to perish but everyone to come to repentance. In Jeremiah 29:11, it says, "For I know the plans I have for you," declares the LORD, "plans to prosper you and not to harm you, plans to give you hope and a future." This was God's message of hope given through Jeremiah to those who were taken captive to Babylon. The Israelites were in despair and lamentation: "We are in despair. We have no hope to live because we have been judged by God." Many of God's people echo such sentiment today.

God wants us to change our thoughts, to change our consciousness. He wants us to know what kind of God he is. The reason we don't evangelize is because we are in despair. We think that we can't do it. You must believe that nothing is impossible in the Lord. God can make dry bones live again. He can attach tendons and flesh to dry bones. We should also say, "So I prophesied as I was commanded." The minister and evangelist of God's word must become a spokesperson of God's Spirit. This is true evangelism. You have to become a preacher of life. You cannot do it by memorization, through learned knowledge. It is true that there is power in words. Which words does God want us to speak? Do you speak the words appropriate for this generation given to you by God through prayer and fellowship with the Holy Spirit, or do you simply share the words you read from a book? The difference is night and day. It is the difference between heaven and hell.

The Bible reads, "So I prophesied as I was commanded. And as I was prophesying, there was a noise, a rattling sound, and the bones came together, bone to bone. I looked, and tendons and flesh appeared on them and skin covered them, but there was no breath in them." Tendons and flesh appeared and skin covered them; they began to have an appearance of man but still had no breath in them. There was no hope for them, still. The evangelist prays yet again. The prophet of God prays one more time. Those who love to hear the voice of God prays. All of you are God's prophets. Prophets are those who receive God's word. When you pray to God on your knees, he will give you his word. He will give you his word for your husband and your children. I challenge you to pray to God on your knees to hear his voice for your children. Then communicate God's word to your children. Their outlook on the future will be changed. Their hope for the world will be transformed, becoming brand new. True evangelism should take place in the home first.

Even though there was no breath, he had faith and he prayed again, "Then he said to me, 'Prophesy to the breath; prophesy, son of man, and say to it, This is what the Sovereign LORD says: Come from the four winds, O breath, and breathe into these slain, that they may live.' "Are we not able to hear God's voice? Who would dare to proclaim such a thing? It is impossible without the voice of the Holy Spirit. However, the Holy Spirit gives us confidence to make the impossible possible. He wants us to proclaim the impossible. We must hear that voice. The evangelist must be victorious in spiritual battle. You are victorious when the voice of God speaks through you.

When the bones came alive, they became a vast army, overflowing with God's anointing and life: "So I prophesied as he commanded me, and breath entered them; they came to life and stood up on their feet—a vast army." God desires his church to be full of life. He wants his church to be more than alive in just the body. He doesn't want our Christian life to stop at stage 1 but he wants our Christian life to enter into stage 2. More than knowledge, we must have the presence of God's spirit. We must pray until His presence becomes so intense that unbelievers will tremble and repent the moment they walk into the church. When that happens, history will be made.

> God speaks the third time. The son of man prays again, "Then he said to me: "Son of man, these bones are the whole house of Israel. They say, 'Our bones are dried up and our hope is gone; we are cut off.' Therefore prophesy and say to them: 'This is what the Sovereign LORD says: O my people, I am going to open your graves and bring you up from them; I will bring you back to the land of Israel. Then you, my people, will know that I am the LORD, when I open your graves and bring you up from them. I will put my Spirit in you and you will live, and I will settle you in your own land. Then you will know that I the LORD have spoken, and I have done it, declares the LORD.' "

Do you know the content of the third prophecy? "My people, Israelites are saying 'There is no hope for church. We have been cut off. The society will not change. We can't do it.' " God has the last word. The Lord Jehovah says, "I will open up your graves. I will remove the doors to your graves. I will bring you up from your graves. I will bring you back to Israel." This is a promise to take them back into the Promised Land. He is saying, "I will return you to the original purpose of your creation. You lost the purpose of your life. Your life has lost meaning. I created you yet you are going down the wrong path, deceived by Satan. I will take you out and return you to the land of Israel. I will return you to the original vision." This is God's proclamation. Evangelism goes beyond the mechanical dimension of simply having people believe in Jesus. To take a soul back into God's original calling is true evangelism. To make it happen is our calling. That is why our prayers are so important. This is what spiritual warfare is all about. Can a soul truly meet the Lord without prayer? No, that is impossible. Is it enough to heal people with God's gift? No. The word of God must enter into them. The power to save souls must be displayed. This is when God's work truly begins.

Therefore, in the first stage, Win, we can use any number of programs. It would be foolish to use just one method. However, it is very important to establish the three people prayer movement. Then start the Alpha Course. No other program is as revolutionarily effective as Alpha in today's soil. It is bearing real fruit all over the world. Over 4.5 million people have accepted Jesus Christ through Alpha. That is not a small number. That is greater than huge crusades because these people have actually accepted Jesus Christ. It is even more precious because they accepted after understanding the gospel clearly. This is the Win Stage.

Second Stage: Connecting

The connection stage functions to solidify one's faith. There must be an encounter with Jesus who hung on the cross. The cross is the most important part of our lives. It is upon the cross our curses were taken away and God's blessing came upon us. We must believe that Jesus truly is the Christ.

God's punishment has disappeared from us and the Salvation of God has come to us. There must be an event where we can come to fully believe in the gospel and we confess that Jesus is Lord. However, this is only possible when we meet Jesus on a personal level. People who have personally met the Lord do not leave Jesus. They can overcome any difficulty. At the first stage, the salvation stage, the most important phrase is "Prayer as Spiritual Warfare." At the second stage, the stage of connection, the most important phrase is "Encounter." It is an encounter with God. It is an encounter with true depth. Through this Encounter, we are made to confess that Jesus is my personal Lord. Apostle Peter's confession, "You are Christ, the son of the living God," was made possible by the working of the Holy Spirit. We have to help people make the same confession. The moment such confession takes place, that person will become someone who will never leave the church. This is why we have the Encounter Weekend, in order to Connect one's faith, and in order to help people meet with Jesus on a personal level. This retreat is designed to encounter God. The duration is 2 nights and 3 days. Let's look at some of the important contents of the retreat.

First, we lead them to true repentance over their sins. Next, two to three sermons are given. Then, two sermons are given to explain about the saving and healing power of the cross and the gospel of the cross. That is followed by a session of inner healing, which is then followed by deliverance ministry. Then comes the filling of the Holy Spirit and finally, we even cast the vision of PRINCIPLE OF 12. That's how an

Encounter Retreat ends. Because the Korean churches emphasize keeping the Lord's Day holy, the program should begin on Thursday evening and end on Saturday afternoon. Most churches in America and Europe start on Friday evening and end Sunday morning. It is effective to rent a retreat center, if possible. This keeps people from being distracted by family matters or children. However, it is difficult to do that in the mission field like my church. It is difficult for people to pay a $20 fee when they only make $100 a month. However, I stubbornly took 100 people to the retreat every week. It is possible when it becomes a movement. People come even if they need to be in debt.

However, after a while, as unbelievers started coming, some people just couldn't afford to pay. Now we have the retreat at the church. People need to go home to sleep at night but it is still very effective. The fact that people are coming together for 2 days and nights is important. Through this Encounter Retreat, people experience radical repentance and the gospel of the cross. They receive inner healing and are set free from evil spirits. They are filled with the Holy Spirit and receive the vision of PRINCIPLE OF 12. They personally experience and meet the Lord in a positive, distinctive way. The key is that their experience with Jesus Christ enables them to grasp the vision in their lives. This is an encounter with Jesus.

However, before going to the Encounter, there is a preparatory stage called a Pre-Encounter Seminar. This consists of 4 simple lectures. The lecture covers assurance of salvation, their need for inner healing, and power of prayer. You can do all three or four lectures in a day or you can spread it out over 4 weeks. This is preparatory work before going to the Encounter Weekend. However, if they have attended the Alpha Course, we do not insist that they attend the Pre-Encounter. They already have a basic understanding of God and salvation through the Alpha Course, so they can go straight to the Encounter Weekend. The Repentance of Sin, the Saving and Healing Power of the Cross, Inner Healing, Deliverance, the Infilling of the Holy Spirit and PRINCIPLE OF 12 Vision are very important parts of Encounter. This is our model today.

After the Encounter Retreat, one thing that my church has experienced is a strong backlash from the Enemy. There will be attacks and temptations. People will experience hardship. Some people get into car accidents and problems arise. Sometimes, strange things happen. This is all the attack of the enemy. Therefore, we hold a Post-Encounter Seminar to help people deal with such attacks. The Post-Encounter Seminar is a 10-week lecture series given to people who have completed the Encounter Retreat to help them overcome the temptations of the world and strengthen their faith. The most important part of the Second Stage is Encounter. We must arrange a personal meeting between the people and God. It is impossible to establish one's faith without it. It is the key to divinely connecting them with the Lord and His church. In most cases, people fall into difficulties, temptations and attacks from Satan without the help of Encounter.

Third Stage: Train

The most important part of making disciples is to equip the disciples with the word of God and mentorship. This is mentoring via the voice of the Holy Spirit and the voice of the prophetic. Disciples are not made with an abundance of knowledge. Some people can't become a disciple with a handful of Ph.D's.

When I was studying theology in the Ph.D. program in Germany, over 40% of students of theology were living together. I couldn't find one professor with Resurrection Faith. I couldn't understand why they even studied theology. They know the Bible better than us. They memorize the original text, word for word. When we would argue about the original text, we would always lose. Yet their faith was worse than an ordinary believer. Knowledge, at times can be dangerous. Wrong knowledge can destroy a person's faith. I ask that you concentrate on hearing God's word for today and proclaiming it, according to the leading of the Holy Spirit.

How is a disciple made? True disciples are made when we mentor or train our disciples with the Rema Word of God that we received through time on our knees. This is the best manual. To facilitate this, we meet for PRINCIPLE OF 12 meetings. My disciples and I meet once a week. Some people ask, "Pastor, what do you teach in a PRINCIPLE OF 12 meeting? Do you have a curriculum? Do you have some materials?"[16] The curriculum is prayer and the Holy Spirit. I

---

[16] This was in the beginning. Now there is excellent curriculum available through BCCN.

pray for my disciples wherever I may be. I pray for their family, even when I don't see them. My twelve disciples pray for me and my family before every meal. This provides the power of protection for me. I am also committed to them in the same way. I continue to pray for their family.

What kind of results are achieved? Before I meet them the following week, the Holy Spirit shows me their circumstances. He lets me know what they must hear from God. That is the sermon I share with them. It can be short. It can get long, over two to three hours. There is no time limit in PRINCIPLE OF 12 meetings. That is mentoring. I am teaching them how to do ministry. These meetings take the place of a seminary.[17] It is taking place between a teacher and his twelve disciples. This is discipleship, but sometimes that alone is not enough. We need the church as well. We need a systematic knowledge of the Bible, but not an unhealthy emphasis.

In order to teach them the word, I established a leadership school.[18] It is divided into 3 semesters, 10 weeks per semester. We meet once a week, with two lectures in two hours. That is a total of 20 lectures. During the 1st semester of the leadership school, 10 lectures involve basic doctrine. The other 10 lectures are special lectures, mostly about the role of a man, a woman and children in a family. That is because the

---

[17] This is druiing their initial training. More on seminars will be discussed when we present leadership development later.

[18] Vision International College and University.

family unit has broken apart in today's society. In the men's network, we teach them about the role of a man. In the women's network, we teach about the function of a woman and the Young Adults are taught the role of children. We also hold pre-marital and marriage seminars. The 1st semester of the leadership school ends by enabling the young adults, women and men to enter a stage where they can form a basic family. This is the basics of educating people in life. The second semester is also 10 weeks. Two lectures are given for an hour each with a total of 20 lectures. The first 10 lectures are about cells. How do you lead a cell? What is needed for explosive growth of a cell? How do you lead a cell meeting? How do you resolve conflicts within the cell? The lectures deal with basic Cell Theory. The following 10 lectures are special lectures. Three lectures are given for intercessory prayer, three for evangelism, two on ministry, and two on service. The 3rd semester of the leadership school is also 2 lectures in 2 hours with 20 lectures total. The first 10 lectures are for Leadership Theory. This is very important. We start with the statement, "Character is everything for Christian Leaders." We talk about the vision a leader must have. The core elements are dealt with here. We try to prepare them to have the basic soil for leadership in the 3rd semester. I know that 10 lectures are not enough. It is not enough even if you teach them during their whole lifetime. However, when we include the core elements in those 10 lectures and teach them through repetition, their faith is deepened and it becomes a lifestyle. What is important is that the cell leaders have full understanding of the lectures. The next 10 lectures are special lectures. We emphasize visitation, Holy Spirit and Christian counseling.

They must complete 30 weeks of 60 lectures in the leadership school. When taking the first semester of the leadership school, as go through the Post-Encounter, they are instructed to pray for three people. After completing Alpha and they go to their cell, they are told to continue to pray for the three people. They must evangelize and send three people to the Alpha Course during their first semester. During the 2nd semester, they open their cell with those people who havecompleted their Alpha Course and during the 3rd semester, they choose their disciples. They are systematically put through 3 stages of discipleship. Remember, true discipleship takes place within the mentoring relationship. Disciples are made when you train them through the prophetic voice of God. Second, each church needs a leadership school. Every member of your church must go through basic education. It should not be overly complicated, but must be strongly emphasized.

Fourth Stage: Send

The fourth stage is the stage of team ministry. Once the twelve disciples are chosen, they try to fulfill the comprehensive vision. For example, let us say the vision is, "Transforming the national consciousness of all the nations through the gospel." Then the young adult's vision needs to be "Transforming the consciousness of the young adults through the gospel." Then the college students' vision becomes "Transforming the consciousness of the college students through the gospel." My twelve disciples, who are in charge of each network, will each pray on their own before the Lord to receive their own vision within the boundary of the greater vision. Their own twelve disciples become the Dream Team that makes their vision a reality. The focus on team ministry is to execute the vision. The team can now begin to function.

Some people have visions but no team. Some people have many disciples but don't have committed people to accomplish the vision. There are many variations of this. Your twelve disciples are your faithful ministry team who will serve as your hands and feet, in order to accomplish the vision of God. In this way, anyone can become a minister. People, who had no vision, hope, or meaning in life, people who did not even know what ministry was, have their eyes openned after becoming a disciple. They begin to discover the meaning of life. They begin to realize why they need to live, where they must invest their lives, and where they must invest their time and money. This is the power of team ministry within the vision.

There is a female doctor called "Muna" at my church. Starting in 2001, we have held the young adults' festival for the Silk Road during the second week of July. We plan to hold this annual festival until the year 2010. Young people from the Silk Road region gather for this festival. They come from

Azerbaijan, Turkmenistan, Tajikistan, Uzbekistan, Kyrgyzstan, and Kazakhstan. The Turkish people who live in the Xingjian region of China also attend. The Turkish people are scattered all over the Silk Road and they live within Muslim areas. So we invite all the young adult representatives from the Muslim region and host a festival every year. We help them go back to their people in the Silk Road and minister to them by casting the vision of Jesus, which is the vision of the twelve disciples. Twenty eight hundred people gathered the first year. In 2002, about 2200 people came. This year, if the sanctuary is completed, about 5000 can attend, but if it is not ready, about 2200 will gather. Next year, we plan to gather about 5000 young adults for a whole week to have a rally. It will last from 7 AM to 10 PM in 30 degree (Celsius) heat without any air conditioning. We will eat, sleep and sweat together. We will be blessed throughout the day.

To be blessed means to be called by God as an intercessor. Muna began to pray for me, Pastor Samsung Kim. As she was interceding, God told her to pray for the Silk Road. That is reasonable. She is given the same vision because she remains within one vision. There is no doubt about it. This is the power of vision. As this female doctor was praying tearfully for the Silk Road, she realized something, "I need a team." When she prayed alone, the evil spirits attacked her constantly. Attacks came from all sides, sicknesses came, difficulties arose, and she would fall into depression. One day, she realized during a sermon, "Ah, it is dangerous to pray alone. I need a team." When she realized it, she realized that it was the power of PRINCIPLE OF 12. Therefore, she pledged to God her life and her intercessory prayer ministry. As a result, she was able to make 12 disciples within 7-8 months.

Now they go all over the Silk Road, nation by nation, and intercede on their behalf; they consider it their highest calling. Her dream is to travel through all the nations of central Asia and into China's Xingjian region through the Silk Road to intercede for each nation. She has received a clear vision from God. Not only that but she shared her vision to create intercessory cells all over the region of Almaty so that they can completely block the powers of darkness in Almaty. Everyone can minister according to God's calling. However, if you do not have specific team members, your ministry can be hindered. She realized that you may have hope, passion and expectation, but that will not necessarily become realized. This simple testimony helps us to understand how important team ministry is. When you go through these four stages, you will experience amazing spiritual transformation in your personal lives and the life of your ministry. Remember this.

In sum, the first stage is the **Win** stage. It is a spiritual battle to win souls. You cannot set God's people free without battle. The second stage is the **Connect** stage. You have to help them meet the Lord through a dynamic personal encounter with Christ. The third stage is the **Train** stage. You must be sensitive to God's voice. You must be able to hear God's voice about each of your disciples to transform their character. Jesus uncovered the hidden motives of his disciples every time he met with them. How? He knew them through the Holy Spirit. We must continue with this ministry. The fourth stage is the **Send** stage. It is the ministry stage. You have to help them make their own teams. To become a part of a team means to become a spiritual family in the truest sense. Such teams will not be shaken. Even if Satan attacks one member, the eleven will rise to protect the one being attacked. The meaning of life will be renewed. "Now I know why I have to live." This is the confession of most of my disciples. You must receive the vision through a team and pray together for the vision. Your ministry will be fruitful only when you stay as a team. As a result, spiritual transformation will take place in your life of ministry.

Thus, your Team Ministry will consist of 12 disciples, men and women who have come through various stages of minisry and now make up a Ministry Network. Each will have an Alpha Course Team, Pre-Encounter Seminar Team, Encounter Weekend Team, Post-Encounter Seminar Team , Leadership School Team (1, 2, 3 Semesters) and Vision Interntional College and University team for chuch extension and planting.

12 steps to Discipling the Nations

How do we save the unbelievers and have them experience the Alpha course, Open Cell and PRINCIPLE OF 12 meetings? Cells go through various stages: Open Cell, Combined Cell, and PRINCIPLE OF 12 Cell. Sometimes, you fill up your PRINCIPLE OF 12 Cell as you run your Open Cell.

You can make new disciples and bring them into your PRINCIPLE OF 12 as you start your Open Cell. You can choose people as the disciples of PRINCIPLE OF 12 as you start an Open Cell. There are many variations. However, in order to save time, we go from Open Cell to combined cell and then move over to G12. Have one anointed PRINCIPLE OF 12 member lead the Alpha Course during the week. Make sure to have the Alpha Course stay connected and operating on Monday, Tuesday and Thursday. Run the Alpha Course in a 4-week interval and run the post-encounter and leadership school on Sundays. Encounter or Leadership School should be carried out as a 10-week course before service or during service. There are 12 classes for Males, Female and Young Adults on Sundays, and 12 stages to discipling the nations. These are stages to make disciples out of unbelievers. All disciples go through the following four stages.

1. **Win: Salvation Stage.**
   - Pray for 3 unbelievers!

Pray everyday for 1-3 months for unbelievers. When you pray for people on your list, their hearts will open. Pray about 10 weeks for 1 prospect.

   - Evangelize three unbelievers and make sure they have assurance of their salvation!

Look for opportunities to evangelize and make opportunities to develop a relationship. Build up the relationship through phone calls or meetings. The moment you begin to pray for three unbelievers (relative, co-worker, friend, etc.), you are creating a spiritual relationship with them. The goal is not to evangelize but to make disciples. Therefore, whenever there is an opportunity, use the time to speak into their lives.

- Meet their needs through phone calls or home visitation.

Visit people who are sick and try to meet their physical and emotional needs. You must remind them that you are praying for them by calling them at least once a week on a regular basis. Make an opportunity to share a meal together if you can.

- Lead them to the Alpha Course and help them to complete it.

Once the relationship is established, you need to encourage them to attend the Alpha Course. Attending the Alpha Course will serve to minimize the stress of attending a church service for the first time. They can hear the core message of the gospel. They can discover Christian life there. If you are planting a church, you can take them straight to PRINCIPLE OF 12 without the cell process from the Alpha course. Alpha Courses serve to establish the faith of unbelievers and new believers but it is difficult to lead them to a committed life in and of itself.

2. **Connect: Stage of establishing the faith**
   - Start your cell with them.

Once people complete Alpha, take them to cell meetings right away. Table leaders or helpers should already look for people to start the cell with. Build up the relationship so the cell can open immediately following the Alpha Course.

- Teach "Pre-Encounter"!

Pre-Encounter is a 4-week preparatory training course before attending the Encounter Retreat. It should be completed in a day during a weekend, from 2-6 PM. People who have completed the Alpha Course do not need to attend Pre-Encounter.

- Have people attend "Encounter Weekend!"
- Have people attend a "Post-Encounter Seminar" and have them pray for three unbelievers!

The most ideal time slot for Post-Encounter is 10 to 11 AM on Sunday morning so that they can attend the service immediately following the Post-Encounter meeting. The person in charge of Post-Encounter must be praying for the 3 people there. Have them read basic biblical literature and the New Testament.

3. **Train: Discipleship Stage**
   - Have them attend the "Leadership School" and have the three people they witnessed to attend the Alpha course!

After finishing the Post-Encounter, the three people they led to the Lord should attend the Alpha Courses. Students in the Leadership School should start the actual ministry at this time. They should put at least 3 people through Alpha Courses before the first semester ends.

- Have them attend the Leadership School and have them open a cell with those three people who completed the Alpha Course!

They must open their cell with those who completed the Alpha course and they need to open a cell before the second semester ends in order to receive the certificate of completion. Even if you heard all the lectures, you cannot complete the semester without opening a cell. If there is no fruit in the practicum, you cannot complete the semester.

- Have them attend the Leadership School and have them choose their 12 disciples!

In this stage, they learn leadership skills and the goal is to select 12 disciples from the Open Cell. They will choose the 12 disciples during the 3rd semester. The entire process takes about one year. From there (or before if qualified), the student begins the Vision International program.

4. **Send: Ministry Stage**
   - Choose your 12 disciples and form your "Ministry Team" with your 12 disciples.

Again, the ministry team consists of your Alpha CourseTeam, The Encounter Ministry Team, and the Leadership School Ministry Team. Your team becomes your permanent family member in the truest sense. You will discover the truths of God's word together, and the meaning and purpose for your life and ministry together. This stage brings the greatest joy, as they reproduce what you have produced in them as a leader.

Chapter 8: Process of Choosing and Developing the 12 Disciples

How do you choose disciples? How can you disciple them? What types of meetings are there in PRINCIPLE OF 12 Ministry? Our answer comes from Christ' life and teaching. First, let's review some princples of scripture.

> ¹²One of those days Jesus went out to a mountainside to pray, and spent the night praying to God. ¹³When morning came, he called his disciples to him and chose twelve of them, whom he also designated apostles: ¹⁴Simon (whom he named Peter), his brother Andrew, James, John, Philip, Bartholomew, ¹⁵Matthew, Thomas, James son of Alphaeus, Simon who was called the Zealot, ¹⁶Judas son of James, and Judas Iscariot, who became a traitor. (Luke 6: 12-16)

How should you choose your disciples? I've said it before; you must trust the power of prayer. There are a few standards in choosing and discerning your people. Obviously, we have Jethro's advice, given to Moses in Exodus 18: "Select capable men from all the people—men who fear God, trustworthy men who hate dishonest gain." However, even this is not always God's heart.[19] There must be a clear realization that comes from the Holy Spirit.

---

[19] For more on Good ideas vs God ideas, see *Visionary Leadership* by Dr. DeKoven

Even though he was the Son of God, Jesus chose his twelve disciples after praying through the night. To see it in more detail, we can read from Mark 3:13-19, which speaks about the same event as discussed above. It tells us that he prayed through the night,

"Jesus went up on a mountainside and called to him those he wanted, and they came to him."

We should not choose according to our own desire, but must choose people who are teachable, and people who love to obey, respect, and follow the Lord's command. When doing the ministry, you can see disobedience on certain people's faces. It is not easy to become a disciple even if you have money and education. Jesus had eyes to see clearly and was able to choose whom he wanted. It is because he prayed throughout the night. The twelve disciples of Jesus were the Vision Team and we also must become this type of Team. What we are thankful for is the fact that he chose Judas Iscariot to comfort us in our moments of weakness. It is great comfort to realize that even after such careful selection, even Jesus had a disciple like Judas.

Jesus prayed through the night and called to him those he wanted after going up on the mountain. Who were the people that Jesus wanted? My personal understanding is that they were people who understood the vision of the cross and believed in the power of the word and prayer. One thing I am certain of is that if you pray and rely on Jesus without ceasing, you will experience character transformation and be successful in ministry. Without prayer, you can make mistakes. You choose people who look good externally; people with a good educational background, money and even good looks you can miss God. It is easy to choose people but once you choose them and they start to cause trouble, they can become a thorn in your side. It is not about choosing who you want but choosing people who have the same vision as you. For example, if a pastor has a vision to minister to a certain area, then his disciple must have the same vision. It is not about someone who is smart or who graduated from seminary. It must be someone who shares the same vision as the pastor, someone who will agree with your vision. You need to create a Vision Team who will risk their lives for the vision. This is a true ministry team. They are useless without such commitment.

You will not be successful by scouting. You must raise them up and they must grow up in-house. You must know about them. If you are to choose an outsider, you ought to scout someone who is willing to risk his life for your vision after getting to know you. You must measure the person carefully. He might agree with you too easily, he might be a prudent person or a person who acts on a whim. It is the same in business. You must become a Vision Team. If you don't, you will fail. It is the same way for churches. God's principle applies equally in every facet of life. You choose the people you want.

Jesus chose twelve, not eleven, not thirteen, not four or even seven, but twelve. God's government is established through the twelve. God accomplished it through the twelve tribes. Twelve pillars are holding up the New Jerusalem, the kingdom of God. Twelve is so important that they replaced the vacant position after Judas. A person who is famous for group dynamics said the dynamic of a group is at its best when there are between 8 to 15 people. Jesus was very wise; he obviously had godly wisdom. He tells us to choose twelve. There is a tremendous difference between choosing twelve and choosing 8-15. There is a difference in the sense of responsibility. Responsibility follows when you are chosen. What kind of responsibility is it? It is the responsibility to be committed to each other. There is a family like contractual relationship that forms. They become a vision and ministry team that is closer than family, willing to risk their lives. This is why the number 12 is important. Not so much the number itself, but the fixed member is more important. This is why he chose the twelve.[20] Do you know what the purpose is?

Why did he want to have them with him? Why did he have them live with him? It was for the purpose of mentorship, so "that they might be with him."

When you look at a person from afar, you do not know his personality. The hidden motives of the heart remain concealed. Opinionated, rash, volatile …these personality traits are hidden within. That is why Jesus wanted to change them by living with them. Jesus knew that Peter was Simon. He was a man who was lacking in many ways. He was like a

---

[20] Along with the obvious focus on fulfilling all righteousness by choosing 12 disciples for the New Covenant, replacing the 12 tribes as God's foundation for His church.

reed, swaying back and forth in opinion and conviction. Yet, Jesus saw that Peter was obedient. Jesus saw that Peter was able to launch the boat into the deep, cast the net in the deep water and was able to repent. Jesus discerned that He would be able to change him allowing him to see Jesus at work. That is why he called the twelve to live together. Why is living together important? It allows for deep mentorship. I am not saying that we should all sell our homes and live in a retreat center together. However, we should meet at least once a week on a regular basis. When you start the PRINCIPLE OF 12 ministry, you are supposed to meet once a week, but you end up meeting many times within a week. You simply love it. Now you have someone to talk to when you have a problem. So you will end up calling and meeting with each other. You don't have to tell them to do it. It will become automatic as people spend time together. When you meet together, true motives surface.

  Earlier I mentioned my disciple named Alok. He has a special fervor but he was way too rough with people. I would tell him, "Alok, if you keep treating them like that, they will all run away. You have zeal but you must be meek. Read the Bible. Take on Jesus' disposition. Jesus did not speak harshly like you. People respect polite people because that is the character of God. You must do as I say." He took my instruction to heart and obeyed. This is what mentoring is. You will never realize and learn about each other without actually being together. People are obedient and kind in front of you. Who would defy the pastor outright? You will learn quickly if a person is the type to talk behind your back. The time spent working together as a ministry team, will bring out all the hidden agenda and true desires of the disciples. Some become confrontational when you fail to praise them. You must point out their shortcomings and transform them as you live together. You must remove those who do not change. You basically have to tell them, "Please go to another church. If not, you must obey and follow me. Choose one or the other." This may seem harsh, but it is necessary to grow healthy leaders.

This is why living together is important. You can find out their motives when you come together often. You can help shape and change their character. Moreover, you become intimate when you live together, building trust to the point where you can share anything and everything. Superficial politeness in a relationship will never lead to discipleship. If you meet only to work, problems will definitely erupt. Complaints will manifest and grow. They will begin to disagree with you not because of that specific issue but because of their personal issues with you. This is why Jesus called his twelve disciples to be with him. The ultimate goal of the calling was "that he might send them out to preach and to have authority to drive out demons."

This passage speaks about two areas of ministry. However, in Luke 9 and 10, and the entire New Testament shows that Jesus always did three types of ministry. When he sent out the disciples in pairs, he sent them out to heal the sick, gave them authority to drive out demons and to proclaim the kingdom of God. The goal is clear. The goal is to commission and to minister. Blessing was not the main goal, but to teach them to minister. One thing you must remember is that the goal is to send them out as soldiers. In other words, the goal is to send out every believer, to minister and to empower them as ministers of the Kingdom. We need to help them to lead people, proclaim the gospel, heal, cast out demons, and infiltrate society by spreading the Good News. This is the goal. We cannot lose sight of it. All members must become witnesses of Christ. You must raise your disciples by personally sharing the gospel with them. You must raise them up. You must impart your anointing to them. Then, they in turn must also raise up their own disciples and impart their gifts.

We must differentiate the roles between a leader and a minister. A leader is someone who sets the direction and casts vision. You need to continuously convey the voice of Jesus. You cannot keep sharing knowledge with mere words. The church cannot become healthy that way. It will become stagnant and the members will not be satisfied. However, once the PRINCIPLE OF 12 system is clearly implemented, once the senior pastor is able to convey the message that the church needs to hear, the eyes of the 12 disciples will be opened wide.

I was once asked, "Pastor, how did you know?" I responded, "How did I know? I came to know through prayer. God gave it to me because I prayed!" When my 12 disciples heard my answer, their eyes opened wide and they went and shared with their own 12 disciples what I had said. Subsequently, it spread through the church quickly and we were experiencing explosive effects. The church transformed quickly and an amazing spiritual movement began to take place. We need this type of spiritual system. Millions of people would begin to move through a simple command given to the twelve tribes by Joshua. They were twelve disciples who became one in vision. This is a tremendous team. There is no way that the explosive work of Jesus could not take place. I bless you to be able to choose such disciples in Jesus' name.

Use the Net

There is an actual net used to catch men. Evangelism must take place first. One on one evangelism is important, as well as evangelism through Alpha courses. In order to catch people, to maintain and disciple them, we need certain nets. We use four methods.

1) Open Cell

We call it Open Cell because anyone can come and it is open to everyone. It is like octopus tentacles. We open these cells in every area, city and work place. People are nurtured in this cell structure and further encouraged to attend the Encounter Retreat. It is a place where people are trained. Open Cells are designed to infiltrate all facets of society for the purpose of evangelizing and nurturing people. Evangelism, consolidation, discipleship and ministry: all four stages must take place within Open Cell but the primary objective of Open Cell is evangelism and spiritual nourishment.

2) PRINCIPLE OF 12 Cell

This is the gathering of PRINCIPLE OF 12 leaders. This can be called the leaders' cell. Only 12 people can attend. If one person leaves (if one is commissioned to another cell church), that person is replaced. You need to maintain the 12. True mentoring and transformation of character takes place here. They receive true vision here. Simply speaking, I do not have too many male cells at my church. There are only about 70 cells. My wife, on the other hand, has over 600 cells under her. There are 12 men under me and these 12 men have cells under them. This is my PRINCIPLE OF 12 cell. This is a closed cell and a leaders' cell. Of the 12 disciples of mine, some have their own PRINCIPLE OF 12 cells. Others have Open Cells until they have a complete PRINCIPLE OF 12 group. Within the Open Cell, about three have opened their own cell and the rest are under training. The nets that we use to attract people are Open Cell, PRINCIPLE OF 12 Cell, Worship according to different Nets, and Sunday Celebration Worship.

3) Worship according to different Nets

The women worship by themselves. Worship services that serve as a Net are Women's service, Men's service, Young Adult service, and Children's service. For example, March 8th is Woman's Day of the World (actually, it is only celebrated in

Russia but they think the whole world celebrates this day) and participants of Women's service prepare many special programs for this day. My wife's twelve disciples prepare programs to draw and win over the women in the city. They hold a Bazaar to attract the local women. They hold it at open markets, at the church, and even at restaurants. They also hold Alpha dinners. We are casting our nets to catch people for Jesus Christ.

4) Sunday Celebration Worship

Sundays must be a celebration. Whoever comes to Sunday service must be able to feel the presence of God. They can make commitments through powerful testimonies. They can enter into the presence of God through worship. In addition, they can experience the power of God through passionate prayer. Celebration worship causes people to be transformed by the powerful message. Sunday services must avoid formality, however. We must cast off formalism. We must pursue the presence of God first. Seek to have the presence of God in your services. Do not be bogged down by formality.

I changed the order of service hundreds of times. I changed it every time there was a lack of the presence of God. What would please God? Does he like formality? He loves dwelling in the midst of his people. There must be his presence.

The reason my church's services are always alive is that my wife and I are sensitive to the Holy Spirit. My wife, in particular, is very sensitive. She is very perceptive about the songs that are sung, and even the order of prayer and offering. Even if the service does well for a while, if I sense that it is becoming ritualistic or habitual, I change it. Why? Because if we do not keep it fresh, worship becomes habitual and the congregation members merely look forward to the sermon. We can't allow that to happen. We must give worship its proper place. The Sunday service must be a celebration.

In sum, we catch people with these four nets: Open Cell, PRINCIPLE OF 12 Cell, group specific Worship services, and Sunday Celebration Worship. When Jesus told Peter to throw the net into the deep water, Peter obeyed. When he caught so many fish that the nets began to break, Jesus said to him, "From now on, I will make you a fisher of men." Peter received the vision at that moment. He saw it with his own eyes. You will become a fisher of men who will catch so many men that the net will begin to break. Cast your net. Cast it with precision. Fix the nets. If the worship is in disarray, change it. Change the worship services so that worship is alive. If the PRINCIPLE OF 12 cell is anemic and the mentoring does not take place, change it so that mentoring occurs. Make Open Cells and use it for effective evangelism. Is the three people prayer movement dead? Set it up again. We continue to throw out nets, but we need to remember that the nets will continue to break. We need to fix the nets. We need to make it new. You can't be looking for a new net just because it is not working well or because it is torn. We must work with persistence and push on until we start bearing fruit.

The purpose of Open Cell is to evangelize and nurture. Of course, we must do all four: Win, Connect, Train, and Send. Leaders are made within the cell. Yet the primary objective is to save them and then to Connect them. In other words, there must be evangelism and guidance. For this purpose, there is a Consolidation Team in PRINCIPLE OF 12's ministry. When a new member comes, they make sure to contact them within 24 hours and visit within 48 hours. We have a manual regarding visitations. I would say it is more of a visitation team than evangelism team. This is how we touch their hearts. We do this because Satan begins to attack them the moment they make a decision to believe in Jesus Christ. This is why a team of intercessors must be able to go out to them to answer basic questions and to pray for them. You must establish this strategically. The meeting time should be limited to 1 hour. It is not easy to finish a visit within one hour. Therefore, at my church, we try to keep it between 1 to 1 and a half hours. We suggest that you not go beyond an hour and a half. In addition, eating is not recommended.These specific guidelines are important because one can easily lose sight of the true goal by focusing on the nonessentials.

So what is the agenda? There are a few basic details. Testimonies and games are essential. You need to have Icebreakers. You can exchange an ice-breaker with a testimony. Also, there must be worship and praise. For the message, we share the Sunday's sermon. Why do we do it this way? The senior pastor's vision is imparted through the Sunday sermon. The spiritual climate flows out from the pastor's mouth. This is a fact. This spiritual climate must be maintained. Weekly sermons become the study material. The senior pastor's sermon is not a sermon that is prepared overnight; it comes from his lifelong faith in God. It comes out of his character, his conviction and his calling. Therefore, it cannot be processed fully within 30 minutes. It must be discussed once again. This is why we have people discuss it in Open Cell during the week. However, if possible, Sunday's sermon must be evangelistic and spiritual in nature. This is the only way the church can grow.

Testimonies, icebreakers, games, praise and worship and Sunday's message are shared in an Open Cell. This is why the sermon cannot be too complicated. The key is for the shepherd to listen to the sermon carefully on Sunday and share with the cell members in areas that has blessed the shepherd. If you get too caught up with questions and answers, the cell seems to lose vitality. It is good, however, to maintain basic questions. That is wise. For some people who do not have such facilitation skills, they can ask three questions regarding the sermon to lead the discussion smoothly. The cell leaders must be blessed deeply from the Sunday's message. They Do not come on Sunday to simply keep the Lord's day should arrive about an hour early to pray that God would give them the heavenly manna through the sermon. Then the pastor's sermon will have a deep impact on their heart. When people are complaining about the sermon, it simply means that they have not prepared their hearts to receive. Pastors must prepare their sermons with all that they have. The title of the message, the main text and the direction of the message should be determined by the prompting of the Holy Spirit. Then they proclaim it. Sometimes the members of the church take the sermon too lightly. They also must prepare for the message. Please prepare your hearts. The cell leaders must pray for the senior pastor at least an hour prior to service time. At my church, there is a prayer room that is open 24 hours a day. It has a maximum capacity of about 400. Nothing else is allowed in that room. A typical service lasts anywhere from two to two and a half hours. My twelve disciples and my wife's twelve disciples take turns praying for me during the 1st, 2nd and 3rd services. They pray for two hours at a time. We do it this way because of spiritual warfare. How can God not work? God works in our services without fail. Even if the preparation is a little lacking, when I go on the altar, there is the presence. The anointing of the Holy Spirit is there. Life giving words gush forth, even if it was not fully prepared. I have a team ministry with my members. They support me by praying for me. I do my part by preparing. This makes it a family-like ministry.

After testimonies, praise and message, there is time for prayer and ministry. We pray for people's needs. We do not seek to get results right then and there, but simply pray in faith. Then we wait. Jesus will come and work. No doubt about it. After the prayer and ministry time, we always do three people evangelism prayer. Always pray together for 3 unsaved people. This is the only way we can experience vitality in the group. A passion for lost souls must flare up within the people. The church cannot grow without it. The leader can share his vision and announcements if there is time remaining. This can be done in an hour. It can be done at a work place. Continued gatherings brings change in people so if there is a need, the meeting can be shortened to 30 minutes. Start the Open Cell and complete the work of God in Jesus' name.

PRINCIPLE OF 12 Cell: Train and Send

There is a need for training and mentoring. Meetings, therefore, lasts 2 to 3 hours, for me, it takes about 3 hours. My wife takes 3 to 4 hours. It is because relationship needs to take place. If there is no personal contact and connection in the PRINCIPLE OF 12 meetings, the group begins to die. What does this mean? We need to help them experience the deep presence of God. You must prepare the words of life. You must pray throughout the week for the disciples to gain understanding about their life's problems and marriage struggles. When you begin your PRINCIPLE OF 12 ministry, you will first realize that you need to restore their families first. You will realize 100% that you need to help them to restore their family relationships. After the restoration of the family, you will discover that you need to restore their character. All family problems are rooted with character issues. From that moment on, you must teach them to pray, "Lord, transform my heart, no matter what the cost." Then the vision will come. Even in this meeting, there needs to be, testimonies, praise and worship, and messages prepared for the disciples. Then you can do ministry that is needed for their life, marriage, family, finances, relationships, and for their character issues. Then you can also prophetically pray for them. The prophetic ministry will flow within this group. If you do prophetic ministry with new Christians and baby Christians, there will be many problems as the ministry becomes a type of psychic encounter. However, within the PRINCIPLE OF 12 ministry, true prophetic ministry can take place. Proclamation through the prompting of the Holy Spirit is a prophecy. Believers must have the power to prophecy. They can hear the voice of the Holy Spirit when they lay hands on people. They can hear words of comfort. Sometimes they can even hear words of rebuke. Transformation takes place. As for my part, I listen to their ministry reports and give them direction, cast vision, and encourage their faith. Then PRINCIPLE OF 12 ministry meeting ends.

Summary

The formation of a Principle of 12 Cell is developed as follows:

1) Establish an Open Cell stage: three people prayer, visitation, Encounter nurture
2) Develop a Mixed Cell Ministry, moving to Connect and Train. Every Cell member as disciples!
3) PRINCIPLE OF 12 Cell Ministry Stage:
When 12 of your members can lead their own cells, hand over

the Open Cell and change to the PRINCIPLE OF 12 Cell.

Following this pattern has been highly successful in our work; int can be in yours as well.

Chapter 9: The Power of Mentoring (John 17) Transform them to make them into Disciples!

The power of mentoring or discipleship can be seen best in the ministry of Christ to His disciples.

In John 17:1-26 we read;
> 1 After Jesus said this, he looked toward heaven and prayed: "Father, the time has come. Glorify your Son, that your Son may glorify you. 2 For you granted him authority over all people that he might give eternal life to all those you have given him. 3 Now this is eternal life: that they may know you, the only true God, and Jesus Christ, whom you have sent. 4 I have brought you glory on earth by completing the work you gave me to do. 5 And now, Father, glorify me in your presence with the glory I had with you before the world began.6 "I have revealed you to those whom you gave me out of the world. They were yours; you gave them to me and they have obeyed your word. 7 Now they know that everything you have given me comes from you. 8 For I gave them the words you gave me and they accepted them. They knew with certainty that I came from you, and they believed that you sent me. 9 I pray for them. I am not praying for the world, but for those you have given me, for they are yours. 10 All I have is yours, and all you have is mine. And glory has come to me through them. 11 I

will remain in the world no longer, but they are still in the world, and I am coming to you. Holy Father, protect them by the power of your name—the name you gave me—so that they may be one as we are one.

12 While I was with them, I protected them and kept them safe by that name you gave me. None has been lost except the one doomed to destruction so that Scripture would be fulfilled. 13 "I am coming to you now, but I say these things while I am still in the world, so that they may have the full measure of my joy within them. 14 I have given them your word and the world has hated them, for they are not of the world any more than I am of the world. 15 My prayer is not that you take them out of the world but that you protect them from the evil one. 16 They are not of the world, even as I am not of it. 17 Sanctify them by the truth; your word is truth. 18 As you sent me into the world, I have sent them into the world. 19 For them I sanctify myself, that they too may be truly sanctified. 20 "My prayer is not for them alone. I pray also for those who will believe in me through their message, 21 that all of them may be one, Father, just as you are in me and I am in you. May they also be in us so that the world may believe that you have sent me. 22 I have given them the glory that you gave me, that they may be one as we are one: 23 I in them and you in me. May they be brought to complete unity to let the world know that you sent me and have loved them

even as you have loved me. 24 "Father, I want those you have given me to be with me where I am, and to see my glory, the glory you have given me because you loved me before the creation of the world. 25 "Righteous Father, though the world does not know you, I know you, and they know that you have sent me. 26 I have made you known to them, and will continue to make you known in order that the love you have for me may be in them and that I myself may be in them."

Mentoring has amazing power. In a word, mentoring is the process whereby a leader turns a pupil or subordinate into a leader, by bringing to surface the potential power of God's image. It is to take them back to their original place where the potential image of God can be developed. It is to help them become leaders. It is to help them become conquerors. It is to help them become affluent. This is mentoring. Worldly people cannot understand the ultimate goal of mentorship.

There are many different kinds of mentoring. For example, there are mentors for businesspeople, where they learn to strategize and ultimately make money. However, mentoring someone to build character helps the person to discover the image of God that is within them and to accomplish the purposes of God; simply, it is to help them achieve their original Calling. This is what mentoring is all about.

Someone asked a famous sculptor, "How can you sculpt a vibrant, lifelike horse from a solid chunk of marble? Then the sculptor answered, "That is not difficult at all. There was already a horse within the marble. I can see the horse. I simply took away the unnecessary pieces, one by one, and then the horse came to be." A person may seem to have unnecessary baggage, look unattractive, lack leadership skills and so on to ordinary people, but people with spiritual eyes can see the horse hidden in the person. If you can see it, then you can chip away the unnecessary parts through mentorship, thus creating a masterpiece. This is the most important goal of mentoring.

The Bible tells us endlessly that we must be conformed to the image of Jesus Christ. In a way, this is the power of continued evangelism. It is about transformation. In fact, everyone can change. However, what one changes from and too is of utmost importance. It has been said that you must be responsible for your face when you turn 40 years of age. Our ultimate task is to transform people so that they can reclaim the original purpose given to them by God. Heroes are never born; they are created.

Here is a brief illustration. I read this in a book once. A young man had admired a great man. He admired him so much that he wanted to see where he was born. He wanted to know the origins of such a great man. He was able to find the small village where the great man was from after much inquiry. When he got to the village, he asked the villagers about the man. No one seemed to know him. On the last day of his visit, as he was about to head home, quite disappointed, he decided to give it one last try. Then he saw an old man with gray hair.

> He thought to himself, "Oh, he must know."
> So, he approached and asked, "Sir, may I ask you something?"
> "What is it, young man? Go ahead and ask," he said.
> "Do you know this great man by such and such name?"
> He replied, "I do. I heard that he was born in this village. Do you happen to know which house?"
> "Look, young man. No great man has ever been born from this village; only babies have been born."

This is a story that holds great truth. No one claims, "I am Napoleon" upon birth. They are created through the circumstances of life. Neither great pastors, great preachers nor great businessmen are created overnight. This is a process. Thus, if we can mentor properly, people can be transformed in an amazing manner and our twelve disciples can become great apostles who can turn the world upside down. I am confident of this. This is why I like the PRINCIPLE OF 12 ministry. And because of this fact, I feel a strong sense of responsibility.

The text tells us the process of "How Jesus mentored his twelve disciples." We can find out the truth from the main text. In John 17:1 says, "After Jesus said this, he looked toward heaven and prayed: 'Father, the time has come. Glorify your Son, that your Son may glorify you.'" Let's focus on "the time has come." Jesus lived 33 years and he knew that he was only given 3 years. The time that was given to him to lay the foundation to accomplish God's will on earth was three years. His task was to evangelize the whole world. Do you know how much time you have been given to accomplish the will of God in your life? We become more earnest when we are facing death. We all must go before the Lord. There is a day when we all must repent. But do you understanding the urgency of the matter? If we are given 30 or 90 years of life, what are we going to do during that time?

Jesus was committed to using his 3 remaining years to mentor his twelve, imparting his character, anointing and vision. This is why he said, "Father, the time has come," as he prayed in the upper room. The time had come. He did accomplish all that he was asked to do during the 3+ years of his ministry. Later in the Bible He declares, "It is finished." It is not that he achieved global evangelism, but he was able to create the basic model to accomplish that goal. He knew exactly what he had to do during the 3+ years of his ministry. We must continue to develop plans regarding the future of Christianity, and participate in evangelizing to the whole world. If we assume that we can serve in a ministry until we turn 65 or 70, it may be fun to think about how much time we have. We can think about where we'll be pastoring or where our church is going to be. As we try to predict Christianity's spiritual movement may evolve, a new vision may emerge. Jesus chose to choose 12 disciples. He chose to prepare the twelve disciples. It is because he understood the times that

He gave his life to develop his disciples. I am simply suggesting that we do the same!

Let's move over to verse 2, "For you granted him authority over all people that he might give eternal life to all those you have given him." Jesus decided to choose only twelve disciples when countless crowds were gathering around him. When he chose the twelve, he believed that they were given to him by God the Father. In verse 6, he says, "I have revealed you to those whom you gave me out of the world." If we can pray for 3 unbelievers and end up with 5, 10, 15, or 20 members in Open Cell, do we understand that God gave them to us? Do you understand that God has entrusted precious souls to you? Without such responsibility, we may quit or kick everyone out of the group during times of difficulty. However, in his heart, Jesus had confidence and faith that even someone like Judas Iscariot was given to him by God.

He prepared each of them with skill and grace. As you mentor through PRINCIPLE OF 12 ministry, you will grow to love each soul. It will lead you to rebuke and endlessly intercede. Where does such power come from? The Father has given it to me, and will give it to you. It is the responsibility that comes with the understanding that this person has been given to me by God. That is where true love arises. It is the same principle when raising children. The concept of sacrifice, so that another may eat is part of the mindset of Jesus.

Without this passion for souls, God's church cannot

thrive. Without it, true relationships are impossible. Jesus showed us this example through his ministry. With what kind of heart did he mentor in John 17? In this passage, we will discover the most important aspects of mentoring. Not only that, he shows us the different stages of mentorship. If we can follow these steps as we nurture disciples as our own spiritual children, God's tremendous work will take place with great speed. Man is able to feel the emotion and sense how the leader feels towards them completely. Therefore, forming relationships is very important. The most important factor within the relationship is responsibility. It is responsibility, and realization that God has given the person to me that is key. So we must think, "I will not lose one single soul. I will pick them up if they fall. I will raise them up again by helping them to repent if they sin." Such plans of heart become the prime power that enables church to be church, and enables church to become God's true family.

In the second stage, Jesus says in verse 6, "I have revealed you to those whom you gave me out of the world. They were yours; you gave them to me and they have obeyed your word." What should we do for the people God has entrusted to us? What is the direction of discipleship? He wants us to reveal the name of the Father to them. The name of the Father means the character of the Father. The disciples not only witnessed healing, deliverance, miracles and power by living with Jesus, but they saw the character of God evident in Jesus. Jesus considered this a most important part of his role and function. God had various names: Jehovah

Rapha (God the healer), Jehovah Shalom (God the Peace), and Jehovah Jireh (God who provides).

One day, the disciples were talking and complaining, "Boy, even as we follow Jesus, there are no miracles or wonders. We ate because of miracles but it is difficult to rely on miracles every day. He doesn't even pay us. In a communist regime, the company gives you an apartment if you work for them, but following Jesus does not guarantee an apartment or even a future. How can we live like this? Our clothes are filthy rags..." Jesus told them, "Look at the birds of the air. Look at the lilies on the ground. God will clothe you with greater splendor than Solomon's. God will feed you all. Are you not much more valuable, you faithless men? Seek first the kingdom of God and his righteousness and all these things will be added unto you." Isn't that enough? God provides for us.

To teach them to believe in Jehovah Jireh is what mentoring is all about. Jesus began to mentor the disciples, with a primary purpose of helping them to know the Father and to trust in him. He was determined to make disciples who were completely connected to God, so that not even poverty or tribulation could overcome them. Thus, the first step reveals the character of God and the name of God.

When you first meet someone who has a rough personality, it is like a diamond that's been dug out of a mine. You must continue to polish the stone until the original shine is restored. Even my present disciples are filled with inconsistencies. They like to avoid responsibility at times and they often lack commitment. People who have strong relationships with other people may still lack deep commitment. I learned a variety of things as I discipled these twelve. In some cases, some were careful and brave on the outside, but very timid on the inside. I thought, Wow, this is a big problem. There exterior is so different that their interior. I must strengthen their inner man, helping them become brave."

I grew as well. I was weak, easily swayed by other people's opinion, and had difficulty making decisions. But God became my mentor. He allowed me to enjoy His special instruction. I was no doubt privileged because I was on the mission field. Holy Spirit mentored me directly, causing me to experience transformation from my core self, little by little. Now he has entrusted me to do the same work for others (of course, with the leading and empowering of Holy Spirit).

There is a young lady, one of the women leaders named Kamshot. She has established 72 cells from 16 cells. She is a native Kazakhstan woman who is an outstanding leader. Though her father was a leader, and an owner of a farm, she had no special skills of note. One of her disciples was named Ashara. Her speech was crude. She was not soft, but in fact, very blunt. Because of Ashara's personality, she had a difficult time growing her cell, even though she prayed with passion and taught the Bible well. A cell may do well for a while, but as people began to build relationships, the cell would break down. Her personality would surface once the relationships were made. So Kamshot challenged her. "You have to change your personality. If your personality doesn't change, you will have difficulty all your life," she told her with a serious look. She talked to her one on one. Ashara acknowledged the truth of her statement, but replied that she tried to change before but it never worked. As a result, she did not want to try anymore. Kamshort retorted, "Then give up your ministry. I will lead that Open Cell. You give it up. People are continuing to get hurt because of your personality. I don't want wounded people increasing in my network. Give it up." When she heard that, Ashara began to pray and fast for a week.

    At times, people need to be treated with tenderness, but some people need to be told the truth in brutal honesty. That is a part of successful mentoring. Kamshot spoke to her harshly, "Look at other people. Among my twelve disciples, you are the only one with one cell. All others have 6, 7, or 8 cells. Why is it that you are the only one who can't grow? I am not rebuking your ministry. I am telling you that the reason why you are not successful in ministry is your personality." Ashara was initially traumatized. However, that trauma caused her to reach out to God. She wrestled with herself. After 6 months, Ashara, having faced the difficulties of her personality head on, was transformed. Soon she was able to open 6 more cells.

    It is a simple story, but it demonstrates the impact of mentorship. Perhaps even her parents wouldn't have been able to speak to her with such impact. Countless numbers of people may have passed through her, being kind to her, saying, "Okay, okay... hallelujah." However, her leader had a responsibility and commitment to help her. She told her that without God's character, God will not work in her life. Because of this truth, she was able to save not only her ministry but her whole life. This is the power of mentorship.

Third, let us look at John 17: 3, "Now this is eternal life: that they may know you, the only true God, and Jesus Christ, whom you have sent." Knowledge is power. It is important to know who Jesus is. To "know" here means to know by experience and not simply by knowledge. Do you have the assurance that your cell members have confessed, "Jesus is my Savior? and declared that Lord, you are Christ, the son of the living God." Many people attend church. However, how many of them have a commitment to obey him because, having recognized that Jesus is the Savior and Lord of their lives?

It is said that there are 10 million Christians in Korea. How many of them tithe, are devoted and submit to the power of the Lord in obedience. Without mentors, they become Sunday Christians. This is the reason why Jesus was interested in finding out whether his twelve disciples knew him as the Christ. In Matthew 16, on the road to Damascus, he asked, "Who do people say the son of man is? Who do you say that I am?" Peter answered, "You are Christ, the son of the living God." How important is the testimony of faith? Healing, deliverance, answered prayer, and increase of ministry can easily take place as long as we stand firm on the confession of faith. If you stand firm, you can overcome anything and anyone. You may have the anointing for ministry and you may have giftings, but without your testimony of faith, you will be shaken. Testimonies are important. Members of the church are people who possess testimonies of faith. The gates of Hades will not prevail against them. When we strengthen the testimony of faith, our inner man is strengthened. You can overcome your tendency to wander and think, "Why do I have so many difficulties when I believe in Jesus? Why did this difficulty come about?"

As I was praying such prayers in the wilderness in Germany, I understood the meaning of the gospel, and that I am such a sinner; I was set free. I was afraid of no one. "I am saved. Jesus has become my Lord. Now I know how long he has waited for me. I know that the Lord will never leave me or abandon me, no matter how difficult things get." This is what I truly believed. After that encounter with God, I feared nothing. I held nothing back. What is more important? This is how we become passionate about sharing the gospel. Disciples must be transformed in this manner. A personal encounter with Jesus must take place in their life. There are many difficulties in the lives of the disciples; however, this is a good thing. We can draw closer to the Lord through adversity. For those of us who do mentoring, let us always remember: do not complain about the way they talk or about the lack of change in their lives. People who change later on are scarier. I pray that you make your faith secure, as you mentor you disciples to Win, Connect, Train, and Send.

Fourth, we must make the dream of Jesus become their dream. In verses 20-21, Jesus prays, "My prayer is not for them alone. I pray also for those who will believe in me through their message, that all of them may be one, Father, just as you are in me and I am in you. May they also be in us so that the world may believe that you have sent me."

The dream of Jesus was to see the Israel, and eventually the nations come back to faith. Therefore, he shared his vision and his dream with the disciples. He not only helped his beloved disciples to be blessed through the witnessing of miracles, but he shared his vision with them so that they could continue to have a heart for the nations. He showed them that the kingdom of God was expanding. This is why Jesus told Peter "Look, from now on you will become fishers of men," from the very first time he saw him. He showed Peter the picture of many souls and many nations coming back to the Lord. He tells him, "You are now Peter. You are not Simon but from now on you are Peter." Why did he re-name Peter? In giving him a new name, he gave him a dream and transformed him to conquer the nations. Peter, who used to be called Simon (small), began to be strengthened in his heart as he heard the name Peter. His heart and mind began to change. He began to think that he could do it. His was a great transformation. If you change your thinking, your body follows. If the spiritual climate changes, then the church changes. "My people perish for lack of knowledge," is the truth. If you have no vision, even after listening to the stories for a long time, you will perish. We must provide the right vision. Jesus presented the right vision from the beginning. "Dream for the nations!" That is why I have a dream for the Silk Road. Why did the Holy Spirit come upon us? What does Acts 2:17-18 tell us about the outpouring of the Holy Spirit in the last days? Holy Spirit has many functions. When we are speaking from the dimension of missions, evangelism, and the will of God, the reason for the outpouring of the Holy Spirit was to give us dreams and visions for the nations. God gave us a prophetic voice to proclaim with our lips. Let us dream. My vision includes that I will become a great evangelist, a great mentor, and an heir of God to transform the world. I will become the successor of Jesus. These are all possible. Yes, I desire to see the world transformed through me. In the truest sense, being successful in life is to accomplish the will of God for your life. This brings true satisfaction and joy. I am overjoyed. I sought the meaning of life for 10 years. My search ended when I met the Lord. I did not want to lose him. Who wants to give up the treasure he found. We'd all sell our possessions to buy the treasure. I have no regrets; in fact, I have never been happy. I went through some difficulties, but I found happiness again, and now I am happier than ever. I can't tell you how wonderful it is to do the work of the Lord. I can't understand why people will not do something that is so satisfying. I pray that you will be able to set your heart and mind in the right direction in your life in Jesus' name. Invest in worthwhile causes in your life. Invest in things that have rewards in return.

There is a lady at my church named Asia. She was a medical student and started a PRINCIPLE OF 12 ministry at my church. I'd been preaching, "Who ever you are, make twelve disciples. That is your team. They will be your co-workers who will help you to achieve your dream. They are your potential. They are your guardians. They will protect you. You will conquer the world with them. You can accomplish the vision that God has given you with them." As she heard my messages, her heart began to swell up with dreams. She began to dream, "I will make twelve disciples out of medical students and transform the medical field of Kazakhstan." She said she was disappointed at times at the grandeur of the dream. Yet she pushed on. "No. Even Pastor Kim said God's vision is difficult. He suffered in Germany." My church members must have heard my stories of Germany about 50 times. Yet they love it because it is so real. She said my testimonies became such an encouragement to her. She continued to pray, "I will overcome, no matter what. I will accomplish my dream. I will serve the Lord. God has given me the medical field of Kazakhstan." As she kept praying, something amazing happened. The American embassy had a contest. The committee was looking to reform the medical field of Kazakhstan. The winner would go to the U.S. for one year as an exchange student. So she simply wrote about the concept of PRINCIPLE OF 12 and proposed to make disciples to transform the Kazakhstan medical field. Her plan was chosen as the number 1 entry. So she was able to complete 1 year of studies in the U.S. Then she was chosen as a lecturer for the best medical school in Kazakhstan. The American embassy invested money to make her project become a reality. Now she boldly proclaims the gospel as a lecturer. She used to be weak, but the moment she captured the vision she was transformed. She continues to proclaim the gospel.

When my wife became sick she was admitted to the hospital. Many people from the hospital ended up joining the Alpha Courses offered at the hospital through Asia. Vision is an amazing thing. A single vision will continue to give birth to more visions. It can change a person's life to the extreme. PRINCIPLE OF 12 ministry is not just about church growth. It enables the church members to infiltrate and transform society. It causes the society to become God's church and God's kingdom. It transforms people's consciousness. I am confident that it helps to usher in the character of God into the world. In that sense, it is the most holistic ministry of God.

What is your dream and vision? Why are you going to church? You may need a special dream and vision from God. Truly, life is much more difficult without a clear vision from the Lord. I pray that you will find and live out your dream in Jesus' Name.

Fifth, what is the greatest mission of Jesus? The greatest mission of Jesus during his 3 years and 6 months of ministry was to preserve and protect his 12 disciples. Jesus said it this way,

"I am not asking that you take them to the father. I am

asking that you protect them." "I will remain in the world no longer, but they are still in the world, and I am coming to you. Holy Father, protect them by the power of your name—the name you gave me—so that they may be one as we are one. While I was with them, I protected them and kept them safe by that name you gave me. None has been lost except the one doomed to destruction so that Scripture would be fulfilled." (John 17:11-12)

The greatest interest of Jesus was to preserve their purity, to protect their faith, to keep them from evil and to protect them by interceding on their behalf. More important than programs, we must invest into people's lives. Jesus invested his life so that his disciples would mature as beautiful children of God. There is a need give special care and consideration for our disciples. They often suffer, and are in need of our support. They are suffering at home and in their marriage due to the temptations of Satan. They are suffering from relational and character issues. They are in conflict because of sin. We must preserve and protect them. That is the only way to produce diamonds. The greatest mission of Jesus was to protect them. What should we do in PRINCIPLE OF 12 meetings? We must do the same as Christ. We must let them realize that we are their spiritual fathers and mothers. Can they expect such devotion from society? They deserve this level of commitment from us as their spiritual leaders.

My wife had a young lady as one of her disciples. She was leading a cell for Jr. High and high school students. In her cell, she had a girl named "Naja," a Kazakh from Korean descendent. She challenged Naja and told her that she had personal problems that needed to be addressed. Naja grew up without significant problems under her Korean parents. During a marriage seminar at our church, she received the highest score in human relationships from a personality test that she took. So she said that she had no personality conflicts. She was outgoing and jovial. She always had people around her, and she felt that she had a wonderful personality. Yet strangely, whenever she started a cell, she began to have problems.

The problems began when she started her PRINCIPLE OF 12 ministry. Everything was well when she was fellowshipping on a superficial level. But when she started the PRINCIPLE OF 12 ministry in February of that year, she began to have problems with her cell members. "What is going on? I never had any problems before PRINCIPLE OF 12. Now that I have started, I am struggling." Yet, she thought that it was other people's problems, since she had a wonderful personality. Things in her leadership deteriorated to such an extent that her only cell broke apart. Everyone in her cell left. That is when her leader challenged her.

"It is my understanding that the problem is with your character." She responded, "That can't be. I have never fought with anyone or even argued. I haven't had any conflicts with anyone. How can this be?" She was forced to analyze the cause and discovered that it was due to her selfishness. She discovered that she was being nice to people formally, but couldn't develop deeper relationships. Some people are nice to others, in mere formality. They laugh a lot but they can never go deep. This girl prayed about her character throughout the night, even weeping. No matter how much she prayed, she was not able to grasp what her problem was in a real significant way, even though she understood the concept. She tried so hard to change but couldn't. She often wondered, "God, why do you torture me? You only give me the difficult people." She felt that she didn't have problems, and it was her cell members who were difficult. Yet, she felt that she needed to pray in the prayer room. She felt that God was telling her to go pray, saying "Pray for one week, for at least an hour a day. Pray earnestly for your disciples."

She was too ashamed to tell others that her cell broke apart. There was no one left in her group. She began to pray for her members one by one, calling out their names. Then God did an amazing thing. As soon as she started to pray for her members, her members started to come to her, one by one, seeking counsel. They began to open up to her about their family and school problems. She realized that it was an opportunity given by God to listen to their stories. She told them, "I don't know anything but I will pray for you. Let's pray together." And she came back and prayed for another week, for an hour a day. Her cells began to open and within four months, her cells had grown to four. This is an amazing story. When we protect and intercede for our twelve disciples, they submit to us. When they are able to trust us, the relationship becomes a committed one. Then we can begin to bear the image of God's church within us.

Lastly, help them to love God above all things, and to love one another! The ultimate goal is in verse 22, "I have given them the glory that you gave me, that they may be one as we are one." There is nothing more dangerous than divided opinions and dissension within the church. Like I said, the church is led by the spiritual climate establishd by the leader. Leader, Cell Leader, Senior Pastor… whoever you are, as a leader of a group or an organization, you must be able to discern what kind of atmosphere it is." If the atmosphere is headed in the wrong direction, you must be able to grasp its origin. You must be able to solve the problem from its roots. You must solve the problem with an atmosphere of love and continue to preserve the unity among the group. If you are able to do that then your church will grow into a strong and stable church of God.

Chapter 10: PRINCIPLE OF 12 Ministry is a Team Ministry

The development of a ministry team was certainly an objective of Jesus. Let's look again at the focus of Jesus ministry, as presented in Mark 3: 13-35.

> 13 Jesus went up on a mountainside and called to him those he wanted, and they came to him. 14 He appointed twelve—designating them apostles—that they might be with him and that he might send them out to preach 15 and to have authority to drive out demons. 16 These are the twelve he appointed: Simon (to whom he gave the name Peter 17 James son of Zebedee and his brother John (to them he gave the name Boanerges, which means Sons of Thunder 18 Andrew, Philip, Bartholomew, Matthew, Thomas, James son of Alphaeus, Thaddaeus, Simon the Zealot 19 and Judas Iscariot, who betrayed him. 20 Then Jesus entered a house, and again a crowd gathered, so that he and his disciples were not even able to eat. 21 When his family heard about this, they went to take charge of him, for they said, "He is out of his mind." 22 And the teachers of the law who came down from Jerusalem said, "He is possessed by Beelzebub! By the prince of demons he is driving out demons." 23 So Jesus called them and spoke to them in parables: "How can Satan drive out Satan? 24 If a kingdom is

divided against itself, that kingdom cannot stand. 25 If a house is divided against itself, that house cannot stand. 26 And if Satan opposes himself and is divided, he cannot stand; his end has come. 27 In fact, no one can enter a strong man's house and carry off his possessions unless he first ties up the strong man. Then he can rob his house. 28 I tell you the truth, all the sins and blasphemies of men will be forgiven them. 29 But whoever blasphemes against the Holy Spirit will never be forgiven; he is guilty of an eternal sin." 30 He said this because they were saying, "He has an evil spirit." 31 Then Jesus' mother and brothers arrived. Standing outside, they sent someone in to call him. 32 A crowd was sitting around him, and they told him, "Your mother and brothers are outside looking for you." 33 "Who are my mother and my brothers?" he asked. 34 Then he looked at those seated in a circle around him and said, "Here are my mother and my brothers! 35 Whoever does God's will is my brother and sister and mother."

In verses 13 through 19, Jesus called "those he wanted" and chose the twelve. The purpose was that "they might be with him." He wanted to mentor them. The purpose was that "he might send them out to preach and to have authority to drive out demons." Verses 31 to 35 tells us that when "Jesus' mother and brothers" came looking for him, he said, "Who are my mother and my brothers? Here are my mother and my brothers. Whoever does God's will is my brother and sister and mother." And he showed the disciples to the people.

We need to form a spiritual family. Jesus came to earth for this very work. He lived within the context of the true kingdom concept, and he lived within the model of the heavenly kingdom's family.

Today's society is broken. Because people are relational beings, we cannot enjoy true happiness or satisfaction when relationships have been broken. People must be taught at home to foster true relationships, but people these days have a difficult time understanding what it means to develop healthy relationships. They simply have not seen it modeled at home. In fact, unfortunately, many come from broken homes. Yet, God has a plan to restore relationships and the spiritual family.

God makes a new family within God's vision, God's dream, God's grace, and God's love. When we belong to God's family, our physical families can also be restored. This world will not be restored with mere words and actions; the spirit needs to be restored. It is meaningless for husbands and wives to say, "Let's try to make it work." We need a fundamental solution. We need to understand where we come from – our original nature.

The time has come for us to realize that, because we have been forgiven by God's deep grace, we also must forgive. The family of God must become stronger so that my physical family can be restored to normal. Jesus said, concerning the true family, "Whoever does God's will is my brother, sister and mother." The twelve disciples became one family under God's will and his clear vision. There was no significant conflict between them. There was one atmosphere, one goal and one community. They became a family with God's will at their core. Jesus continues to want to make such teams. This type of team is needed in your life, ministry, work and relationships. You need a team of committed people. What are some of the factors we need in order to prepare a true team? The Bible provides for us many clear answers. The true meaning of team ministry is found in the relationhip between Jesus and his twelve disciples.

Jesus and the twelve disciples

First, the relationship between Jesus and the twelve was one between teacher and disciple. It was a relationship that continued through mentoring in relationship. There was a relationship of total authority (which of course, only Jesus has), where the teacher taught and the disciple learned through the course of ministry and through living together. People tend to hate authority. However, in my PRINCIPLE OF 12's discipleship group, there is a tremendous amount of respect from my disciples and the feelings are mutual. Even when I say something totally off (by mistake or as a joke), they take it seriously. It has come to a point where if I were to say, "Let's stop doing this and do something instead starting tomorrow," they would believe me and follow. This demonstrates our unity. It also shows how much they respect me. This respect is important.

The twelve disciples were able to believe in what Jesus said. Only through such relationships can a team be formed. Your business should function this way. You need to share your vision and others will be blessed through it. When they realize that your relationship is not just about making the business work, but it is about helping each other, they will join you and be committed to your ministry. This is a picture of Christian community.

Second, the relationship between Jesus and his disciples was one of an anointed leader and committed disciples. The leader must equip the disciples under the anointing of the Holy Spirit. It is a difficult task for a few equal leaders to lead a team together, or if the team does not have a leader.

I have made many relationships with missionaries from the mission agency called Intercorp in Korea. We are working together to evangelize the entire Silk Road region. When I went to Turkey, three missionaries planted a church as a united effort. In the beginning, because it was so hard to be alone, it was good to lead the church together. However, as time passed, they began to run into problems. I asked them what kind of problems they had. One of the three told me, "Because three of us are leaders, in order to keep peace, in order to not hurt each other's feelings, we couldn't get anything accomplished. We can present ideas generally, but we could not assert our own ideas. We found it difficult not only to stress our own ideas, but even to present them in the first place. We feared that if the others did not agree with the idea, then feelings would be hurt. For the sake of unity, we denied ourselves, we denied each other and we ended up denying the ministry."

The second problem according to a local member was, "Because the pastors take turns giving the sermon, there are discrepancies between the messages. One pastor says that this is right but the other pastor says that that is right. Yet, I could not express that because the three of them were working so peacefully. It has been years, but they have not yet decided who the leader is" When three people lead together, there is no leadership. When one of the three approaches a member to show interest or provide mentoring, the other two are concerned that he is trying to stand out. They faced these difficulties. I said, "Let's look at the twelve, and the discipleship model of Jesus. Let's look at what team ministry is all about. Let us throw away the worldly terminology of 'Team Ministry' and think about biblical 'Team Ministry.' In that team, Jesus was the center. He selected the ones he chose. He cast his vision. The team was led according to his vision. The twelve functioned as the hands and feet of the team to help and accomplish the vision of their teacher. However, they were not passive. Rather, they were willing to risk their lives for the vision that had become their own vision through the impartation of their leader. This is team ministry. There cannot be two leaders. The body will be confused. You cannot have two or three heads. That is a monster." Fortunately, two of the missionaries planted their own churches and the other missionary stayed on as the senior pastor. They didn't separate; they returned to normal. Now they are committed to finding their own twelve.

I led a PRINCIPLE OF 12 seminar in Uzbekistan as well. The biggest local church in Uzbekistan has about 4000 members. Along with 20 of the other local churches, I led a PRINCIPLE OF 12 seminar. The missionaries had been there for over 10 years as professional bi-vocational missionaries. As professionals, they did computer work, dentistry, and other ministries. Yet they were without disciples for over ten years. They were in despair.

I gathered them together in Almaty last August and held a PRINCIPLE OF 12 seminar and Encounter Retreat. They changed completely and caught the vision. Now they are starting their own PRINCIPLE OF 12 ministries with the local people. I later led an Encounter Retreat and the locals were completely changed. 4 dentists had built a hospital together. They were doing well in their hospital ministry. After the Encounter, they now want to do church ministry. All four of them split up to find their own 12 disciples, leading Encounters and Alpha courses. Four churches were planted as a result. The twelve disciples are the church. When those twelve disciples give birth to their own twelve disciples, the church will continue to grow. The work will be accomplished if the vision can be imparted clearly.

When there is a team of one anointed leader and committed disciples, that team is a perfectly formed Dream Team. It is the team with a dream. It is a team with vision and goals. The team burns and yearns with hope and vision. If the members of the team can all be committed and grow stronger to accomplish the vision, then they can become a great set who can experience the accomplishment of God's will and also share in the joy of working together. It is the same for the Alpha Team. Twelve people can form the Alpha Team. The twelve can serve as group leaders and helpers. As they serve together, they grow stronger. They will begin to bear new fruit and new souls will be saved. They will become disciples. More people will become disciples through the new disciples and an amazing work of God will take place. Alpha ministry and PRINCIPLE OF 12 ministry are team ministries. God's kingdom is expanded in a limitless fashion through team ministry.

Therefore, when reflecting on the true definition of team ministry, today's definition must be amended. Just because you have many leaders in a team, it does not mean that they can provide more leadership. Only one leader can provide leadership. Team ministry occurs when all of the team members take on the leader's vision as their own and work together to accomplish the vision. The Alpha Course Team, the Encounter Team, and the Leadership School Team have clear goals that God has already given them. They all run together to accomplish the goal. Every 10 weeks and every year, clear results are visible. Fruit is produced. The teams are filled with joy as the result of attaining the vision. This is what team ministry is all about. It does not work just because people gather.

The first element of the team is family. The team gathers as a complete family. The team leader has an understanding that the twelve disciples are people given to him or her by God. It is a relationship of responsibility. It is a relationship of commitment. Beyond ministry, the leader should be responsible for the disciples. Without such family like relationships, the team will crumble.

Therefore, today's definition of team ministry needs to change to a more biblical concept. We must develop a team that functions like a family. Jesus loved and was truly commited to his disciples. Even though they abandoned him at the crucial hour, even on the cross, he continued to love them. Why? He understood the concept that God brought them to Jesus. This becomes the driving force behind uniting the team as a family. If you chose your twelve disciples and make a commitment to give your life to them, they will probably give you more than that. They will give you faithfulness and commitment. They will invest their time in you. They will become the hands and feet that accomplish your vision. This is the element of a true team ministry.

Second, team ministry becomes like a band of soldiers. When the team is united as a family, you can accomplish your mission. You can minister together when your hearts are made one. Yet, the team does not become a simple army system. Things don't always work out just because you implement the system. If you are a small church, transitioning from Alpha to PRINCIPLE OF 12 may not be that difficult. If you are a big church, you may find it more complex.

The reason it may be difficult is due to the relationship of family members. Big churches can quickly implement the system by putting twelve people under you and then having them place twelve people under them. However, this system will almost always fail. Why? Because they are not the people you have chosen, nurtured and poured your life into. The PRINCPLE OF 12 program is not done systematically. It is accomplished through heart, commitment, and relationship.

I always advise the senior pastor to choose her/his twelve disciples first. It is okay if it takes 1-2 years. Do not be in a hurry. Show them your love and commitment. Korean pastors are usually seen as strong authority figures. Sometimes, there is a deep chasm between the pastor and a congregation member, between the pulpit and the pew. You must narrow that gap. At least with the twelve disciples, you must narrow that gap to the point of becoming one. Then the twelve, chosen by the senior pastor will, in the same spirit, choose their own twelve. This is not the quickest way, but is the most effective. You will fail if you create the organization too quickly. You must love and pour your life into these people as if they were your own children.

As Paul the apostle said, there are many teachers but few fathers. If you can be a father to them, then they can become soldiers. Why is this? It is like my own child. I have and continue to pour my life nto him. My children feel my love, so they are ready to hear and obey no matter what I say. I have four children of my own. I try to pour into my son, investing into him as much as I can. I try to take him wherever I go. I even took him to China. I plan to take my son to Afghanistan and Tajikistan also. He may be only fourteen, but when I treat him like a young adult and speak to him with respect, he responds to me on the same level. It may be strange if a child acts like an adult, but he is so thankful that I am teaching him godly principles at an early age. He is happy that I have conversations with him about the deep things of God, and everyday life as well. He is thankful that I ask for his opinion on certain matters, I ask him to go with me on trips and ask him to share his testimony.

My fourteen-year-old son was actually leading his Open Cell. I asked him to share his difficulties, because one time he came home early from his cell meeting. I asked him why he was home so early and he answered, "Dad, nobody came." I told him, "You need to pray a lot. It does not happen on its own. You need to pray for each and every one of them. Then one will come and then two and so on. Think about what you will share with them as you pray for your members." So he prayed for his cell members throughout the week. As he was leaving to lead his cell the next Thursday, I asked him, "Did you prepare the word?" He said yes, so I asked him to share what he prepared. He told me that he chose the passage during his time of prayer. As he was reading the passage, he felt that the passage spoke about what his members may be going through. I felt that it was good so I said, "Okay, go." He told me one person came. "What did Daddy tell you? When I was fasting, God told me to preach as if I am preaching in front of a million people even if there is only one person in front of you. You need to do the same. This is the only way you can become a great pastor." I am so thankful to see my son go through this phase.

Think about how you would feel if you gave birth to your twelve disciples in this way. It is the greatest blessing of my life to have met my PRINCIPLE OF 12 members. I wish that I'd found out about these princples a little sooner. I believe God allowed me to find out about it at the right time, after preparing the foundation.

The PRINCIPLE OF 12 is truly the strategy to transform Central Asia and the entire Silk Road. I will continue to raise up my twelve disciples. By God's grace I will teach this principle to all the members of my church and make everyone into disciples of Jesus Christ. The church will become more and more like soldiers that way. God led the entire Israelites through one man Moses. When they became the church in the wilderness, God showed them the model of Cell Church through Jethro. Appoint people as officials over thousands, hundreds, fifties and tens. When that was not enough, a little later in Numbers 1, God commanded them to make an Army based on the twelve tribes. Later in Numbers, God have him the 70, men who carried the same spirit and vision of Moses, and together they prepared the people to fulfill God's purposes.

He is telling us that we will not be able to defeat our enemies if we do not have a strategy. We fall because we fight as individuals when the enemy attacks as a joint force. Come together. In order to be united, be united under one vision and make spiritual children by giving birth to your team. If any church desires to become a strong church, then make sure that your associates are the ones you have trained and raised yourself. This is a basic principle.

Fourth, the unity of the team is very important. There must be an atmosphere of unity within the team. Where does true unity come from? Many people hear about unity and talk about the need to be united. Leadership networks are developing all over the world. Unless we are careful, the network meetings will end up being just another meeting. People meet, but there is no persistence. It is because there is no driving force behind such meetings to bind everyone together. There is no motive.

The power that leads to continuous meetings is vision. Vision has the power to bind millions, tens of millions, and hundreds of millions of people together regardless of number. The Chinese went through amazing growth as they went through harsh persecution. It is said that there are 100 million Christians among 1.2 billion people in China. This is an incredible number. I have been doing mission work in China and have seen much progress. However, when the Beijing Olympics opens in 2008, there will be huge problems. Christianity will be shaken as secular culture comes flooding in through the gates. They were able to maintain their passion underground but once the secular wave comes crashing through; the Christians who go into the cities will fall. They will fail in their attempts to make money and attain material goods.

It is the same way in Kazakhstan. It is very difficult. There are existing pressures from Muslims and materialism. Now there are added pressures from immoral mores that have come in from the West. Now we are ministering in a society addicted to drugs and alcohol. How can we change these people? This is a very important question. It is impossible without vision. Chinese churches are facing a great crisis due to Western culture. What is one way for the Chinese church to survive? Will they simply fade away as other nations have after blossoming? Or will they fight the uphill battle? The Chinese church was in deep anguish as they faced denominational differences, the separation of the underground church network and pressures from all areas. They could not imagine how they could unite the church again. Yet, God raised a great vision in their midst. God began to show his vision to a few leaders, beginning from the 1930's to 1990's.

It was the "Back to Jerusalem" vision. The gospel started from Jerusalem and has come full circle. Now the gospel has to make its way back to Jerusalem. All the idols and gods have made their way through the Silk Road to the East from the West. Now there is a movement to resend the gospel back to the West from the East. It is not one person's vision. God gave this vision to a few leaders, and this vision is now spreading throughout the underground churches, and the three self-churches, reaching the hearts of all the believers. Back to Jerusalem - Back to Jerusalem - Back to Jerusalem. This movement is beginning to take place. We must go forward. Once the doors open, we must share the gospel all the way to Jerusalem through the Silk Road. An unseen coalition has begun to take place. There was a gathering of leaders from the Chinese underground churches and the leaders of the 3 self churches. They made a decision to send 100,000 missionaries Back to Jerusalem by the year 2008. They want to send missionaries through the Silk Road, to the South through India. They have already sent out hundreds of missionaries.

In a certain meeting, God gave us the Back to Jerusalem vision. What should we do? As we were praying, one person stood up and said, "The Holy Spirit says that one of us should go out as a missionary." Everyone fell silent. "Let's pray together. Let's hear the voice of God to find out which one of us should go out as a missionary." We were praying but no one stood up. A day passed, and another. One evening, a woman stood up. She said she is a doctor and God told her that she should go. Then how can we send her? In the west, they would have done a lot of research about the amount of financial support she would need, cultural training, which route to take, getting a visa, so on and so forth, so it would've taken some time. After I heard her story, I looked for her because I wanted to help her to go out as a missionary. But she was gone. She left for missions. When I asked where she went, they didn't know. She simply left because God told her to go. Where about is she right now? They didn't know. They simply took up an offering for her at that meeting. It was barely enough money to live on for a month and for her travels. The rest was up to her to receive from God through prayer. What commitment. It is because they had a vision. That vision brought Christians who didn't know each other together. Vision has great power. If you don't have a vision, people cannot continue to stay in your ministry. You cannot accomplish your goals. You must proclaim your vision to people endlessly but you must receive that vision first.

    A true team ministry begins with vision. Vision helps you to set goals. Vision gives you new strength. Vision is the element that gives us faith. People without vision are truly without faith. They don't have the faith to accomplish the work. I cannot grow weary because God has given me the vision to conquer the Silk Road. I cannot stop the faith. Why? Because this is a vision given to me by God and faith continues to rise within me. God speaks to me when we are low on materials. "Is it not the vision I have given you? Didn't I tell you that you will see my glory if you believe?" I pray that you would own your vision.

    People commit to a leader for reasons. First is the leader's vision and the second is the leader's character. The team can be a powerful team when both are present. The relationship between vision and love is that vision has the power to pull people to one direction. It continues to pull people, having the power to make people move. Many pastors say that their members are not willing to move. However, if you continue to proclaim the vision, the dry bones of Ezekiel's valley will begin to form flesh and receive life. They will begin to move like an army. This is the power of vision.

When you pray, God gives you a prophetic vision. Vision is the power to pull people in a direction. Love is the power to bind people's hearts together. You must have these two elements. Some people have an overabundance of love and have great character, but they cannot seem to accomplish many good works. Why? It is because they lack vision. Some people may have great vision, but due to a lack of character and love, people keep dropping out, or they have a high turnover rate. Therefore, these two elements must be present.

My dream is to see all my children serve the Lord. I told my wife, "I don't want to send my children to universities in England, Korea, or America. I want them to go to a university in Kazakhstan and learn about ministry and leadership from me. I learned from life experience that a top-notch university does not make one happy or even successful in life. Instead, they must grow up in God's word. I want to raise my children up as servants of God. I know that I still have much to learn. I will have to continue to listen to God's voice, but that is how I want to raise my children. I want them to grow up with vision and purpose.

Fifth, you must discern and know the source of your strength. Of course, God leads and supplies the strength through the leade,r but the true leader and supplier of the team is the Holy Spirit. You must absolutely acknowledge this. Holy Spirit is the one who completely reigns over our lives. If we want to be led by God and walk in victory, we must have the willingness to obey the Holy Spirit and have the humility to submit our own desires, knowledge and logic to the Lord. We must be completely sensitive to the Holy Spirit.

Vision was given to the Israelites. God gave them a vision to go forward to Canaan, the land flowing with milk and honey. God spoke to them consistently in the wilderness, as seen in Hebrews 3:7-19. In the wilderness, the Holy Spirit spoke to the church. What did he say to them? Of course, we do not know, other than what has been recorded in scripture. But I can only surmise that He probably spoke to them about the vision, especially holding onto the vision of the Promised Land, even when faced with difficulties. The best way to overcome hardship is to remember the vision. He spoke of vision when enemies attacked; essentially assuring them that they would win the battle because He told them that He would give them the land of Canaan.

The Holy Spirit spoke. Holy Spirit is the true leader of the team. I pray that you welcome the Holy Spirit. Holy Spirit is the one who can bring the leader and the disciples together. What did Jesus teach his disciples? He taught everything in the Father's will, as he intently heard from the Holy Spirit. If we can align our lives according to the Holy Spirit's power, guidance and wisdom, a wonderful spiritual transformation will take place in our lives and the entire team will experience spiritual transformation. Holy Spirit even worked within Jesus. Jesus prayed "as usual" to hear the voice of the Holy Spirit. Holy Spirit is the source of power. In Luke 4:14, Jesus returned to his place of ministry with the power of the Holy Spirit after being tempted. In verse 18, Jesus speaks about his ministry as he proclaims that "the Spirit of the Lord is on me." Holy Spirit is the source of power. We must personally welcome him into our lives.

Sixth, the power of the same gender ministry team is powerful. Women are to minister to women while men minister to men. Young adults must also have the same gender ministry team that binds the young adults together. When the teams are intertwined, there is a tendency for women to hide behind the men, for men to hide behind the women, for older adults to hide behind young adults, or for young adults to hide behind the older adults. You cannot maximize each member's full potential if everyone is hiding.

When women, men, and young adults meet on their own respectively, true relationships can form. Effective mentoring is possible and open hearted relationships are formed. Real conversation becomes possible.

Further, lay ministry (non-paid clergy) is activated. When the same gender meets together, more people can be mobilized. Imagine if the pastor's wife begins to lead the women's meeting. The women's interest will be piqued, even if it is just a prayer meeting. Most women are very interested in family matters. So have a prayer meeting among women to restore the families. They could pray for 9 months for the babies in their wombs. When women come together and begin to form ministry teams with one heart, incredible changes will occur.

Also, families are strengthened. When men gather as men, they are transformed as men. When women meet together, they develop into true women. My church prepares separate seminars for each specific group. For example, we hold a family seminar for men, for women, and for young adults, because they all have different roles and different functions in their respective families. Often, after the men's family seminar, many women would come to me to share that their husbands have dramatically changed (for the better). What do you think the men talked about? I challenge the men during the seminar. I say, "Let us be like men. Let us not lose our tempers when our wives nag. Let us lead with a vision. The women have a hard time acknowledging us as their men because we are not acting like men." I tell them about how my wife would nag me, how I was comforted, and also about conflicts in our relationships. As I shared transparently, the men listened with tears streaming down their faces. They realized that I am a man just like them. This is how the change takes place. True transformation takes place when people meet and share commonalities. Many families have been transformed at my church. We cannot count how many divorced families have reunited and reconciled.

The results of this include effective evangelism, which occur naturally. It is much more effective when a woman evangelizes to a woman and a man evangelizes a man. They are able to have a frank talk that is effective for evangelism.

Further, gender specific impartation of vision is effective. Men and women have slight differences in how they receive the vision. They are wired differently. After sharing the vision for a season, I noticed that men and women react differently. The vision is imparted clearly when a man imparts to man and a woman imparts to a woman.

In all things we must bear fruit. For a long time, men were not participating in the zones at my church. We had a difficult time evangelizing them. I mistakenly thought that men just do not want to come to church. However, when we started cells for the men, 160 cells formed within a year and a half. Now the men's understanding of who they are, the meaning of a man's life and goals have changed. This is an amazing transformation. The women were even more excited because we grew from 200 zones to 800 zones. They were so happy; they cried, "Freedom!"

After separating the young adult's network, transformation began to take place in their lives as well. Their vision for the PRINCIPLE OF 12 and the Silk Road became more detailed. They are now being highly creative. In the past, the young adults had many besetting problems. They were broken here and there due to gambling addictions, broken families, broken businesses, etc. Now, they are being healed of their brokenness. The young adults are strong and resilient. When I cast the vision for the PRINCIPLE OF 12 and the Silk Road, the young adults began to dream their own dreams. One particular young man wants to form a young men's center to aid the young people of Kazakhstan. He wants to create computer centers, language classes, and English classes to bring in young people so he can hold the Alpha courses with them. The effectiveness of Alpha Courses within our society as an evangelism tool is amazing.

Incredible things are happening. Society is being changed and tremendous spiritual changes are taking place.

Lastly, why do we need to create gender specific teams? In my opinion, a pastor cannot counsel a woman deacon. If you meet together too often, a problem will definitely arise. When I first went into Kazakhstan, women members wanted to come in for counseling. As I sat there listening to them, I turned red. Russian women are so explicit. They have no inhibitions about sharing their problems. They tell me about their discontentment with their husbands and married life. What do they want me to do? How am I supposed to counsel them? I am a man. After that, I asked my wife to take over the counseling for women. I had no clue as to what to say. No matter how long I would listen to them, I had no answers. So I turned it over to my wife. My wife, once she goes into a counseling session, doesn't come out for hours. I didn't have much to listen to. After listening for 10 minutes, I would come to the conclusion that I had no answers. But my wife would stay in the room for one, two even three hours. I'd hear them praying, crying and laughing. Three hours later, they emerge with their make up gone and faces flushed. Then the woman would tell my wife, "Thank you." Nowadays, women members at my church do not look for me. If a woman is looking for me that means that she is either an unbeliever or a new believer. She doesn't know any better. When people come to me, I tell them, "This church has two senior pastors. Your senior pastor is my wife so please go to her." Then they go to her for counseling. In similar manner, men must be counseled by a man. They will become uncomfortable when a woman counsels them. I think this is a common male tendency. So men receive counseling from me. As a man, I mentor and advise the men around me. This is why gender specific ministry is so vital. It makes men men and women women. It allows young adults to be themselves also. This is the way to recover the society, and God's work will continue on. My only concern is that even though this is a great principle, you may be disappointed if no one follows the principle. You must choose what is right and push on with perseverance.

Make disciples. You must start early. Without making disciples, there is no way to restore the church. If you cannot restore the church, you cannot restore society, and God's church will become a museum. The only way to restore biblical Christianity is through mentoring. Do not let this vision slip by you. Catch it! Put it into practice. If at all possible, gather with co-workers with the same vision and pray together.

Chapter 11: How to Convert to PRINCIPLE OF 12?

Habakkuk 2:1-3 states;

> 1 I will stand at my watch
> and station myself on the ramparts;
> I will look to see what he will say to me,
> and what answer I am to give to this complaint.
>
> 2 Then the LORD replied:
> "Write down the revelation
> and make it plain on tablets
> so that a herald may run with it.
>
> 3 For the revelation awaits an appointed time;
> it speaks of the end
> and will not prove false.
> Though it linger, wait for it;
> it will certainly come and will not delay.

When I teach, many come to me to get my signature. Many are praying to become missionaries and many to plant churches. Some are leading their own churches. I want to tell you that there is still a lot of time if you want to make the decision to start your own PRINCIPLE OF 12 church. When I made the decision to convert to a cell church, the Holy Spirit spoke very clearly to me. I also realized that I absolutely could not do it by myself. Therefore, for me, it was a radical decision. I want you to know that it will be a revolutionary decision for you. I had the determination to go after it no matter what. I also had the mindset that this is the only way. Then I went before the Lord to ask without ceasing and the Lord gave me his confirmation. If you truly want to convert to PRINCIPLE OF 12 ministry, you need to realize that it is all about unshakeable leadership. Everything rests on the leader. The spiritual leader's radical decision and clear vision is the most important. Once that is taken care of, you will need wisdom, patience, research, and a willingness to be challenged in your faith. Once again, you need wisdom. You need wisdom because you will run into much opposition. You will also need patience. People will have a difficult time understanding. Please remember that you must make clear the vision that you received from the Lord. Not only that, but when your church is moving ahead as a PRINCIPLE OF 12 church, you will need to have a clear picture of which direction your church is going to go. People will not follow you just because you are converting to the PRINCIPLE OF 12 model. The members will understand when you have a clear vision and when you explain to them that in order to accomplish this vision it has to be through the PRINCIPLE OF 12 method. They question is what kind of vision do you have? The Bible is clear that God's vision for the nation rests on discipleship. Once I understood it, I proclaimed it to the church members endlessly. The important thing is that everyone understands that discipling of the nations is the will of God. Then the question becomes is PRINCIPLE OF 12 the only way? Many will ask this question. For you, it may be clear. You should have realized by now that making twelve disciples and imparting your vision, your whole life, your whole character and anointing is the only way to reproduce more disciples. This is the only way to become a true disciple. You should have realized the importance of team ministry by now as well. However, your church members may not have reached such a level of understanding. This is why you will need tremendous patience. It is most important for you to impart this vision through the Sunday sermons, leadership group meetings and other meetings.

After I first encountered a PRINCIPLE OF 12 church in January of 2000, I spent the next 1 year and 6 months to 2 years, sharing about the PRINCIPLE OF 12 system and the spirituality of PRINCIPLE OF 12. Even before introducing it to the church, I shared it with the people who were in leadership every time we met. They were a little bit skeptical. They could not understand why I would abandon the cell church system overnight after developing and producing it in Russian. However, after much persistence and consistent preaching, they finally began to realize, "Aha! This is it."

After making the proclamation to the church that we were starting PRINCIPLE OF 12, we began to hold an Encounter Retreat every week, beginning from January 1 of last year. Thousands have attended the Encounter Retreat from my church. When it was done, the spiritual atmosphere of the church was completely changed, and actually improved. How shall I say...there was so much enthusiasm. It felt as though the whole church was floating in the air. Everyone felt that they could do something. They wanted to take part in what God was doing. Next, I proclaimed that we would plant churches. Suddenly, the number of cells grew from 375 to 950. This will not necessarily happen in the exact manner. You will need much wisdom in implementing the PRINCIPLE OF 12.

What are some of the elements that are needed in order to convert to a PRINCIPLE OF 12 church? There are nine stages needed for implementation. First, you must attend a PRINCIPLE OF 12 Conference at least once a year. This is my personal suggestion. There will be four PRINCIPLE OF 12 Conferences this year. If you truly want to convert your church to a PRINCIPLE OF 12 church, attend every PRINCIPLE OF 12 Conference and seminar. You cannot accomplish anything if you are chasing different methods and models one after another. You may have a good understanding of the concept of PRINCIPLE OF 12 but once you attend a seminar, you will realize, "Aha, I didn't understand it after all." Then at the next seminar, while listening to the same lecture, you will come to say, "Ah, so this is how it works." You will begin to have ideas on how to implement it in your church. It is not something I can explain or share with you one on one.

There are certain stages you need to go through. During the time between conferences, you need to seriously review and brainstorm how you are to establish everything you've heard at your church. If you forget about what you've learned, you'll remain at the same level at the next conference. This is a serious problem. I found that many people attend the conferences but do not end up applying it at their church. It seems as though many are called but only a few are chosen. You need to attend the PRINCIPLE OF 12 Conference at least once a year. I advise you to attend two to three times consecutively until you can implement it at your church. Please think about why it needs to be this way.

I continue to try to improve myself. Many people have told me that each conference is better than the last one. The reason is that I have learned something new since the last one as well. In other words, I am learning more and more about the different factors that are truly important, as well as learning to teach them in an easier and more effective way. This is why I like consistency and repetition. We are in the process of learning together. You may feel that it will become tedious when things are continuously repeated. In actuality, it gets deeper and broader. It allows for detailed application. This is why you must attend the PRINCIPLE OF 12 Conference at least once a year. However, even that will not be enough. Once a year means that there is a 1-year gap before the next one. You will not be able to ask questions during those times and you are more likely to grow colder in your conviction. There is a need to manage your level of excitement because it needs to be long lasting.

Second, you must understand PRINCIPLE OF 12 as God's governing order. Without the understanding of PRINCIPLE OF 12, without clear an understanding of why Jesus chose 12 disciples, you will not be able to start a PRINCIPLE OF 12 church model.

Of course, some leaders, after attending the PRINCIPLE OF 12 Conference will realize limitations in their gifts and abilities. They may start with a lessed number, say three or four disciples. Though the number of government is 12, we must start where we are; with a view to increase as God give us strength and abilty.

Many ask "Why is the number12 so important? Why must we do it that way?" I told myself, "Let's believe what is stated in scripture. There must be a reason behind it. The church experienced growth through the PRINCIPLE OF 12. That is good enough reason for me. I have a considerable amount of members but I still must learn some more. I must learn from the pastor of a bigger church."

Therefore, I researched and discovered a theological basis from the Bible. I asked many questions but decided to study the Bible on my own to see why the PRINCIPLE OF 12 was so important. You need to read the Bible, keeping the number 12 in mind. I am just telling you a general concept that is needed for implementing PRINCIPLE OF 12.

Third, understand the difference between an Open Cell and PRINCIPLE OF 12 Cell, completely. What is Open Cell and what is PRINCIPLE OF 12 Cell? For example, let's say I became a Christian and went through the Alpha Course at my church. Then I attended the Encounter Retreat and the school of leadership. After that, I attended the cell seminar and realized, "Ah, this is how to lead a cell." Then I opened a cell and invited unbelieving friends. I am now leading their cell. I am now a shepherd; I am a cell leader. I hope that people are being saved. I send them to Alpha Courses and then to the Encounter Retreat. In the meanwhile, their cells are growing in numbers: three people, then five people, 8 people, 10 people, 15 people and so one. As the number begins to grow, some people are completing the Alpha Courses and the Encounter Retreat, moving on to the leadership school. They begin to have a desire to open their own zone. One person opens the first zone. A second person opens one and a third one opens as well. Yet, I continue to meet with these cell members. I meet people who became zone leaders. I also meet people who have not become zone leaders yet. It is because the zone leaders who newly opened up their zones do not know how to lead their groups yet. Thus, they need to keep coming to my zone in order to continue to learn.

For example, let us say I have my Open Cell meeting on Thursdays. Then, one of my cell members starts his Open Cell. Then his cell meetings will be on Wednesday. Mine is on Thursdays. And as he comes out on Thursdays, he will learn, "Ah, I was inexperienced in this area. I need to learn more." Then within my cell, one, two, three…more and more people begin to open their zones. When the twelfth person opens his zone, I pull out all twelve people from my Open Cell and put the rest of my cell members into the zone of the twelve. This is possible. People who have not opened their own cells are invited to attend another zone. They do obey and become a part of their zone. From that point on, these 12 people who opened their own zones are my disciples. You will remember that on the first day of the lecture, I said that only those who open their own zones can become disciples. Once these twelve people are formed, I close the cell. I do not take in anymore people. I put the rest of the members into the zones of my twelve disciples. I now concentrate my ministry on these twelve. This is the PRINCIPLE OF 12 Cell. Therefore, on Thursday evenings, I take only the twelve and devote myself to them for all my life. I help them to form their own twelve disciples and with their problems and difficulties in leading their own zones. I do hope this is clear. Therefore, it is necessary to understand the difference between Open Cell and PRINCIPLE OF 12 Cell.

Fourth, in order to establish the PRINCIPLE OF 12 Church, you must understand the four stages of PRINCIPLE OF 12. In other words, you must know the stages of fostering and nurturing people within church. There are four stages in the ladder of success. The first stage is Win; the second, is the Consolidation stage; the third stage is Discipleship and the fourth stage is Send. You must understand these four stages completely and must progressively establish these four stages in your church. You must have in mind how you are going to establish these stages in your church.

First, you must establish the Alpha course. Then you follow with the Encounter retreats. After this, you must build up the leadership school. Fourth, you devlop a ministry team and help these teams carry out all these ministries. Finally, you establish your Vision Center, to continue to educate and train your leaders to reach their fullest potential in the Lord. This is why it is important to understand the four stages of

PRINCIPLE OF 12.

    Fifth, you must establish the Alpha Course in order to win people to Christ. Then you must successfully establish the Encounter Weekend. When you establish the Alpha Course, the church can learn the dynamics of small groups. Have every member of your church complete the Alpha Course, even if some of them have been coming to church for a long time. You must help them to learn about Cell and Zone life, specifically how to build relationships and how to discuss certain content. It will take about a year to establish the Alpha course. Afterwards, you need to establish the Encounter weekend. Spirituality is very important at the Encounter retreat. The manual for the leaders and participants should be prepared by July. However, you need more than just the manuals. That is why my wife and I plan to lead an Encounter Retreat for pastors and their wives. Once it is established, the spiritual climate of your church will be completely renovated. The worship will be changed, prayer will be changed, and many other areas will be changed. Some people make mistakes after establishing the Encounter Weekend at their church. Some people believe, "Encounter Weekend is everything in PRINCIPLE OF 12. The church will come alive once you do it." No! That is not true. You must open zones. You cannot do it alone with just passion and fervor. In addition, in order to open the zones, we need to establish the leadership schools successfully. We must foster the environment so that zone leaders can be continually produced through seminars and leadership training. Then the zones will continuously grow and new believers can be challenged to begin their own process. It is designed to continue turning like a set of cogwheels.

As these stages are beginning to settle in, one thing you must be mindful of is the need to have a successful spiritual Sunday service. In many cases, pastors who return from vision trips and seminars claim to have fully understood the whole concept but what is amazing to me is that when I attend their Sunday service, I feel that "this church is still a traditional church." I understand that it is impossible to change everything all at once. However, it is important to prepare for the presence of God through passionate worship and prayer, even if your church is singing hymns. You must revive the prayer movement that is dead. When worship comes alive, people's spirit begin to come alive as well and prayer is made possible. Thus, you must establish the worship movement first in the church and then work to establish a prayer movement. When that happens, the church's spiritual climate will begin to come alive and Sunday service will begin to reflect this heightened spirituality. The church members will begin to say that there is something different about Sunday service. That will lead to the strengthening of the authority in the senior pastor's word. That is, the congregation will begin to give ear to his message. When you start casting your vision at this point, they will begin to accept it. Please remember that we are not able to do anything when the people are sleeping, when there is no momentum in the church, or when the church is in a state of slumber.

I want to share with you about my church's Sunday service. At Grace church, the Sunday service lasts 2 to 2 and ½ hours. We start with a passionate time of praise and worship, for 30 to 40 minutes. I am not talking about ritualistic worship but the kind of worship where the whole congregation can take part in. There is no such thing as "preparation worship." How can there be "preparation worship?" Even that time of praise is worship. Why is it "preparation worship?" This is where you must stake your life. The worship leader must become a "true worshipper." The worship leader is very important especially when the church is transitioning to the PRINCIPLE OF 12. Furtehr, the worship leader must become an awesome man or woman of prayer. They must be able to feel the presence of God and be very careful when selecting songs - fast songs, slow songs. He/she must be very sensitive in selecting these songs. You may have selected certain songs for a worship set but there may be a need to sing just one song for the entire hour. That is how sensitive you need to be.

It is so important to give life to the congregation's soul. This is why we worship for 30 to 40 minutes at my church. The worship team (we do not have a traditional choir) leads the Sunday service. The worship team consists of 5-6 singers, musicians and 50 to 100 worshippers. It is a little different than a choir. They are up there to worship. I try to help the entire congregation to participate. I make the training for the worship team very intense. The members of the church try very hard to become part of the team. Why? Because they realize that it is a blessing in and of itself to be a part of the worship team. They also receive healing during the training session for the worship team. In general, their practice time lasts anywhere from 3 to 5 hours. This is how I prepare them for one service. I prepare the technical aspect as well as the spiritual.

If the spirituality is not evident during practice, I have them do it over and over again, along with more prayer and training. Worship brings in the presence of God. After worshipping God for 30 to 40 minutes, two to three people give their testimonies about their lives. Many new believers open up their hearts at this time. There are so many extreme changes, even by my standards, which the worshippers and congregants experience. If they can continue to experience such change in their lives, the existing believers as well as the new believers will not want to live a life of mediocrity. In order to foster such a climate, we continue to make testimonies a part of our services. Before the testimonies, we briefly make a couple of very important announcements. Then the associate pastor comes up to lead the congregation in a time of corporate prayer. We have them pray for a couple of themes. We pray for the Silk Road because it is our vision. Sometimes we pray for the three unbelievers in our lives. At other times, we pray for the salvation of families or for the restoration of men. After prayer time, I go to the front. I either have them pray once more or depending on the need I have them join hands with others and minister to each other. Then I go straight into my message. My sermon used to last more than an hour, but I've been trying to limit the time to about 40 minutes. It has been very difficult to reduce the length of my sermon, however. Sometimes, I used to give two-hour sermons. I reduced it down to one hour at my wife's recommendation. I realize that the congregation finds it very difficult to sit through lengthy sermons. Now my sermons last between 40 to 50 minutes, but closer to 50 minutes.

After the sermon, I always give an invitation to receive Christ. I say, "Please rise if you want to give your life to Jesus Christ." I have them stand up, and then come to the front. After leading them through the prayer of acceptance, we sing a song of blessing over them and guide them directly to the new believer's bible study. Then I give the benediction and end the service. This is the worship climate of my church.

The most important thing that we do is thoroughly change the order of service if the presence of the Holy Spirit is not evident. Why? It is because the presence of the Holy Spirit is the most essential part of worship. How unfortunate would it be for the congregation to go back home without experiencing the presence of God, especially when they have invested their precious time to attend Sunday service. Also, it becomes difficult for them to live the following week in victory.

Sixth, you must maintain the presence of the Holy Spirit within the cell meetings. You must examine the cells. Is the Holy Spirit moving within the zone meetings? Is the ministry of healing continuing? Are people experiencing the Holy Spirit as they pray together? Are people open to sharing testimonies in the cells? Is the prayer movement alive? You must monitor this checklist at all times to ensure that a certain level of the presence of the Holy Spirit is maintained at all times.

First, it is important for the Senior Pastor to start his Open Cell. It may be a little difficult if you are a mega church. However, you need an Open Cell with 20-30 members so that you can choose your future 12 disciples. It is necessary to run your Open Cell, even if it is to identify who is able to clearly understand your vision. You need to lead it. No matter how big your church is, if you simply organize it by placing twelve here and twelve there, you will fail. Your vision must be imparted through your leadership. Imagine if the twelve people you have with you either do not know your vision or are opposed to it. Then the second and third generation will fail. Further, the church will not understand God's vision. Rather, conflicts will arise. For this reason, the senior pastor must launch his Open Cell and his vision must be imparted within the Open Cell. The senior pastor needs to keep communicating to his 20 - 30 male members of the church. If possible, the senior pastor's wife must also gather dedicated prospects from the female congregation and continuously impart the vision of the senior pastor. This is vision impartation. The senior pastor must open his Cell so that he can continuously impart his vision. He must communicate the vision, define the PRINCIPLE OF 12 church, and watch and identify those who are able to understand and commit to the vision. This is an important stage. This is the senior pastor's Open Cell stage.

The second stage is to make the vision of the church clear. If you continue to communicate your vision, you will discover that your vision becomes more logical and graspable. What is interesting is that when we try to convey what we think we know, we realize that we really do not know much. In my case, there were times the vision I received from God was correct but was not too precise. However, the vision becomes more defined during the process of conveying the message. *You must be able to precisely put your vision into writing.* The time to present this vision to the church must come. Such a time should come while the senior pastor is running his Open Cell. The message must be mission minded and action oriented. It cannot be abstract. At my church, the vision is to plant 1000 churches by the year 2010 and to preach the gospel all the way back to Jerusalem through the Silk Road. Because the vision is so clear and precise, the people have no room to doubt. The vision is very distinct. You must be able to present such a vision to the church.

Third, the senior pastor must start his PRINCIPLE OF 12 cell. You can choose your twelve disciples, but these people must open their own cells. In choosing the twelve, you must help them to open their own cells. Even if they have yet to start, it is important to receive confirmation from them that they will. It is important to form a team which will develop strategies together and follow through with them.

Fourth, once the team of twelve is formed, you must establish the Alpha Course within the church. This is very important. Alpha is the starting point for a church to move towards becoming a PRINCIPLE OF 12 church. It is the stepping stone. If your church is able to run the Alpha Courses, your church will be able to learn how to manage and interact in a small group setting. For this reason, your chosen twelve disciples must attend the Alpha seminar at least twice consecutively, in order to run it in its original form. I find that many people who are doing it all wrong claim that they know what they are doing. The Alpha seminar is very enlightening because it will help you fix and change any problems you may have.

Once the Alpha Courses are established, the next thing you must do is to have all the church members attend the Encounter Retreat. This stage may seem easy but it is not. The senior pastor starts his Open Cell and begins sharing the vision together. He starts teaching PRINCIPLE OF 12 and presents his vision to the church. Next, he chooses his twelve and establishes the Alpha course with those disciples. If your church can have the Encounter Retreat as the next stage, the church's spiritual climate will come alive. In the previous stages, only the leaders were excited, but following the encounter retreat, the whole church started to get excited. The church as a whole will be excited about God's ministry and people will be committed to discipleship. These things take place when you hold Encounter Retreats.

Next, you must establish the Leadership School. It is the leadership school system that continuously prepares future shepherds. I have recently added seventh stage to extend and to strengthen the team ministry. This is accomplished through our partnership with Vision International University.

Thus, your team will go through the Alpha courses together as a team of twelve. However, as cells begin to grow, each of your disciples may have their own Alpha Course and they may lead their own Encounter Retreat, especially if the church is large. In such cases, you must have the team ministry actively help out every team. This will ensure the natural growth and operation of the PRINCIPLE OF 12 church. From what I have experienced, this process will help you systematically establish the PRINCIPLE OF 12 in your church.

Evangelism is important to all churches, as souls are on the heart of the Father. However, if you are not sharing the gospel, then there is no need for Leadership Schools, Alpha Courses or Encounter Retreats. There are some strategies or what we call nets that can help "catch" people for Christ. What are those nets? There are three important nets.

First is the Open Cell. Anyone can come into the family of Open Cell, including unbelievers. People may find it uncomfortable to come to church so it is easier to attend a smaller, more intimate setting. It is actually illegal to invite a Muslim to a Christian church in a Muslim country. That is why we use the Open Cell to draw them in. Once they are part of the Open Cell, some go straight to the Alpha Course. In most cases, they attend the Alpha Course first and then become part of the Cell before settling down in the church. Nevertheless, the Open Cell is used as a net to catch people, a strong tool for evangelism.

Second is the Sunday Celebration Service. I purposely use the expression "Celebration Service" for Sunday service. Sunday service must become a celebration. I believe that one Holy Spirit-filled service can supply enough strength to live throughout the week for most believers. A large number of worship services are not what fills us with the Spirit. The spirit is not revived, no matter how many times we attend services, especially if the service stays traditional or if the members are inhibited. However, worshipping God even once a week in a manner that is completely committed and filled with the Holy Spirit has the power to liberate and open up the spirits of believers. At my church, we only hold the service once, the Sunday service. Still, I am confident that the believers are living Spirit filled lives. Part of the reason is that people are actively participating in bringing people to Christ. Recently, we bought a kindergarten school to build our sanctuary. The place is filled with church members from Monday to Sunday. There are people coming to pray at 5 p.m. and at 5:30, people who lead the Alpha Courses stand in front of the church greeting the believers and unbelievers alike. The church is always packed. It is so wonderful. There is no time to rest. The church goes round and round. It is so nice and comfortable for me because I only have to give a sermon once a week. You must be successful in turning the Sunday service into a celebration service.

I always give an call for response to my message at Sunday celebration services. Generally, Koreans never learned to invite people to accept Jesus Christ as their Savior, especially in Presbyterian denominations (I grew up in a Presbyterian church). We live according to how we were taught.

When I first arrived on the mission field, I set the worship order according to what I learned in Korea for the first service. Something was not right, especially in a new culture. They love to dance and jump around; it did not fit. I had a problem, because I did not know how to get people to commit their lives to Christ. In reality, I was not trained in Evangelism Explosion or CCC training. I never even opened a cell. Yet I became a missionary. A few famous pastors from America would visit my church because it was the mission field. However, after preaching their message I felt that their messages were not very great. It was not too interesting and it was not even about Jesus. They would always have an altar call. At first, I thought, "those people are strange." What was stranger was that people raised their hands every time they asked, "Whoever wants to accept Jesus today raise your hands." I was so shocked. "This is not right." It was not an isolated incident. Whoever came, especially the Pentecostal pastors would always preach and give an invitation. It was so simple. Jesus is our Lord. They would give a very simple gospel message and they would ask people to stand. And people would stand up. I asked myself, "Why don't I do this?" Yet, when I tried to do it, it was awkward and uncomfortable; I'd never done it before. I wanted to learn, so I took Billy Graham's tapes and wrote out his invitation for salvation in English, and then translated it into Korean. Then I got Pastor Yongi Cho's invitation prayer. My church still uses his prayer. I like his the best. I got other pastors' invitation prayers, including Derek Prince's. I got about ten different prayers of invitation. After studying the different prayers, I felt that Pastor Yongi Cho's was the best for new believers. I used his prayer as the model. After each Sunday service, I asked the new believers to come forward and had them repeat the prayer. Then I'd pray for them. That's how I did it. What is amazing is that when I visited the cells, the cell leaders were doing it just like me. All the Full Gospel church pastors have the same invitations because of Pastor Yonghi Cho. I was so surprised. When I first met people at my home, we prayed for healing and for the filling of the Holy Spirit. I would not leave them alone without seeing the confirmation of salvation. God sent a soul to me and I could not let them go. I prayed until they would get saved. It became my lifestyle and model. As a result, my disciples pray for the salvation of the newcomers in the cells. The prayer for salvation is the same. I am truly thankful. It is important to be a role model. We were able to set the example during the Sunday service.

Open Cell, nets, and networks: What are these? My twelve disciples and my wife's twelve disciples are all leaders of networks. They are the leaders of PRINCIPLE OF 12 but because they have twelve disciples who also have their own twelve disciples, they are considered network leaders. Their networks have their own ministry as well. For example, one of my twelve disciples planted a church near Almaty. He was still attending my church. They opened an Alpha Course at an orphanage and a ministry for the homeless. They all have a ministry of their own. They are beginning to unfold their nets to bring in countless numbers of unbelievers through his ministry. He and his disciples constitute a network.

These three important nets to catch people are very effective. Ministry according to networks is very important. Each of my disciples started to pray before the Lord with their vision, asking how they can bring more people to Christ and in turn, make them their disciples. Their vision began to go forth through their prayers and they were able to begin their ministry of saving lives and making disciples. This is ministry according to networks.

I have previously shared with you briefly about Open Cell and PRINCIPLE OF 12 Cell. How do you lead a meeting in an Open Cell? The purpose is mostly to evangelize and nurture. The pure purpose of Open Cell is to invite unbelievers, and to help them accept Jesus. The most important thing for unbelievers is to hear a testimony. Testimonies must become a lifestyle in the Open Cell. There must be prayers for unbelievers and prayers for their needs. There will be people that have all sorts of issues including illnesses, financial difficulties, people with marital problems, etc. Therefore, we must concentrate our efforts to pray for all these problems. The next thing Open Cell needs is the Word. The Word needs to be short. It needs to be short, clear and in the form of a testimony. I have the leaders of Open Cell share for about 10 to 15 minutes only, related to the Sunday sermon.

It is not recommended for Open Cell leaders to give long sermons. Then they have a short discussion about applying the message.

Prayer and the Word is always needed. Praying for the needs of the people and praying for three unbelievers needs to become a lifestyle within the cell. Testimony, praise, prayer, and word should be a part of the meeting but the order in itself is not that important. We must follow the leading of the Holy Spirit. If you begin to follow formality, the flow of the Holy Spirit may be disrupted. In certain cases, in an Open Cell meeting, praise time can last 30 minutes with an abbreviated prayer time and the sermon can be cut short. In some instances, you can go straight into the sermon. If the atmosphere is right, you can share a testimony without praise time. We should not be too restricted by formality. We must be sensitive to the leading of the Holy Spirit. However, testimony, prayer, praise and word: these four must never be skipped. At times, the vision of the church and cell, and the vision of the network must be communicated regularly. Testimonies and reports should be present at all times within the cell. I always emphasize that these meetings should end in about an hour. At the latest, it should not exceed an hour and a half. It becomes a big burden to an unbeliever or a new believer. Especially in a Muslim nation, if a woman goes home late because the meeting ran late, she can literally be beaten and kicked out of her home. The young adult meeting should not be too long either. In Open Cell, problems can arise if meetings run longer. For example, people without prophetic gifts might try to prophecy. Others will interrupt the sermon to say what they want to say. It is best to stick to the point and have them share their testimonies and end it with a strong emotional impact.

The PRINCIPLE OF 12 Cell is most important. Where are the disciples made? They are made in the PRINCIPLE OF 12 cells; they can mature and grow most efficiently in that setting. This is why at times we call the PRINCIPLE OF 12 Cell a Discipleship Cell. It is a cell that leads to discipleship. Within the PRINCIPLE OF 12 cell, discipleship and ministry takes place at the same time. That is why this meeting takes over three hours. I meet with my disciples and my wife meets with her disciples. Our average meeting time is about three hours. Less than three hours are a rarity. There is so much to talk about. There are so many problems discuss and deal with, from personal issues to strategies for further outreach.

When you first form the PRINCIPLE OF 12 cell, before you can cast your vision, you have to help settle their family problems first. As you continue to meet, it will become evident that their family problems are due to their character problems. After leading a meeting for 12 men, the most common interest among these men was how to solve their marital issues. As we began to deal with problems, we all came to the same conclusion; we are not prepared as men. We lack character. Therefore, we would repent, share new ideas, and study the Bible. A simple word might come but we would wrestle with it and try to apply the word to our lives. As we did, we realized that two hours were not enough. For example, one would complain that his wife has certain shortcomings that make it difficult for him. He says that it is impossible to change her. I listen but do not give my response right away. I ask the others to weigh in on what they think. One of the disciples of PRINCIPLE OF 12 shares his answer. Then another shares what he thinks. There are times when that is all that is needed. At times, I have to draw the conclusion for them. Sometimes, when the Holy Spirit gives me the word, I may preach on it for an hour, an hour and a half or even two hours. It is truly freeing because there is no formality. We know each other so well we can share openly. We know each other's problems. In addition, we strengthen the PRINCIPLE OF 12 cell by going to their homes to bless and encourage their wives and family members. In the PRINCIPLE OF 12 cell, testimonies, praise, prayer, the Holy Spirit's message, ministry reports, and discussions about our vision are continuously discussed. Not only that, but we also address administrative issues. For example, we would discuss the following lecturers for the next Encounter Retreat. Even though we meet once a week, it feels as though we are very short on time.

Final Thoughts

The PRINCIPLE OF 12 has been a most effective tool for the development of my own local congregation, and has become the foundation for a true church planting movement for the Silk Road. The same is happening in many parts of the world. For example, my friend, Dr. Steve Mills, the Director of the Global 12 Project and Director of Strategic Planning for Vision International University is actively involved in training and releasing leaders to plant churches in Western Africa. Through his network of disciples, over 1000 churches were planted, using the PRINCIPLE OF 12 discussed in this book, in his region of the world. This is most exciting, and similar reports are being given around the world.

Let me say that THE PRINCIPLE OF 12 is not for everyone, and it is certainly not for the maintenance oriented pastor. However, for those with a heart to see the Kingdom of God expanded throughout the world, it is dynamic. My pray is that you will take these principles and actively apply them, under the leading of the Holy Spirit, with expectation that God will indeed increase your influence and His name in the earth.

Questions and Answers

Over the years, I have responded gto many excellent questions which relate o the PRINCIPLE OF 12. Here are some of the most common questions and responses.

Q) How do you divide the Young Adults into same gender groups?

A) In some places where the PRINCIPLE OF 12 is used, they do not divide the genders. So I asked them, "Why didn't you divide them into same genders? Don't you have any problems?" Their only reason was, "They need to get together in order to get married."

At my church, they are divided. They are excessively liberal when it comes to sex in the Old Soviet nations. If you allow them to interact together, it will definitely lead to problems. Therefore, we separate them by genders and train them. Certain activities, such as the young adult family seminars, are held together. We just started the young adult Encounter Retreat with both genders together. We'll examine the effects some time later. In that sense, I think that you can take the original PRINCIPLE OF 12 model and apply it at your church for a few test runs. If it is truly difficult to implement, it is possible to make a few changes while keeping the original frame. At my church, young adults are separated by genders.

Q) Do you lead the Young Adult PRINCIPLE OF 12 by yourself or do you lead it with your wife?

A) I have twelve male young adults with me and my wife has her female 12. To add to the question, why must you as the senior pastor lead them directly? It is because they are the next generation of my church. If the next generation does not receive the same vision from the senior pastor, they cannot run the church.

There is a missionary that came from America. He had a successful ministry in Chicago and also planted seven churches on his own. He came to my church and asked to serve under me. When he came in, I asked him to take over the young adult ministry but he was not able to clearly impart my vision. So I called him in and said, "I am sorry but this is about the future of this church. I will need to directly lead the young adult group." I meet with the young adults once a week and my wife does the same with her girls. In some cases, it is very difficult but because you are imparting your vision to the next generation, it is very important.

Q) What is the age limit for your church's young adult group? If they get married, do they need to be replaced?

A) There is no specific age limit at my church's young adult group. However, ages range from 16, 17 to about 30 years old. There is a cultural element here. In Central Asia, once they reach 16, they are able to get along well with people in the

20's and 30's. They can converse well and their thinking process is also very mature. If this is not the case in another culture, you may need to separate them. At our church, the young adult group has their own PRINCIPLE OF 12 ministry. Some people want to stay with the young adult group even after they get married. We allow them to do that. We have people who are 30, 32, and 35 years old who are part of the young adult group. Or, if they want to transition over to the adult PRINCIPLE OF 12, we help them to make the transition as well. There is a man who is 50 years old, who is a part of the Young Adults' PRINCIPLE OF 12 network. We don't put an age limit. If they feel that they want to belong to the young adult group because they are young at heart, then we allow them to do that. Moreover, we have some women who insist that they belong to the male PRINCIPLE OF 12. They just don't find it interesting to be a part of women's PRINCIPLE OF 12 and only find it interesting to do male PRINCIPLE OF 12. Those women are actually leading men's cell. As you can see, we do not sent age and gender limits. We leave the door open quite a bit without restricting people.

Q) Everyone has a different spiritual level. Do you make everyone go through the four stages of discipleship from the beginning? Alternatively, do you allow some to transfer into the mid level stage?

A) When you become a part of a church's system, even if you have been going to that church for a long time, it is important to go through every stage because you are helping to create the spiritual atmosphere and lifestyle of the church. Wisdom is needed to set the right spiritual climate. Most people breathe a sigh of relief once they finish a seminar or a course but the PRINCIPLE OF 12 courses do not necessarily end because we emphasize this as a lifestyle. People continuously participate in the same program as they experience the birth of new believers and transformations in the lives of fellow Christians. This brings fullness and joy to the lives of the church body. No matter what the programs may be, the helpers tend to be blessed more once they participate in the four stages of Discipleship.

Q) Can you maintain a relationship with a female leader or believer who has a higher spiritual level than the senior pastor's wife?

A) In the PRINCIPLE OF 12 ministry, it is recommended for senior pastors' wife lead the women's ministry. It is most ideal if the senior pastor's wife can become an intercessor who can hear God's prophetic voice. If that is not the case and someone else ends up leading the women's ministry, there will be some difficulties. If the senior pastor's wife completely gives up on the ministry, then the senior pastor has to train a female member from the congregation as the leader. In such a case, I do not think that it would last long. My wife actually hates to be in front of people. She likes to stay in the background, supporting me. She is excellent at administrative work and organizing conferences. However, if I ask her to come out and preach or lead a meeting, she has a difficult time with it. Even so, I prayed to the Lord for over 3 months in fasting and prayer. I prayed, "Lord, allow my wife to have her ministry. Have her minister to the women."

We have four children. We have a seventeen year old daughter, a fourteen year old son, eight year old son, and a two year old son. She ministers even with those four children. There is a lot for her to do especially since my church is made up mostly of women. She oversees 850 cells. Her ministry is bigger than mine and women talk more. She was the one who thoroughly set up the worship ministry at my church since she graduated from a music university, majored in piano and did music ministry at her church. She also leads the intercession ministry. It is as if she laid the foundations of our church, while I simply gave sermons. When I asked her to lead women's ministry on top of all she was doing, she asked if I wanted to kill her. Yet the more I prayed, the more I felt that the she would come alive if she would involve herself in the ministry full force. I did my best to get her involved in the ministry. At one time, she was so burdened that she told me, "You are using me to the maximum." I responded, "I am definitely not trying to use you. When you are involved in the ministry, you will become busy, find your worth before the Lord and find satisfaction in the maturation process of your disciples." Because she is a sensitive woman, it does get problematic at times. However, I involve her in the ministry, even with such drawbacks. The purpose is to walk together on the same level of spirituality and to become true co-workers.

Only the wife can counsel the pastor and give meaningful advice. No one can touch the senior pastor. Many times a senior pastor can become stubborn and dictatorial, when the wife does not say anything. It is a good sign when the pastor's wife nags a lot. First, it is proof that she is alive (if she doesn't nag, she is already dead). Second, her advice is truly precious. Men can see far but women have the ability to see the present with detail and take care of minute details with wisdom and accuracy. I do 100% of listening and 100% of the decision-making. This is my family's principle.[21] My wife wants it that way as well. When a woman begins to lead, things go haywire. It absolutely cannot work. It is because God has set the man up as the leader of the family. I raised my wife up as the leader under the principle that a woman has to lead the women. Before she's ever given a single sermon, I announced, "Starting next week, the 1st service will be strictly men. The 2nd service will be strictly all women and the 3rd all young adults." The following week, the first service was less than half-full. It was a depressing sight for the 1st service. Yet the men were happy to be with other men.

I was curious to see how many people would gather for the 2nd service. I didn't go in just in case I'd make my wife nervous. I peeked in from the back to find the sanctuary filled

---

[21] Also a major factor in Korean culture; not all cultures will be the same.

to the railings. The praise time was so intense; it felt as though the sermon wasn't even needed. When she gave her message, people responded explosively. To me the sermon wasn't that great. Then I realized, "Ah! This is the power of same gender ministry." As I was listening to my wife's sermon, I realized that she was touching the areas I was not able to touch. Women's hearts were being opened and people were weeping and being healed. "This is it. We must minister this way," I thought. Now I make the same proclamation from time to time. "Next week, the 1st service will be strictly men. The 2nd service will be strictly all women and the 3rd all young adults." A woman should lead the women's ministry as a fundamental rule but the senior pastor's wife should have the priority to lead. There is great power within the pastor's wife. She can certainly do it.

Q) Once the senior pastor chooses his twelve disciples, should you keep the relationship for a lifetime and mentor them?

A) My answer would be "Yes," based on principle. I plan to be with my twelve disciples for the rest of my life. However, there are some people whose personalities are so strong and independent that they cannot remain under someone. You desire to come along side him and mentor him but there will be people who want to be on their own, in an independent ministry. You should identify such people early and help to plant a church with them. That person will be very successful and love you even more. The relationship will become even better. In such cases, the top disciple should fill the space left void by the disciple. If no such disciples exist, then you may choose a top disciple from the best performing disciple of your remaining eleven. For example, if one of your eleven has 100 cells and the other 10 cells, and another 2 cells, then you should choose the top disciple of the one who has 100 cells to fill that spot. When you pray to the Holy Spirit, moment by moment, he will give you wisdom to lead your twelve disciples with wonderful leadership. However, the principle is lifetime relationship. It is because we keep growing in the Lord. We learn throughout our lives. I keep learning new things about the ministry as well, which means that the disciples can learn throughout their lives as well. We must grow at all times. This is why I make lifetime relationships a principle.

Q) Does the senior pastor continue to make twelve disciples?

A) Once you choose your twelve disciples, then those are the only ones you stay with. You only need to help them to make their own twelve disciples. However, in the case of some churches, the senior pastor's twelve disciples have reached a certain level and are doing very well. There is no need to meet on a weekly basis. In such cases, there is a need to choose another set of twelve. The reasoning is that it is so easy to become complacent. The fresh wind stops blowing and we fall into traditionalism. However, when you choose new people and start a new work, the church experiences renewal. With that reasoning, I heard that the senior pastor of some large PRINCIPLE OF 12 churches have chosen a new set of twelve disciples even though he already has twelve disciples, because they have grown so well and are maturing on their own. The PRINCIPLE OF 12 church system is a relatively new system. Therefore, as long as we hold on to the basic principles, problems that arise from moment to moment can be solved by the wisdom of the Holy Spirit.

Q) Can you start discipleship even if you do not have twelve members?

A) Of course. The point of fostering disciples is to make disciples and to fill the twelve positions. It is not that we nurture the disciples after they become disciples. Whoever can open an Open Cell can become one of the twelve disciples. There are Open Cell and PRINCIPLE OF 12 Cell. PRINCIPLE OF 12 Cell includes the leader and twelve zone leaders. That is the PRINCIPLE OF 12 cell. It is a closed cell. Open Cell is a place where unbelievers or new believers can come and be blessed. This is Open Cell.

Q) Where are the meetings taking place?

A) At home. Even with my twelve disciples, we take turns at one of the disciples' home. This way, I can learn of their family situation and their relationship with their wives. Just by the way the wife greets us, I can tell something about their relationship. I can tell by how the shoes are arranged. There is no doubt about it. I can tell by how the food was prepared. I can tell how much she respects me, whether she prepared it with all of her heart. I can tell by the way she addresses me. I can then discern what message to share. I can grasp what type of relationship I need to make with that particular disciple. In that sense, PRINCIPLE OF 12 cells should move from house to house. However, Open Cells where mostly new believers gather should meet at one place. This reduces confusion. It prevents people from quitting due to confusion over where to go after being absent.

Q) Are you in charge of just one team at a time? How long is the duration of a team?

A) Yes, you look at the twelve disciples as a team. You hold on to a team of twelve disciples for a lifetime, transforming them continuously. However, it is different when you make a team for the Alpha course. In my wife's case, three of her twelve disciples each have their own Alpha course team. They are doing so well. Another disciple is in charge of the Encounter Retreat. Such team's length of continuance is about one year. This helps other teams to be trained as well. However, if one is very good and would like to invest their entire life in a certain team, we allow them to do that as well.

Q) Can you be in charge of Adult, Children and Young Adults at the same time?

A) When a church considers PRINCIPLE OF 12 ministry, the senior pastor should focus on making 12 disciples, 1 for young adult ministry, and 1 for children's ministry, one for women's ministry, etc. You may be able to do that initially but I would not recommend it. I think it would be prudent to have adults separately, young adults separately and children separately.

www.ingramcontent.com/pod-product-compliance
Lightning Source LLC
Chambersburg PA
CBHW050121170426
43197CB00011B/1674